DATE DUE

Books by Blake Ehrlich

PARIS ON THE SEINE

RESISTANCE
France 1940–1945

RESISTANCE
France 1940-1945

ENGLAND

BELGIUM

GERMANY

LUX

Amiens

Le Havre

RHINE R.

MOSELLE R.

Reims

SEINE R.

Paris

Nancy

Brest

Rennes

Le Mans

Orléans

SEINE R.

RHINE R.

Nantes

Tours

LOIRE

Nevers

SWITZERLAND

LOIRE R.

JURA

RHÔNE R.

Vichy

Geneva

HAUTE SAVOIE

AIN

Clermont-Ferrand

Lyon

ALLIER

SAVOIE

Grenoble

ITALY

ISÈRE

Bordeaux

Valence

RHÔNE R.

DRÔME

HAUTES ALPES

GARONNE R.

Nîmes

VAU-
CLUSE

BASSES
ALPES

Toulouse

BOUCHES-
DU-RHÔNE

VAR

ALPES
MARITIMES

SPAIN

Perpignan

Marseille

Toulon

FRANCE ∗ 1944

Occupation zone

0 20   100 Miles

0   100 Kilometers

RESISTANCE
France 1940-1945

by BLAKE EHRLICH

with maps and photos

Little, Brown and Company · Boston · Toronto

Published simultaneously in Canada
by Little, Brown & Company (Canada) Limited

PRINTED IN THE UNITED STATES OF AMERICA

*A mon ami Pierrot, qui m'a ouvert sa porte
et tant d'autres*

Contents

RESISTANCE
France 1940-1945

Two Weeks in Paris — All Expenses Paid

T*he German Army ended the eight months' "phony war" by attacking across the Low Countries May 10, 1940. Exactly thirty-five days later to the hour and minute, at 5:30 a.m., June 14, they entered Paris.*

JUNE 1:   Schools ordered closed. "All those whose work does not require them to stay in Paris should leave the capital." However, the Paris evacuation plan is not invoked, since transport, supplies and personnel were never arranged for. A few thousand evacuate privately, by automobile and train. They follow refugees from Belgium and northern France who began passing through two weeks ago.

JUNE 2:   "I have toured the defenses of Paris," Premier Paul Reynaud reports. Having seen the few blockhouses and machine-gun emplacements, the scanty trenches and anti-tank constructions, he adds, "I was struck by the insufficiency of the works."

JUNE 5:   Germans attack along the Somme.

The Military Governor of Paris appeals to the vigilance of the population to notify without delay the military authorities, the gendarmerie or the police of the appearance of parachutists or enemy aircraft landing in the region. Also to report the presence of suspicious persons in the area of military establishments or factories, tunnels or bridges.

Railway stations inundated by departing Parisians.

JUNE 6:   Exodus continues. Ministry of Public Works brings in one hundred thousand construction workers from provinces to build Paris defenses. Military governor's chief of staff comments, "It might have been expedient to put this program into action during the autumn of 1939 . . . These laborers serve no purpose except to complicate the task of combat units." Somme front breaks.

JUNE 7:   The Aisne front collapses. Disorganized remnants of French units begin to appear in Paris. There are not enough officers or NCO's to form them into new units, and no weapons to re-arm them. There is no transportation to the rear where they could be regrouped. The chief of staff observes, "They no longer have the slightest discipline," and characterizes them as "an immense horde."

The sight of these disarrayed, disarmed and haggard soldiers accelerates the panic among Parisians, who bolt for the exits in ever greater numbers.

JUNE 8:   At the morning press conference, the spokesman assures the world that the Government will stand fast. In the afternoon, having commandeered trucks, automobiles and even river barges without regard for military requirements, the Government picks up its files and flees to Tours. Paris municipal council ordered out as well.

JUNE 9:   Farmers from surrounding countryside begin driving livestock through city.

JUNE 10:   Government accepts General Weygand's recommendation that Paris be spared bombardment and combat by declaring it an open city. They neglect to make this declaration public or even to inform General Héring, military governor of Paris, who orders all draft-deferred war-plant workers to join their army units.

JUNE 11: General Héring collects military odds and ends to form an "Army of Paris." Tells prefect of Seine and prefect of police, remaining civil authority, he will "defend Paris house by house."

JUNE 12: During the night Weygand telephones Héring to tell him Paris is an open city.

JUNE 13: Notices posted telling Parisians there will be no combat in their city. All the same, they flee in even greater numbers. Shops are shuttered, restaurants and cafés closed, and food and drink become difficult to find. Subway stops running as bosses and workers leave. Buses all commandeered, taxicabs vanished. Private cars have headed south. Even garbage trucks and sprinkler wagons have been taken south. Garbage piles up, streets littered with lost baggage, broken furniture. Railway workers stick to their posts, but there is not enough rolling stock to absorb the masses of terrified people.

A mad rush of bicycles, handcarts from Les Halles, baby carriages, delivery wagons. Piled high with household treasures, invalids and infants, they make for the highway to join the seeping mass of motor vehicles which includes even patrol wagons and fire engines from suburban towns.

To add to the sense of terror, flames roll across the sky and smoke palls the city as the stocks of oil and gas burn in the depots of seven river towns around Paris.

JUNE 14: More than three million Parisians have fled. On the quais by the Seine, lost cattle low. The Germans enter a deserted city and occupy abandoned buildings. Their spearhead pushes through Paris, aiming for Angoulême, 250 miles to the south.

The impenetrable mass of French soldiers and civilians and their grotesque parade of vehicles is stalled, backed up from

fifty miles ahead where the French Army has blown up the
Loire bridges (some of the bridges thick with frantic, unheed-
ing refugees as they were blown apart).

The German Army wants the road cleared. They send the
Luftwaffe to sweep it clean with cannon and machine-gun
fire. After the first wave of planes has passed, nothing remains
on the road except an occasional burning car. Half a million
refugees crouch in the ditches and fields.

A stunned silence stretches until it is snapped by the first
German column, led by motorcycles and tanks, which thunders
down the highway. Military police are dropped off every two
hundred yards. With disdain, they point the refugees back
toward Paris. The sun has risen. This will be a long day.

I Lay Me Down
to Bleed a While Then
Rise to Fight Again . . .

Aᴼᴛᴇʀ the armistice of June 25, 1940, the Gemans made every effort to show themselves to be "correct." Although only a measure to insure tranquillity in their new territory, to excite no opposition, it was also a masterly rebuke to the French. The French had not been "correct" among themselves.

The serenity, the charity, the unity of the Germans, even the radiant health, elegant uniforms and superb machines of the soldiery, left the French with little resource. They, the French, had been riven with political dissent. They, the French, had panicked and run. There had been millions of small, ignoble tragedies enacted on the routes of the exodus.

While whole armies were intact, their military leaders had counseled surrender, and the people, cornered and terrified, had been happy to accept the counsel. Everywhere private interests had taken shameful precedence over national interests. The French had not been "correct."

The armistice did not end the frantic scrabbling which the exodus had produced. How will I get out of this? How will I live? Will I get my old job back? Where will I find food? Can I get back home? Where is the rest of the family? Are they dead or sick or simply stranded somewhere without

money? And the soldiers? Are they dead or wounded or safely
prisoners? The telephone is out of order. The post office is not
functioning. The railroad lines are torn up. The telegraph wires
are down. Where is everybody? How will I live? Is there any
food?

The Germans showed themselves to be correct. They provided gasoline for the trip back home for those refugees who
had cars — if the cars had not been abandoned or stolen or
destroyed by gunfire. They pushed the repair of the railways.
They facilitated the return of familiar French authorities. In
some places, they even provided food.

One of the first posters the Germans put up showed a smiling, bareheaded Wehrmacht trooper holding a grinning French
kid in the crook of his arm. The child was joyfully chomping
a piece of buttered bread. Two little French girls looked up
in apparent adoration. *Abandoned population, put your trust
in the German soldier!* said the text.

And there was still a French government. No longer the
French Republic, it was the French State, and its head, with
the title of "Chef d'Etat," was the greatest living French war
hero, the Victor of Verdun, Marshal Henri Philippe Pétain.
He spoke to his people:

"I make the gift of my person to France to attenuate her
misfortune." He assured them, "It is not I who will mislead
you with deceptive words. I hate the lies which have done you
so much harm." He assured them further, "The Government
remains free. France will be administered only by Frenchmen."

The rationing and distribution of supplies would be decided
by the French, not the Germans. The French police would still
see to order. French courts would insure justice. French schools
would still inculcate French culture. French postmen would deliver the mail, French railways would be run by Frenchmen.
The newspapers and the radio would remain in French hands.

The Marshall gave them villains on which to blame their
defeat: the liars who had run the Third Republic, and the

voters who had elected them — the people themselves. He reminded them and reminded them that they had warred and lost and should now drink defeat to the bitter dregs. Not, of course, without deriving some beneficial moral lessons.

They had been naughty, and now they must accept their punishment. They had been spoiled and self-indulgent. They must acknowledge the error of their ways. Back to the soil, he urged them, back to religion, back to the healthy basic realities: *Travail, Famille, Patrie* — Work, Family, Country.

The Germans supplied some auxiliary villains: the Jews and the English. When the British attacked French naval units harbored at Mers-el-Kébir, Oran, on the third of July, all the organs of propaganda opened at full throttle in the occupied zone. Two days later there appeared a poster ("Don't forget Oran!" it said) which showed a drowning French sailor sinking in the blood-dyed waves, holding aloft with his dying strength the tattered French flag. From the left-hand upper corner, the Royal Navy bore down on him like sharks.

The same day this tricolored poster appeared, alongside it in Paris was posted a simple announcement: the eight o'clock curfew was forthwith pushed back all the way to 11 P.M. (The British hate you, the Germans like you.)

Another anti-English poster showed a street of smoking ruins. In the middle ground a thin, weeping mother held a babe in arms. A frail girl child in soiled dress sat staring beside her. In the background the ghost of a British officer, pipe in mouth, fists on hips, riding crop in fist, sneered over the scene. In the foreground, a French soldier, arm in sling, face a mask of battle fatigue, eyes starting from his head (no German poster in France from now to the end of the war would ever show a Frenchman fighting, except in German uniform), declaimed, *"C'est l'Anglais qui nous a fait ça!"* — It's the English who have done this to us.

This was a theme to which the Germans returned again and again, to persuade the French that the English were still the traditional enemy. Joan of Arc and Napoleon were put to this propaganda use, apparently without fear of arousing a patriotic reaction which would include the Germans as enemies, too.

It was a tidal wave of propaganda, but still, it failed to sweep the whole population with it. Eight weeks later, there was a new poster, much smaller, in simple black and white:

> All persons harboring English soldiers must deliver same to the nearest Kommandantur not later than 20 October 1940. Those persons who continue to harbor Englishmen after this date without having notified the authorities will be shot.

Saving these Englishmen, saving Frenchmen escaped from POW camps, saving Jews and other anti-Nazi fugitives was the first task of the Resistance.

THE UNDERGROUND RAILWAY

At this moment, immediately after the collapse of France, there was nothing which could be called "the Resistance," but there were individuals who refused to accept defeat, or who at least wanted to help those who could not accept defeat.

Out of their linked gestures of charity in an uncharitable time, some of the future organized resistance was born. Among the great leaders of the Resistance-to-be were many who got away from prison camps. The role of escaped POW's in the foundation of the resistance and the liberation of France was a leading one.

It took resolution and initiative to escape from German surveillance in those early days, but it was not enormously difficult. The conquerors found themselves with almost two million French prisoners on their hands, and, certain as they had been of victory, they were not prepared for this overwhelming windfall. The first stockades were improvised, and a determined man could break out, provided he was not shot as he made the attempt. But once he was out, he was far from free.

Most of the prisoners were held in compounds in the east and northeast of France, the area which, until that moment, had bordered Germany and Belgium. Now the *départements* which made up the old provinces of Alsace and Lorraine were no longer French. They had been annexed to Germany.

French evacuees returning via Strasbourg were met at the station by German bands playing the "Horst Wessel Lied" and "Deutschland Uber Alles." Stretched across gates to the station hall were huge banners: WILKOMMEN IN DER DEUTSCHEN HEIMAT. The street signs on the Place de la République now read, "Bismarck Platz." Thus, the Franco-German frontier now began at the western borders of Alsace and Lorraine.

To the north other *départements* had been declared a forbidden zone. These regions Hitler was planning to colonize. He had a dream of reconstituting a Flemish State by unifying French Flanders and the Low Countries.

Before the fighting had begun the French Government had evacuated large sections of the border regions. Now, in the Ardennes, for example, the owners of farms were not allowed to return. Their farms were turned over to the Ostdeutsche Landbewirtschaftungsgesellschaft, known as Ostland, later renamed Reichland.

The purpose of the organization: to *colonize* — to settle German colonists on the farms. "The French have abandoned their soil, and it is now the duty of the Germans to exploit this resource."

The *départements* of Pas-de-Calais and Nord were not annexed to Germany, but to Belgium, and formed part of the Belgian Occupation Command.

Once over any of these heavily patrolled borders, the escapee was where? He was in occupied France, beetling with Germans.

In the first month or so, even in the occupied zone, he would be all right once he got home and slipped back into his habitual prewar routine. (At least, he would be all right for a year or so, when he would be stopped, as everyone was at some time, and asked for his papers. He wouldn't be able to produce a demobilization certificate.)

If the escapee's home was in the Vichy zone, the southern one-third of France (except for the Atlantic coastal strip, very alertly held by the Germans), he had one more border to cross. This was the demarcation line which marked off the two zones.

If the fugitive were an Allied military man, or an anti-Nazi refugee, then there was no real hiding place. He had to be smuggled out of the country. He could go across the Swiss border or the Spanish border, or go by sea to Spain or to England.

On his travels he would need identity papers, food, lodging, clothing and, very often, a guide. In short, he would need friends, and these would have to be prepared to lay down their lives as part of their charity.

Berthe Marquaille took in Allied soldiers left behind after Dunkerque. She hid them, fed them, and helped them to escape. One of her neighbors in the village of Lézennes (Nord Department) denounced her in February of 1941, and she was condemned to death by the Germans. By waiting until February, the informer gave her a full six months to save scores of soldiers.

In the same area of France, in Béthune, one man was able to rescue fifty-seven French and British soldiers, most of whom had been hidden for months by farmers who didn't know how to pass them along. M. Assart (in 1944, Resistance Captain Assart, killed in the liberation fighting) worked out an escape route, the basis for the Resistance network he would later lead.

There was a group in the city of Nancy, the capital of Lorraine, which passed on 6781 escaped prisoners in a year and a half. This group stayed together to become the Resistance réseau Lorraine. (The word "réseau" can be literally translated as "network," but network has connotations of vastness and prosperity which don't apply to the Resistance.)

Through the hamlet of Champagne-sur-Loue (Jura Department), four miles from the demarcation line, 150 escaping prisoners a night were slipped across the line. The population of Champagne-sur-Loue was 145.

At the beginning of 1942, the Germans in a border village arrested an Alsatian woodcutter named Weissenbach. When they turned out his pockets they found a dozen compasses and letters of thanks from boys he had helped across the line. Backtracking, the Germans unearthed a réseau which had been started in 1940 in Strasbourg by one girl, working alone. Other people, mostly girls, had sent her escapees from other points. She would meet them kneeling before the statue of the Virgin in the Church of St. John. They would give her a simple password, and she would lead them out of the town, through the fields and to an unguarded spot on the border.

By the time the Germans got to it, it was a well-founded organization. It had reception and outlet centers around the province, and by 1942 was aiding the escape of young Alsatians drafted into labor battalions in June of 1941. The girl, Lucienne Welschinger, and four of her aides were condemned to death.

Foreigners as well as Frenchmen helped. A band of American Quakers in Marseille aided refugees of many nationalities. The American consul there and the U.S. military attaché at Vichy stretched the word "neutral" as far as they could without causing an international incident.

A lone British officer, Ian Garrow, with the help of French friends, forged a genuine escape route all the way down from Paris to the Spanish border. This was not a matter of one friend simply handing on a fugitive to another friend, but a relay of safe houses and guides. When Garrow was betrayed by one of his group, his place was taken by a Belgian physician,

Dr. Albert Guérisse, known as Lieutenant Commander Pat O'Leary.

Later, the O'Leary organization grew to be very large. It did not content itself merely with sending fugitives (principally crews of crashed British and U.S. aircraft) out of the country. It developed techniques for jailbreaks, for bribing prison guards and corrupting German officials to save their men. In urgent cases, their radios could summon submarines, fishing vessels and even motor torpedo boats to pick up "packages" along the Mediterranean coast.

Mrs. Etta Shiber, widow of an American journalist, impulsively hid an English officer in the trunk of her car as she returned to Paris after the exodus. Involved by happenstance, she took seriously to rescue work. Using her Red Cross papers, she spirited British and French prisoners out of military hospitals.

Using the name of one of her clandestine English passengers, she even put ads in the papers. In this way she came upon several isolated soldiers in hiding, and an entire contingent of British hiding in a forest since Dunkerque.

She got them all on their way with the help of several highly placed French friends, but she ran her operation with such innocent club-lady fervor that she was bound to be caught. Before that happened, an informer turned her in for a German reward, and she spent long months in prison before her government — still a neutral — could arrange to exchange her for a minor German spy.

The least arduous and least difficult of the passages was across the Swiss frontier. Along a stretch of twenty-five miles all one has to do is cross Lake Geneva, unfortunately a wide and extremely deep lake. Then there is the simple matter of wading across the little Foron River near Geneva. Unfortunately, the corridor between the two countries is very narrow here and easily policed. Far more difficult, and rarely attempted, were mountain passages, over the Jura from the west, or over the Alps from the south.

The French jump-off town for Geneva was Annemasse, four miles away. The Gestapo, the Vichy police, the gendarmerie, the Gardes Mobiles, the customs service all kept watch on those who came and went at Annemasse and its surrounding hamlets.

If the fugitive were not arrested as he got off the train ("Your identity papers?"), not apprehended as he looked for a "passer," and did not try to cross without help, then the crossing was not hard. It could be a fairly simple, cautious stroll, perhaps with a little cowboy-and-Indian dodging from bush to bush. Nevertheless, it had to be well prepared, and those being passed across had to master their panic as they stood in the shadows and let a patrol pass. There was barbed wire on both sides of the Foron, and the banks were rather steep and could be slippery in wet weather. The patrols followed each other in quick succession.

Later on, many of the Resistance organizations had their regular contacts with Allied agents in Switzerland and chiefs and couriers crossed in the Annemasse region every night, in both directions. The Swiss were not very neutral toward the Germans, whom they eternally suspected of planning an attack. They weren't neutral toward the Resistance, either, but unneutral in the most hospitable way; and the Resistance gave the Swiss up-to-the-minute reports on German troop dispositions inside France.

Within a year, the entire French customs brigade in the Annemasse region was working with the Resistance. As the Resistance men made contact with the French gendarmerie and with police officials (the gendarmerie is national, the police municipal and departmental), they found more allies. Between 1943 and 1945, dozens of these patriots were arrested by Gestapo agents and by collaborationist French authorities. Whether detected or betrayed, they died.

The Spanish crossing was extremely hazardous, even with a

"passer." There are roads, but these are useless to the escapee. There are railroads too, at either end of the Pyrenees, but these can be used only with the complicity of a railroad crew. It was the rare fugitive who had the necessary connections to allow him to ride as assistant baggage man or brakeman to the end of the French line, where he'd go off to the railroad hostel with the rest of the crew, a few hundred yards from Spain. The only "practical" way to go was by smugglers' trails over the worst part of the mountains.

Most of the illegal travelers came laden with baggage, with the wrong clothes, and shoes too new (black market) or too light for the climb, which could take as long as three nights (hiding out by day). Almost all came with the wrong bodies. It was not only a grueling climb, but a high-speed scramble as well.

Those not being convoyed by some underground group paid out exhorbitant sums to the "travel agency," only to be told halfway across by their guide that he had not been paid his share and would lead them no farther until they gave him money. Foreigners were always conspicuous while waiting, and always in danger. Thousands were scooped up while waiting in summer hotels in the dead of winter. It has been estimated that in four years some thirty thousand managed to get across into Spain (often to be interned). This is probably one-third of the number that started out.

There were deaths on the mountain, some from the usual dangers: avalanches, rock slides, falls from heights. Here and there — but the cases are rare — a passer killed a client who, with a broken ankle or leg, could not go on and who could not be carried. ("I could not leave him there to die like a dog" — Lazare Cabrero, acquitted 1953 of the charge of murdering Jacques Grumbacher, an editor of the Socialist paper *Populaire,* in the mountains in November 1942.)

At least one passer was found guilty of surrendering his whole party to the Germans in return for the reward. But other passers lost their lives on the trail, and others were arrested and deported to death camps by the Germans. And there were many passers who worked without fee.

Some who started for Spain never got out of Paris. Some made arrangements with Dr. Petiot, steered to him by a hairdresser and a beautician, each of whom got 5000 francs commission for each new client. The clients were buying a trip straight through to South America, a trip only for the very rich, and the prices were enormous. But after all, South America . . .

The nearest subway station was, appropriately, Argentine. It was a chic district, not far from the Etoile. Arriving at the doctor's office with baggage and all their valuables, the men and women were embarked. From the evidence, between twenty-seven and thirty of them were first asphyxiated, then carved into small pieces and burned in the basement furnace. If a man said he'd found passage to South America and then disappeared it was nothing strange in those days. People dropped out of sight all the time. The law did not catch up with Petiot until March of 1944.

The German border line that gave the most trouble to the most people was the line of demarcation severing occupied France from Vichy France (also called "the Southern Zone," also called "the Non-Occupied Zone," also called "the So-called Free Zone"). It was established June 25, 1940.

Although refugees were encouraged to return northward over the line, anyone wanting to go south needed an *Ausweis* from the Germans, who issued very few of these. Postal communication across the line was closed. Millions of people were frantically seeking lost relatives, but mail could go through only when it was smuggled through. Many benevolent border dwellers, whose names were soon known throughout the occupied zone, took thousands of letters and packages across in both directions, to be mailed on the other side.

After three months, the Germans allowed mail between

families to cross the line. The dispensation was the same for everyone: one printed postcard of thirteen lines, with short blanks that could be filled in and words that could be left or crossed out. The first five lines: the date (line one) followed by

(2) blank in good health, blank fatigued.
(3) blank lightly, gravely, ill, wounded.
(4) blank killed, blank prisoner.
(5) blank dead, blank without news of blank.

Stark and sterile as they were, between three hundred thousand and half a million of these "family cards" went across the line every day. In May 1941, "free correspondence" was re-established, with permission to send unillustrated postcards with whatever message the sender wanted to write.

Inspection of those crossing the demarcation line was severe, especially of railroad passengers, who were often made to get off the train with their hand baggage and pass through police and customs inspection at the station. In some places the inspection included all the linings of the clothing and all the apertures of the voyager.

Crossing was considerably simpler in those towns where the demarcation line wandered through streets and across buildings. Out in the country, it sliced across farms. Still, on either side of the border on any surfaced road, there were apt to be roadblocks for spot checks.

All this made it necessary for those passing the line illegally to have false papers which could pass a cursory examination. In the latter years of the occupation (the line was not abolished until February 1943, even though the Germans occupied the whole of France November 11, 1942) it would be necessary to have papers which would stand up to a complete examination, including a check with the issuing authority.

Every possible dodge for crossing the interior "frontiers" of

France, short of going over the line in a balloon, was tried at one time or another. Following a funeral cortege, crashing the barrier in a truck, hiding behind the merchandise of a supplier regularly crossing the line, playing the role of corpse in a hearse, seducing a border guard, floating across rivers behind logs, wearing German uniform, playing feebleminded or deaf and dumb, secreted in a compartment in a locomotive tender, all these and variations on them were tried. They worked hundreds of thousands of times.

THE PEN AND THE SWORD

The escape routes were essential not only to those who had to get out, but also to those who wanted to get out to join General de Gaulle.

This tank-corps officer had been pulled out of battle (his unit scored the single successful offensive by French arms against the Germans) and put into Premier Reynaud's cabinet. It cannot be explained exactly what kind of thinking produced this vacancy for the General. He had long made enemies among politicians and his senior officers by his advocacy of a mechanized army coordinated with air power. His theories had been adopted in toto by the German Army. The Third Republic, having rejected his theories, had no such armies, but they did have the theoretician, and they called upon him.

After thirteen days in the post of undersecretary of state for war, some of it spent on missions to Churchill, de Gaulle rejected the defeatism of the Government and the General Staff. On the seventeenth of June, he left Bordeaux by air for London, to carry on France's war — alone, if he had to.

Next night he spoke over the London radio:

France has lost a battle!
But France has not lost the war!
The men who happen to head the government may have capitu-

lated, yielding to panic, forgetting honor, delivering the land over to servitude. Yet nothing is lost!

Nothing is lost because this war is a world war. In the free universe, tremendous forces have not yet been brought into play. Some day these forces will crush the enemy. On that day, France must be present at her victory. Then she will recover her liberty and her greatness. Such is my aim, my only aim!

This is why I invite all Frenchmen, wherever they may be, to join me in action, in sacrifice and in hope.

Our country is in mortal peril. Let us all fight to save her.

Vive la France!

It was a magnificent speech, an historic rallying cry. But it was heard by almost nobody to whom it was addressed. Millions of French soldiers were either being marched off as prisoners or retreating, or, here and there, still fighting. Millions upon millions of civilians were out on the roads of France, hungry, frightened and frightful. Of those who were at home, few heard the call: the habit of listening to British broadcasts, like other habits of the occupation years, had not yet been formed.

Vichy brought de Gaulle's Free French movement to the attention of the French. They condemned him in a communiqué after his radio appeal. Not long after, in absentia, he was condemned to death as a traitor.

There was no rush to answer his call. Thousands of French troops in the British Isles were given the choice of joining de Gaulle or going back to France. Most of them went home.

There was General Charbonneau, whose own idea it was to remain and fight alongside the British with the odds and ends of French troops pulled out of Norway, out of Dunkerque, Normandy and Brittany. Charbonneau thought it was unseemly of Charles de Gaulle to seek to take command over him, his senior in every respect. The relationship between the two generals festered quickly. Charbonneau asked British permission to go back to France with his men. Permission was granted.

According to Admiral Auphand's Vichy figures, repatriated French personnel numbered thirty thousand. The Navy — with an evergreen anti-British sentiment — brought home twenty thousand, the Army about eight thousand, the Merchant Marine, two thousand.

Who stayed with de Gaulle? Seven weeks after his appeal, he had 98 officers, 113 NCO's, 716 soldiers and sailors and 1188 civilians. Greatly encouraging was the arrival of several small groups who came out of France at great hazard to answer the call. Some half-dozen were aviators who stole planes. A couple of dozen were young men from the Atlantic and Channel coasts who came in small boats. Virtually the entire male population of the Ile de Sein, 133 of them between the ages of fourteen and fifty, arrived in their six fishing boats. They had left behind on their treeless rock off the Breton coast all the women, young boys and old men, with little money, few supplies and no means whatever of making a living.

In these first months of the French defeat de Gaulle did not collect an army, did not effect a national uprising. But he did speak the word "resistance," and he did give the lie to the Pétainist line.

This line was described by Massotte, an early resistant, as follows: "*Mea culpa, mea maxima culpa!* We are horses' asses and we richly deserve the way we've wound up, as the *salauds* that we are."

The German and Vichy propaganda were both designed to persuade the French that defeat was their natural environment, that resistance was criminal, and that the enemy was not Hitler. Everything was the fault of somebody other than the Vichyites and the Nazis. Blame the Jews, blame the British, blame the Third Republic, blame the Socialists, Communists, trade unions, blame yourselves. Shut up. Suffer. Obey.

Wrenching human beings from the physical grasp of the Germans was the first Resistance task. Simultaneously, there was another mission to accomplish: to stop the brainwashing, to combat the propaganda.

The day after de Gaulle spoke, stickers appeared on walls in different sections of Paris. They were hand printed on gummed paper, the kind being sold to protect windows in air raids. The first said *A single foe — the invader.* The next said *Liberty — Equality — Fraternity — Vive de Gaulle!* Paulin Bertrand and three friends lettered thousands of these and others, and went all around Paris pasting them on the sides of bridges and on lampposts. They even had a series of taunts in German which they plastered on German automobiles.

In July 1940 Jean Texier produced a brochure, "Counsel to the Occupied." The printer, Keller on the rue Rochechouart in Paris, did a loving letterpress job, though he did it in secret. The "counsels" were thirty-three short, numbered paragraphs. Their style was extremely light, but direct. In supple, simple French, they made an elegant contrast with the bombast launched by the Germans and the collaborators. This gave them wide readership, this and the fact that they continued to think of Frenchmen as the true inhabitants of their own country, and the invader as the invader. They were really a guide to the preservation of individual dignity, guide to a French conduct more icily "correct" than the German.

For example, No. 8: "Ever since they have 'occupied' you, they parade in your dishonor. Will you stay to watch? Interest yourselves rather in the window displays. This is much more moving, because at the rate they are filling up their trucks, you will soon find nothing left to buy."

The brochure was copied on typewriters, by hand, mimeographed, circulated all around the country. In September, the Counsels were read over the London radio, having been smuggled back by the first Gaullist secret agent sent to France.

Counsel No. 30: "You grumble because they oblige you to

get back home by exactly 11 P.M. Innocent, haven't you understood this is to let you listen to the English radio?"

In September Texier put out a second series, and later published several other clandestine brochures. Later he became editor of one of the great underground papers, *Libération*, which began appearing the first of December, 1940, typed out in Paris by Christian Pineau.

In October, *Pantagruel* appeared. It was the work of Raymond Deiss, the music publisher to whom credit has been given for "discovering" the young composers Milhaud, Honneger, Auric, and Poulenc. His printers, the brothers René and Robert Blanc on the rue Dauphine, produced the four-page monthly which summarized the BBC news broadcasts. Deiss published sixteen numbers before he was arrested in October 1941. The printers were arrested too.

This same month *L'Université Libre* appeared for the first time, and kept on throughout the war. Another Sorbonne underground paper was the student-published *Maintenir*.

France, Libère-toi was a hand-copied paper in the forbidden region of the Vosges. In the Nord Department, the Socialist action committee issued *L'Homme Libre,* whose first editor was arrested in June 1941.

In December 1940 appeared the first news sheet to be called *Résistance,* badly mimeographed on both sides of two pages. It was subtitled "Official Bulletin of the National Committee for Public Safety."

Resist! This is the cry in all of your hearts. . . . But you feel yourselves isolated and disarmed, and in the chaos of ideas, opinions and systems you look for where your duty lies. To resist is to keep your heart and your head. But it is above all to act, to do something which yields positive results through useful and reasoned action. Many have tried and have been discouraged, seeing themselves powerless. Others have formed groups. But often their groups have found themselves in their turn isolated and impotent. Patiently

and with difficulty, we have sought one another out and have
united. . . . The method? Form groups in your homes with those
whom you know. Those whom you designate will be your chiefs . . .

With discernment, enroll resolute men, and staff them with your
best. Strengthen and comfort those who doubt and those who no
longer dare hope. Every day, gather and transmit information which
can be of use to your leaders. Practice an inflexible discipline, a
constant prudence, an absolute discretion. Beware of lightweights,
those who talk too much, and traitors. Never boast, never make
confidences. Steel yourselves and face up to your own needs.

Our committee, in order to coordinate your efforts with those
of unoccupied France and those who fight alongside our allies,
will command. Your immediate task is to organize so that you may,
on the day when you receive the order, take up the combat again.

We have only one ambition, one passion, one wish: to accomplish
the rebirth of a France that is pure and free.

What was this National Committee for Public Safety? It was
a group of scholars at the Museum of Man. They were not a
coordinating nor a command group because there was not yet
anything to coordinate or to command, but they hoped to be.
(Eventually, through others, the hope would be a reality.)
Their dream gave hope and strength to others. They seemed
to be tangible proof that the Resistance did exist and was,
what is more, organized.

In January 1941, Léon Maurice Nordmann, a Paris lawyer,
was arrested for "diffusion of the tract *Résistance.*" Boris Vildé,
co-founder of the paper, was implored by his friends to leave
Paris, and went south to Marseille. But when the other co-
founder, Anatole Levitsky, was arrested in February, along
with the museum's librarian, Yvonne Oddon, Vildé insisted on
returning to Paris. He hoped to convince the Germans that
he alone was responsible, and that the others would be released. He failed, and seven of them were shot. Vildé insisted
that he be the one to endure waiting, and was the last to go
before the firing squad at Mont-Valérien.

Others took up the work, and the chain for distributing the paper did become an effective resistance network. However, the Germans struck again at the leadership in July 1941, and again in November 1942, when six were shot, five decapitated and others deported. After that, what was left of the membership joined either a different, new organization called Résistance or another group, Ceux de la Résistance.

In the Vichy zone, where there were no German uniforms, no *Bekanntmachungen* from German rulers, and where the region was rapt in gratitude to Marshal Pétain, resistance nevertheless began. It was not widespread, nor did it immediately affect many persons, but it was there.

Air Force General Cochet, who went to his home in the Auvergne after the armistice, sat down and began writing letters. He wrote ceaselessly and sent them in all directions. They were open letters, meant to be passed on to as many readers as possible. They were full of a general's fury at the acceptance of defeat, of treating with the enemy, of all the Vichy head-in-the-sand policies. An organization of young enthusiasts sprang up to circulate the general's letters.

General Cochet made one tactical error: he *signed* his letters. Vichy authorities were reluctant to do anything at that early moment, to do anything to blemish the image of the high military in their zone, but eventually, reluctantly, in 1941 they were forced to arrest him. After two months, they released him. He resumed his activities instantly, adding to his epistolary activities the gathering and stocking of weapons. They arrested him again in September of '42, he escaped and was taken to London. His réseau joined Combat, by then a growing organization with scores of réseaux.

Combat grew out of the fusion of two groups, Liberté and Vérités, both of which began in 1940 in Marseille. *Liberté* was the name of a clandestine publication run by three professors of law, François de Menthon, Paul Coste-Floret, Pierre-Henri Teitgen, and a well-known journalist, Remy Roure.

Vérités began with the idea that propaganda was just words, that what was needed was action. The action would be planned, however, and required detailed preparation first, and then recruitment of an organization. Last would come equipment of the membership for warfare. Its founder thought of his fighting wing as the Secret Army, a name that stuck with it through the underground years. The organization owed its existence to one man, Captain Henri Frenay. At the end, it was a fighting machine with something like seventy thousand members.

There were a dozen other groups in both zones which began fighting against the counsels of defeat and of collaboration. Their pamphlets, leaflets, bulletins, newspapers cut through the fog of fear and confusion, the desperate wish that everything would be all right in the end, that everything would be as it was before. The German "correctness" and the old Marshal's platitudes initially had spread a layer of soothing froth over the physical and moral suffering.

In view of the Stalin-Hitler peace pact, the Communist Party issued no call for resistance. When the Germans took over Paris, some Party leaders presented themselves to the occupation officials and were promptly jailed, joining other Communists imprisoned by the frightened Third Republic in 1939. The Communist newspaper *L'Humanité* asked permission to come up from underground. The occupation authorities chose to view its publishers as French revolutionaries rather than as auxiliaries of the Soviet ally.

After this rebuff, Communist leaflets, stickers and newspapers continued to flow from underground. They castigated all war efforts and denounced the Vichy authoritarian state with as much vigor as they lambasted de Gaulle, a mercenary in the pay of the British imperialists.

Ignoring Party directives, however, there were hundreds of Communists who rose up with other Frenchmen to say "No!" to the invaders. They joined with non-Communist resistance pioneers; individuals and small groups took action by themselves. The first resistant to be shot during the occupation was a Communist, Pierre Roche, nineteen years old.

Pierre was a sheet-metal worker in the closely guarded Atlantic port of Royan. Two detectives came up from the Bordeaux Police Department after the German telephone cable had been cut between Royan and its sister port of La Rochelle, and they found their man. He was sentenced to two years at hard labor by the French court, which then turned him over to the local German military court, which took a more serious view of his crime. On September 7, 1940, he was shot.

Between July and the end of the first week in September, the Paris police arrested 1141 Communists, announced the smashing of thirty-seven different leaflet-producing groups and the seizure of their printing machines.

From July to the end of 1940, there were forty published accounts of sabotage in the occupied zone: cutting of telephone lines and long-distance cables installed by the Germans; derailment of trains by forcing switch points and by unbolting rails; the burning of German motor pools, of a flour mill on the outskirts of Paris, of a military bedding depot in the center of Paris, of a warehouse on the edge of Paris. In widely separated spots, men were arrested for possessing arms, for stealing guns and dynamite.

The Germans drafted Frenchmen of military age to guard roads and cables. In the town of Evreux, all males born between 1915 and 1922 had to report nightly to the local armory, where they were locked in until morning. Town after town saw the curfew extended to twelve hours — 7 P.M. to 7 A.M. — during which period no one was allowed on the streets. Town after town was hit with huge collective fines — two million, three million, five million francs — to "pay" for sabotage.

In the early days after the armistice, the Mediterranean ports were receiving shiploads of minerals and food from North Africa. Although the British blockade closed Atlantic ports to merchant shipping, it was not rigorously applied in the Mediterranean. The dock workers, along with escaped prisoners, were among the first to see behind the mask of *Korrektion.*

They were ordered to sort the food cargoes arriving in Sète, Port Bouc and other ports, the good stuff for Germany, the rejects for France. By dumping in a few basketsful of rotten vegetables among the good, dock workers insured the spoilage of pretty much the whole shipment by the time the train was unloaded in Germany. "A bottle of acid poured over a truck-load of good vegetables would create a sort of V-shaped wedge of decay on the journey."

Railroad men, among the first resistants, among the bravest, staunchest, and most effective of all who made the Resistance, soon evolved techniques for thwarting the Nazis. By switching the bills of lading attached to each car, they could "lose" cars. Those in higher echelons could "lose" whole trains, and those at the top caused serious shortages of freight cars by "losing" empties.

Little "accidents" in the yard, the kind that happen every day, began happening in greater number, delaying trains, spoiling timetables. Shipments were misrouted, fragile articles were dropped in loading. As the years passed, the railroaders developed new techniques and refined their skills.

There were always the small but deadly acts of sabotage impossible to trace back to the source: sand and emery in the axle grease boxes, three lumps of coal dropped on the ballast for every lump tossed into the fire box, the fouling of water lines.

On October 30, 1940, all over France, including the occupied zone (the Germans did not often allow Vichy posters in their territory), red-white-and-blue posters appeared. In the center was a stern paternal photo of Pétain, seen from below, from child's eye level.

In this announcement there appeared for the first time, officially, the word "collaboration." The Marshal had been to see Hitler, October 24. He intimated that this was quite an achievement:

Such an interview has been possible, four months after the defeat of our arms, only by grace of the dignity of the French in the face of their ordeal, by grace of the immense effort of regeneration to which they have lent themselves. . . .

France has found herself. This first encounter between victor and vanquished marks the first step upward for our country. . . .

A collaboration has been envisaged between our two countries. I have accepted it in principle. The details will be worked out later. . . .

It is in all honor and in order to maintain French unity — a unity of ten centuries — in the framework of a constructive activity in the new European order that I enter today on the way of collaboration. . . .

This collaboration should be sincere. It should be exclusive of all thought of aggression. It must comport a patient and confident effort. . . .

This policy is mine. The ministers are responsible only to me. It is I alone that History will judge.

Until now, I have used with you the language of a father. Today I speak to you in the language of a Chief.

Follow me. Keep your confidence in *la France éternelle.*

The meeting took place at Montoire. In the newsreels, the French could see him taking the salute of three German generals, reviewing a battalion of Hitler's guard posted as guard of honor, and on the station platform, the manly handshake with Adolf Hitler.

For the millions who continued to esteem the Marshal, to believe that they owed him fealty because he had saved a fragment of France from direct German rule, it provoked fur-

ther agonies of conscience. For some, the handshake and all
that it represented was a horrid revelation. They rejected collaboration; some now undertook resistance. Still, for others,
the handshake was a seal that guaranteed the correctness and
respectability of collaboration, confirmed the criminality of
resistance.

The French programs of the British Broadcasting Company
hammered at the Montoire meeting as they did at all of the
Marshal's moves closer to Hitler. The news broadcasts came
on the air at fixed intervals, twelve times a day. The nine-
thirty evening programs were followed by five minutes of
Gaullist propaganda, and a half-hour variety program, "Frenchmen Speaking to Frenchmen." Later on, three times a day,
there were a total of sixteen minutes air time for "Personal
Messages." These were signal phrases for parachute drops of
agents and supplies, for airplane landings, for submarine or
surface craft arrivals, for specific Resistance actions. They were
not coded sentences, but arbitrary password phrases which
meant, "The plane you were expecting tonight cannot come"
or "Okay to set fire to the two barges by the bridge." They
were such phrases as "Marianne detests oysters," or "My wife
has sharp eyes."

The occupying power quickly recognized the danger in this
dissemination of truthful news and in the daily injection of hope
from the Gaullist speakers. During the first autumn they decreed: "Listening to foreign radio stations as well as the deliberate diffusion of news from foreign radio stations is
forbidden."

The decree listed those stations which Frenchmen were
permitted to hear. These included any German stations, and
broadcasts from occupied Czechoslovakia, Norway, Poland, the
Low Countries and France. Listening to the three Vichy stations was allowed as well.

Not long after, the Paris police posted a notice.

BEWARE OF RUMORS

The surveillance exercised in public places has led in the past few days to the arrest of persons who spread news which is entirely false and of a nature to provoke disquiet among the population. The Prefect of Police puts the public on guard against such actions, which will be the subject of severe prosecution and penalties.

The "entirely false" and disquieting news spread by the rumor mongers (the police eavesdropping, the arrests, did not stop Frenchmen from talking, especially in food queues where irritation ran high) — these came from the BBC.

During a broadcast beamed to France on July 14, the first of five Bastille Days under the occupation, Winston Churchill said: "This is the war of the unknown soldiers."

At that moment, all over France, the first handful of unknown soldiers had already begun to fight.

The Enemy

VICHY

Maréchal, nous voila!
Devant toi, le sauveur de la France,
Nous jurons, nous, les gars,
De servir et de suivre tes pas.

Marshal, we are here!
Before you, the savior of France,
We fellows, we all swear
To serve, in your steps, anywhere.

THIS song, one of dozens composed in honor of Henri Philippe Pétain, was virtually the national anthem of Vichy. At the outset, millions of Frenchmen believed that the aged Marshal was the embodiment not only of all virtue, but of all virtue which was traditionally French. Honor, courage, loyalty, dignity, piety, vigor, national pride and personal humility, these were all personified in the Marshal. His photograph not only was on sale in all the shops, but could be conveniently purchased right at home through the postman: a choice of five views at 5 francs (13 cents) each, and many took all five.

It was a perfect orgy of flags, portraits, bugle calls, parades, pledges, orations, dedications and re-dedications. It was an eternal camp meeting of fellowship in a great cause under a great leader in a great tradition. Much was made of morality, motherhood (Mother's Day in France was a Vichy promotion. It survives.) and religious devotion (Down with the Freemasons!).

The family, always of signal anthropological importance in France, was spread to cover the whole population (excepting Jews, Communists, Gaullists and Freemasons) and Pétain was the Daddy of Them All. Father knew best, and his watchwords were Order, Obedience, Service, Faith.

There were no elections under the Vichy regime. There were no strikes and no labor unions. No military conscription. The news on the radio and in the newspapers was all good news: the editors were told which items to feature and how to feature them.

There was the resoundingly phrased Charter of Labor, there was the Army, and the Navy, and the knowledge that the Marshal — he said so himself in his first speech — would not tell you any lies.

Pétain's Army was limited by armistice terms to one hundred thousand men (a figure not then published), exactly what the Germans had been permitted by the Treaty of Versailles. The Navy was to stay in port.

For unemployed young men, there were the Chantiers de Jeunesse (Youth Work Centers) for the healthy mind in the healthy body. Something more than Boy Scouts and something considerably less than soldiers, they lived in cabins in the woods practicing forestry and allegiance to the Marshal. The term was eight months, and at the end of every period, some ninety thousand youths passed through.

For those who wanted the sensation of belonging actively to the Marshal's "great work in the renovation of France," there was the Légion des Combattants (Veterans' Legion). This group, nine-tenths of them veterans of the First World

War, had the effect of making every crossroads village a happily boiling cauldron of Pétainism.

For the New France, there were two new political parties, both "more royalist than the king." The Rassemblement National Populaire was led by Marcel Déat, later Secretary of State for Labor and National Solidarity. The Parti Populaire Français was a native fascist party directed by one-time Communist Jacques Doriot. It attempted to foment a French brand of national socialism, which appealed to the pride of the prejudiced: for the capitalists no more strikes, for the workers a theoretical say in the running of the businesses which employed them.

Since both of these were absolutely projections of the Nazi creed, they were encouraged in the occupied zone. The Légion des Combattants, deliriously Pétainist and Old France, was not able to organize in the north.

Once the authoritarian Etat Français had been substituted for the République Français, the Vichy regime spread its attack on democracy. Mayors and town councils who did not satisfy the government, who were not ardently enough Pétainist, were removed from office (seventy municipal councils suspended, two-thirds of the mayors of towns over ten thousand population). By November, new decrees abolished election of these local authorities.

All trade unions were dissolved and, under the Charter of Labor, workers were incorporated in the State Union.

A Police Service for Secret Societies was instituted, not to attack resistance organizations, but to destroy Freemasonry. The Grand Orient, governing body of the Masons, was dissolved and the society declared illegal. Freemasons were denounced in Vichy propaganda as among the most fearsome enemies of the State.

Jews, though not obliged to wear the yellow star (for which each surrendered one coupon from the textile ration card) as they were in the occupied zone, were banished from government jobs, from the professions, and from some forms of business. A special branch of police for Jewish questions was set up. There was some embarrassment when the pro-church government found its anti-Semitic tactics publicly opposed by the authorities of both Catholic and Protestant churches of the unoccupied zone.

The schools were attacked, too, as hotbeds of democracy. Normal schools were closed as anti-religious. School teachers were fired for being too laic and not sufficiently "patriotic." Later, school books by known Gaullists were forbidden.

The Vichy police were more than zealous in their search for Gaullists, and those whom they caught trying to escape to join the General were given long prison terms. Former officers of the armed services, viewed as traitors, received especially brutal treatment. There was, of course, the Special Anti-Communist Police Service, too.

Within a year, the Légion des Combattants had become La Légion Française des Combattants et des Volontaires de la Révolution Nationale. By 1942, it was decided to add shock troops to the organization, since the organization itself was diminishing and showed less ardor for the National Revolution. Thus the Service d'Ordre de la Légion, for the young, eager and muscular, was formed. The oath: "I swear to fight against democracy, against Gaullist dissidence and against the Jewish leprosy."

In 1943, when it had attracted twenty-five thousand members, it was dissolved and replaced by the Milice, who were hated even more than the Germans. They were a fully equipped little army of young Frenchmen, with special spy services to uncover resistants and to infiltrate resistance movements. They were noted for their joyous viciousness. Auxiliaries of the German Army, they had a license to kill, and in the closing year of the war they used it at whim.

In 1941 Pétain found himself blessing the Légion des Volontaires Français Contre le Bolchevism. This recruited Frenchmen of military age into the Wehrmacht. As an anti-Communist and a collaborationist, there was no way for the Marshal not to endorse the LVF. About five thousand Frenchmen enlisted in this way, to fight as German soldiers. Later on, the Waffen SS, Himmler's own army, also recruited Frenchmen.

Nevertheless, there was a widespread belief — which persisted a quarter of a century later — that the old Marshal was playing a subtle double game. To some extent, he was. Certainly his government was in close contact with the Allies. The moment his tiny army was formed, it began at once to conceal vehicles and weapons not allowed under the armistice, and which were supposed to be surrendered to the Germans.

The Army's intelligence branch, outlawed under the armistice, continued to function, in both zones and inside Germany. Counterintelligence operatives arrested every German spy they could find in the Vichy zone, and Vichy courts jailed the spies.

Pétain was credited with saving what he could from the debacle, with maintaining a French state on French soil, with doing what losers throughout the ages have done — humoring the conqueror in order to survive as a people, and then, when the chance to doublecross him came, rising to the occasion. The occasion arose, but not the Marshal.

The Armistice Army had its sealed orders for combat ready. When the Allies landed in North Africa, November 1942, the secret alert was given. Some units would withdraw onto high ground and hold out against the Germans as long as they could. Others would drive toward targets of attack. Meanwhile, Pétain would go to Algiers and sign a treaty of alliance with the Allies, and declare war on Germany. Then the Allies could land on the French Mediterranean coast, coming to the aid of the ten-thousand-man Vichy Army.

The Army waited for Pétain, who astonished them by saying no. He had promised to remain with the French people, come what may, he said, and he wouldn't desert them now. The orders were cancelled. Only General de Lattre de Tassigny ordered his troops to prepare to march. He set out ahead for the assigned secret command post. Almost the moment he was gone, a brace of Vichy generals swooped down on the barracks and countermanded de Lattre's orders. De Lattre spent some time in prison before breaking out to join de Gaulle. (De Gaulle: "Well! You look the same as ever." De Lattre: "You are much bigger.") The Armistice Army was dissolved, and its caches of arms either spotted by the Germans or revealed by mercenary civilians. Literally thousands of officers, freed from their obligation to the Marshal, joined the Resistance.

Those former soldiers who had been assigned to lead the youth camps joined the Resistance, too, when STO (compulsory labor service, for work in Germany) was instituted by the Germans in 1943. Those eight months of outdoor work, solid food and military-patriotic indoctrination had turned a potential army of delinquents into a corps of reliable young men. When Vichy signed the pact delivering them to the German slavers, they sought out their old leaders and took to the hills, to the maquis.

The French Home Fleet, one of the great prizes of the war, and the one really strong card in the Vichy hand, scuttled itself in Toulon harbor rather than be taken by the Germans. This was hailed by the Resistance and by the Free French as a major victory. But as a victory, it was negative. Had the Navy not been so insulated by its other-worldly sense of prestige, not been so blindly anti-British, it could have steamed out of port and joined the Allied armada a week earlier.

Other services of the Vichy government worked with the Allies. Every single branch had some members working with the Resistance, though certainly not officially, as with the Allies.

The magistrature and the bar (with some exceptions, naturally) refused to give a cloak of legality to actions outside French law, and the Government was forced to set up "special tribunals," the identity of whose members was kept secret. These anonymous judges had one sole function: to hear charges of "terrorist activity" preferred against French prisoners and to condemn to death those so charged.

The last Premier of the Third Republic had warned those who urged surrender in 1940: "You take Hitler for Wilhelm I, an old gentleman who took Alsace-Lorraine away from us. Well, Hitler — Hitler is Genghis Khan."

Even after the men of Vichy found out how horribly true this was, they continued their policy of collaboration. Up until the very end, the trumpets blew and the sentries snapped to attention every time the Marshal went through the doors of the requisitioned Hôtel du Parc in Vichy. The charade of sovereignty continued until the Germans told them that the game was over. They had known, the Vichyites, for some time that the game was up, that indeed the whole party was over. But they kept on playing because they could not stop: there was nowhere else to go.

For a while, it was a glorious epoch for those lesser fry who all their lives had been unrecognized big fish. Here at last was the moment when they stood revealed as persons of consequence. All their lives they had been muttering, "I'll show them." And now they showed them.

THE GESTAPO

Having conquered France, the German Army wanted to run the occupied territory in its own way, though other of Hitler's satraps coveted the power and the plunder. The German Army General Staff was engaged in a power struggle against Heinrich Himmler. Himmler felt that he, like Hitler, was perfectly capable of conducting a war, and wanted to build his SS units into an army of his own.

The Gestapo too was Himmler's. The Army didn't want it spying on its officers and encroaching on its authority in the conquered province. But the Gestapo came to Paris nevertheless, sneaking in among the very first troops, disguised as

Geheime Feld Polizei. There were only twenty of them, but they were experts hand picked by Heydrich under direct orders from Himmler.

The Army was obliged to accept the accreditation of Otto Abetz as German Ambassador to France, and then discovered he had been assigned to Paris with official responsibility for security and propaganda, both civilian and military. The Army had the Abwehr (German Intelligence) and its own security police (Feldgendarmerie). It also was assured of the cooperation of the French police, and installed liaison men in the Prefecture.

The Army's system for keeping order in France was to issue orders to be enforced by the French authorities (excepting the anti-Jewish campaign, which they left to Eichmann's specialists). The Army's policy did not produce the German idea of order. At a continuously accelerating tempo, stabbings, stranglings, shootings, bombings of occupation personnel continued from the beginning and through 1941. Mass trials, large rewards, community fines, extension of curfew hours, savage reprisals with the slaughter of hundreds of hostages did not curb the "terrorists" of the Resistance.

In part, it went this way in 1941:

July 19   Paris mechanic executed for "insults to German Army" during forbidden Bastille Day manifestation, Place de la République.

     24   A second July 14th celebrant executed. His crime — singing "Marseillaise."

Aug. 13   German officer killed near Porte d'Orléans. At opposite end of Paris, Porte St. Denis, street riot, with demonstrators shouting for food.

     15   Another street demonstration.

     16   Another.

19 Two Communist organizers of Porte St. Denis executed.

21 German naval officer shot dead in subway station in Montmartre. Attempted assassination of Pierre Laval and Marcel Déat, head of collaborationist party, Rassemblement National Populaire.

27 Three more street agitators executed.

29 Count d'Estienne d'Orves and two colleagues, on secret mission from Gaullist London headquarters, executed. Under sentence of death for some time, these men were shot in reprisal for subway murder.

Sept. 3 German noncom shot on doorstep of his Paris hotel.

4 Marcel Gitton, working for Germans, shot dead by Communist underground. Was former secretary, French Communist Party.

6 Another German soldier shot. Three hostages executed.

10 German petty officer shot dead in subway corridor.

11 German soldier killed.

16 Another German soldier killed. Ten hostages shot.

20 Another dozen hostages executed.

24 Jean Catelas, Communist central committeeman, guillotined.

Oct. 21 Commander of German forces at Nantes killed in main square. Three days later forty-eight hostages shot. Reward for killers is 15 million francs.

23 Kriegsverwaltungsrat Reiners killed in Bordeaux. Fifty hostages executed.

Nov. 21 German propaganda bookstore near Sorbonne bombed.

26   Two German-requisitioned restaurants bombed.

29   German medical officer killed, Boulevard Magenta. Three soldiers killed, eight wounded in another restaurant explosion. Hostages executed December 15, 23 and 27.

The struggle for authority over the French grew sharper between the Army and the Himmler apparatus. There was only one area in which they worked together: the black market. For Himmler's men it meant power, profit, and an excellent means of corrupting and compromising leading members of the French commercial community. For the Abwehr it meant new sources of valuable information.

Almost every branch of the German Government had procurement offices in Paris which passed their orders for a staggering variety of goods (perfume, pick handles, barbed wire, butter) through a central bureau. This was known as the "Otto Bureau," after the boss, Captain Hermann Brandl of the Abwehr, who was known as Monsieur Otto. The dirty work was carried out by Wilhelm Radecke, who worked intimately with the Gestapo.

Radecke recruited as Gestapo agents some of the slimiest Parisian gangsters who had switched their operations to the black market. It was he who brought in Henri Chamberlin, known as Lafont. The prewar manager of the canteen at the Police Prefecture, Chamberlin had turned to crime and was in jail when the Nazis entered Paris. He was able to recommend twenty talented jailmates to the Gestapo, who forthwith had them released.

Working with former Police Inspector Bony, Chamberlin had his own little Gestapo branch operating from 11 rue Lauriston. Some of his recruits also had their own separate branches. Two of the most notorious were Rudy de Merode and George (Masuy) Delfane, whose torture shop was on the elegant rue Henri-Martin. In their free time, with absolute immunity, they operated in their old nonpolitical fashion, stealing whatever interested them.

In addition to the immense fortunes to be made out of ordinary black market operations — which also produced needed goods for the Germans — the Otto office had other uses. Jewelry, loose stones, and gold (usually stolen or extorted) were bought. Stock certificates either seized or stolen by the Gestapo were passed through Otto to be handled on the Paris Bourse through respectable Frenchmen in the toils of the organization, their patriotism and respectability not having been equal to their passion for a smart deal.

Through threats, economic pressure and blackmail, the Gestapo was able to acquire blocks of stock in major French corporations. These were signed over to major German corporations in which the Himmler organization already had large interests.

To make themselves more agreeable to the Germans, the French money men talked, and supplied information to the Abwehr. As a friendly gesture, they would find the answers to certain questions Otto wanted answered. And sometimes, when they could not refuse without serious risk, they simply did as they were told.

By April of 1942 Himmler won his power struggle with the German Army in France. Hitler made him, rather than the Army, responsible for German police work in occupied territory. He sent his personal representative, SS General Karl Oberg to take charge. The Army commander, Otto von Stülpnagel, gave up and ceded his command to his cousin, Heinrich von Stülpnagel. For some time, Parisians knew nothing of the change in command, since proclamations continued to be signed Der Militärbefehlshaber in Frankreich, von Stülpnagel.

Reinhard Heydrich himself came to Paris, acting for Himmler, to install the Höhere SS und Polizeiführer (Supreme Chief of the SS and the Police). To underscore the Himmler victory, Heydrich gave a reception at the Ritz, to which all German bigwigs and several high Vichy officials were invited. During the reception, Heydrich made it clear to René Bousquet, new secretary general of the French police, that he expected Bousquet's forces to be from now on a dependency of the Gestapo.

Astonishingly, Bousquet said no. He said that if the Germans would abolish their system of random hostage-taking and execution, the French police would be perfectly capable of handling order in their own country. He said his administration would cooperate with the new German police chief only if no Germans were actually installed inside the French force and the two forces were to operate separately.

It is equally astonishing that Heydrich replied that he would have to check with his superiors, and left Paris. Karl Oberg began expanding the Himmler establishment in France, leaving the Army its Abwehr spies and its control of prisons, customs and military police. The twenty-five groups of Army Security Police were reduced to two.

Then the heavy industry of dictatorship was installed, that enormous and intricately meshed police and secret police machine commonly called the Gestapo, but of which the Gestapo was but one specialized section.

Seven regional offices were added to the three that the Gestapo had managed to put into operation at Bordeaux, Dijon and Rouen, and each regional center had branches in the principal towns of its area. When the Germans took all of France in November 1942, the organization spread to cover it all: the Gestapo had 131 branch establishments plus the command posts of its special commandos and the French auxiliary units. The Army's Abwehr had sixty-nine offices of its own. The whole huge apparatus was directed toward one primary goal — destruction of the Resistance.

The Paris headquarters was reorganized when Oberg was installed. There were two main groups, Orpo and Sipo-SD. The

Orpo was the Ordnungs Polizei, police for maintaining order, the Sipo was the Sicherheitspolizei, security police specializing in investigation, and the SD was the Sicherheitsdienst des Reichsführers SS, the security service of the German SS Chief, Heinrich Himmler.

Following the Berlin model, Sipo-SD was composed of seven sections and numerous subsections. The actual Gestapo (Geheime Staats Polizei — State Secret Police) was Section IV, with the encompassing mission of "fighting enemies of the State." Its subsections and commandos handled such assignments as deportation of Jews, penetration of resistance organizations, and the development of French auxiliaries for work that even the Gestapo considered dirty.

Section V was the Kripo (criminal police) ostensibly there to combat the black market, but in reality performing laboratory and identification police routine for the Gestapo. Section IV studied French political groups with special attention to their foreign contacts, and its subsections were concerned with such varied tasks as protection of Axis VIP's visiting France, recruitment of prostitutes for German personnel, visa control, and the cultivation of Parisian high society.

The two French annexes to the Gestapo were the Intervention-Referat and Section IV Police de Secours. The first, largely recruited from French rightist political parties, operated teams for assassination, kidnapping, and raids. The second, directed by an Alsatian, ran a special training school for French agents and was responsible for the shock troops of gangsters in German pay.

Section VI also housed the Funkspiel Commando. The word "Funkspiel" is literally "radio play" but in this sense means "radio plot" or "radio trap." Direction-finder units for locating clandestine broadcast sets were disguised as ambulances or repair trucks. Dozens of these filtered across the demarcation line to operate against the underground some weeks before the Allied landings in North Africa. They did so with the complete accord of the Pétain government.

Once this new, finely fretted grid was laid over France, Oberg swiftly peopled it with agents. Critical points, such as Paris, Lyon, Marseille, and border towns such as Annemasse were saturated with operatives. The campaign against the underground was intensified by every means. Corruption was more assiduously promoted. Terror was more widely, more savagely employed. Astutely cultivated, treason flowered.

The blows against the Resistance were constant and brutal. Sometimes, through superior detective work, often through treason, sometimes as a product of the routine search and interrogation which blanketed the nation, they were able to smash at network after network.

Opposed to this vast, but nevertheless sensitive machine, was — what? The wits and the courage of the Resistance, whose members were largely unarmed until the summer of 1944.

The Resistance stiffened security and planted counter-espionage operatives of its own inside the Vichy and even inside the German services.

The Germans took a grievous toll all the same. However, the response to their increased repression was an increased resistance. In the heat of their witch cauldrons, the magic stuff of folk legend came alive. Very ordinary men were transmuted into heroes. From the fields of the slain rose up armies of vengeance. Patriotism became a living force, a manna which sustained fighters when all reasonable sustenance had been destroyed.

Vivre Dans la Defaite
C'est Mourir Tous
les Jours *

THE Resistance started spontaneously. In both zones there were those who would not be beaten. It took some time for leaders to find men of the proper caliber. It took some time for lone resisters to locate groups they could join.

After the initial fistful of men had rallied, it took some time for them to decide just what they should do to resist the conqueror. At first it was to do something, anything. Only later was it to do something useful. Since almost all of them were novices in secret warfare they did not really know what "useful" was.

Those few who were professionals, formerly officers of French Army intelligence, began gathering military information and sending it to Vichy where it could be leaked to Allied missions by Armistice Army intelligence playing the double game. But for the rest, while there was no doubt of the value of their clandestine press nor of their escape routes, they wanted more to do. They wanted to hurt the Nazis.

If they were to be spies, they needed somewhere to send their information. If they were to be saboteurs, they needed tools and explosives, and they wanted their targets to be

* "To live in defeat is to die every day." — Napoleon. The epigraph of the clandestine newspaper *Résistance*.

meaningful military objectives. If they were to be an army they needed weapons. If they had to exist underground, they needed money.

Where would all this support and direction come from? From the Allies in London, naturally. From General de Gaulle.

But curiously enough, the professionals of London did not believe in the amateurs of France. Men had to come out of France and bang on doors and thump on tables and persuade them. Substantial aid and effective liaison did not come out of London until 1942.

Some of the most enterprising groups established their own contacts with American and British intelligence, first through the diplomatic missions accredited to Vichy, later through Switzerland. Regarding their own military potential, the thinking of Resistance leaders was in advance of London all through the war. The two great concepts of unification of underground forces and of using Resistance troops as "airborne regiments already landed," were developed by the Resistance. These ideas were eventually embraced by London, but late, very late. On D-Day less than half the Resistance troops were armed.

Until the very end there existed a gulf between Free French Headquarters and interior Resistance forces. Forward troops traditionally feel misunderstood — as they often in fact are — by Headquarters. In this instance, each had problems of survival and strategy the other failed to understand. Despite the disputes, the recriminations and the reproaches to which this lack of comprehension led, the final result was victory together. The heads of the Resistance marched down the Champs-Elysées behind General de Gaulle.

Not only were there differences between the Resistance and Free French Headquarters, but there were differences between the British and the French concerning the Resistance. There were differences between the French Communist resistants and almost everybody else.

The entire Free French organization was dependent on

Great Britain for its existence. To Anthony Eden, General de
Gaulle said, "I am too poor to beg, too weak to bow." The
British found him a fatiguing guest and an astonishingly im-
perious pauper. They had kings and queens of exile govern-
ments in London who were more flexible and gracious than he.
And he was just a two-star general (temporary appointment).

That, of course, was exactly the difference so far as de Gaulle
was concerned. The kings and queens were their nations'
sovereigns. Charles de Gaulle was the self-appointed and in-
transigent defender of French sovereignty and of French
equality with other major powers.

Both of these pretentions, honest though they were, were
concepts which at times were incomprehensible to his allies.*
The Americans from the beginning looked for some other
leader. They sounded out General Weygand, they talked to
Vichy General de la Laurencie, they entertained a plan cen-
tering on Edouard Herriot, President of the Chamber of Deputies which had voted itself out of existence in favor of Marshal
Pétain, they made a deal with Admiral Darlan of the Vichy
Navy, they tried to impose General Henri Giraud on the Resistance, and even at the moment liberation began, they did not
take de Gaulle very seriously.

THE BRITISH

The British practiced some artful dodging, but they stuck
to their bargain with the prickly General. Without consulting
him, they proceeded to form their own French underground.

The British Government officially adopted a volunteer and
unofficial Scarlet Pimpernel outfit which had been organized to
rescue scientists and other notables from Hitler. It was added

* It rankled. On New Year's Eve, 1964, President de Gaulle said, "In this
year France will find the political independence she has not had since 1940."
It was the final fruit of the seeds he had planted and so fiercely guarded in
London.

to the Army's intelligence apparatus under the title of Special Operations Executive. Gradually it was expanded to direct and supply subversive groups in all the occupied countries. Section SOE/F (for France) was established early in 1941. Its aim was to deliver agents to France by parachute, light plane, boat or submarine. Its prime purpose: to organize compact information réseaux, and to aid established escape lines.

Section SOE R/F (for Resistance, France) was established some months later. It was erected to serve the Free French exclusively. Although it was a French service, it was entirely dependent on the British SOE for funds, training, equipment, transportation to and from France, and the France-England radio link. Its mission was exactly the same as that of the SOE, except that its agents served Free French intelligence, the BCRA (Central Bureau of Information and Action).

The rivalry between the SOE and the BCRA continued all through the war, so that British officers assigned to run the R/F liaison often became ardent Gaullists, sometimes critics of their British superiors. The most noted of these, Wing Commander Yeo-Thomas, not only went on secret missions for the Free French, but went over the heads of the entire British Army at the end of 1943 to plead (successfully) with Winston Churchill for more parachute drops of supplies.

For their part, the SOE operatives, when running security examinations on French men and women newly arrived in London from all over the world, strove constantly to recruit likely candidates for their own service.

Inside France, constructing réseaux, they let many a Frenchman believe that he was fighting under the banner of Free France, although he was, all unknowing, enrolled under the Union Jack. The SOE was not above trying to lure entire organizations into their service by suggesting that the British could deliver supplies and money, something the Free French were not able to do, they said.

The parachute drops of arms and funds for SOE started in June of 1941. Those for the Gaullists started the third week of January, 1942.

After the liberation of the South of France, two British officers, each in command of "private" armies of the maquis, refused to obey orders of officials of de Gaulle's Provisional Government. One of them, Captain George Scott ("Hilaire") actually stood up to de Gaulle himself when the General arrived in Toulouse. But not for very many minutes.

On the other hand, there were hundreds of other Britons dropped just before and after D-Day as instructors in weaponry, demolition and guerilla tactics. These men worked with great efficacy and complete harmony with units of the SOE, the BCRA, and the FTP (Communist), and also with units which professed no allegiance except to France and their own local hero-leaders.

Support commando units of thirty to fifty men, some with jeeps as well as bazookas and heavy machine guns, were dropped by the British-American Special Forces Headquarters to stiffen the maquis. Command liaison teams, "Jedburghs," were also dropped: one French, one British, one American officer. (The Americans merged their OSS personnel destined for France into the SOE operation when they came to England in 1943.)

Was the British "perfidious Albion" action inside France a purely military policy, a matter of keeping control of forces they organized and/or maintained? Or was it political, an attempt to remove from de Gaulle essential support of embattled French on French soil? Was it perhaps a dislike and a distrust of the Free French organization with which the British had so many sharp conflicts in London? The memoirs of the great men do not touch on this aspect of de Gaulle vs. his allies. The state papers are locked away for decades to come.

In the end, it did not make any difference, and perhaps that is why the subject is not brought up. De Gaulle persisted in his unforgivable habit of being right. His utterances, which seemed at the time to be inflated with grandiosity, proved to have been illuminated with grandeur.

In the end, the Resistance was de Gaulle's, and France was the province of its citizens, not of its liberators.

DE GAULLE AND LA RÉSISTANCE

When General de Gaulle launched his appeals from London in June of 1940, his sole aim was to keep French armed forces in the war. While summoning the French not to give up the fight, he privately offered his services to General Noguès in North Africa and to General Weygand, who could still get out of France. No reply. To General Mittelhauser (Eastern Mediterranean Command), to General Catroux (Indo-China), to High Commissioner Puaux (Syria–the Levant), to Resident General Peyrouton (Tunisia). No reply.

He persisted, nevertheless. He knit together a minuscule organization which contained not a single French personality of renown, including General Charles de Gaulle. Military intelligence was confided to a young captain, André Dewavrin, who took for his nom-de-guerre the name of a Paris subway station, Passy.

The first mission of this infant espionage office was — at the urgent demand of the British — to put some of their officers ashore in France. They were to report what preparations the Germans were making to invade the British Isles. How they were to get their messages out, or to bring back their information, was not arranged for, and the first man, after two errant months in Brittany, got back only by recruiting a fisherman (and his boat) to the Gaullist cause. He was away two months.

The second two, sent out August 3, 1940, got back via Portugal in January of 1941. Another group, headed by Count d'Estienne d'Orves, left London in December of '40 with a

radio transmitter. They never got back at all, having been betrayed by the radio operator.

Military information, like fish, is worthless when stale. The
Free French undercover men had four tries and four failures.
This score of zero did not enhance their reputation with the
British. The failure of the Free French expedition to Dakar
(the French there not only failed to rally to the General but
opened fire), engendered grave Allied doubts about de Gaulle's
support among the French and about Free French military
security.

The first réseaux-forming mission was sent out by the Free
French in May 1941, and radio sets — these first models weighed
thirty-five pounds and, though ponderous, were fragile — were
parachuted for its use in August '41. The first SOE radio operator had already landed in May, three months earlier. Also in
August, the BCRA sent out Mission Ronsard to scout landing
sites for Lysander light aircraft. The British had already com-
pleted their reconnaissance, and their first SOE-Mission Lysander
landed in France a few weeks later.

Persuaded at last by German reprisals, by copies of underground newspapers, by reports of returning agents and by
volunteers escaping from France that there really was a Resistance, a serviceable secret weapon inside occupied territory,
the Free French took action. Of the eleven BCRA missions
sent to France in 1941, six in the last quarter of the year were
sent to contact the Resistance.

This sudden rise in interest and activity from London was
largely due to the violent character of the resistance embarked
upon — finally — by the Communist Party.

De Gaulle's first direct order to the underground forces,
October 23, 1941, was a non-battle cry. It caused no little dis-
may in the Resistance: "There are tactics in war. The war should
be conducted by those in charge. . . . Now the order I give
for the occupied territory is not to kill Germans. This is for

one single reason: at this moment it is easy for the enemy to answer with the massacre of our combatants, momentarily unarmed. But as soon as we are fit to move to the attack, orders will be given."

Now that it was clear that there were organized groups fighting the Germans, that interior resistance was a fact, it was de Gaulle's duty to take command of it. The leaders of the Resistance groups wanted official as well as physical existence, and they wanted liaison and a great deal of material aid.

It must be remembered that in 1940 those who rose to fight acted in the face of public opinion which was grateful that the fighting and the destruction had stopped. In 1941, public opinion in the north was in favor of not provoking German wrath. In the south, there was general loyalty to the Maréchal, "with his sky-blue eyes," to quote one of the hymns of praise. Thus, the number who fought and the number who helped them was tiny, appallingly tiny. A year after the defeat, there were perhaps a thousand resistants.

They were volunteers in the war against the invader. Of all the troops they were the most feeble, the most vulnerable. All things considered, they were the most valorous.

Actions which mean medals for heroism in the regular forces were simply the conditions of life for the men and women of the Resistance. That is, extreme resourcefulness and efficacy in the face of overwhelming odds, alone and with no hope of reinforcements.

THE COMMUNISTS

When Hitler broke his pact with Stalin, June 22, 1941, the Communist Party officially discovered itself to be French, patriotic and resistant. The Party had been operating underground ever since it had been declared illegal by the late Third Republic. It had at its disposal a small but efficient band of international Party operatives whose whole existence was anonymous and subterranean. This restricted elite included organizers, tacticians, saboteurs and assassins.

The Soviet Union had agents of its own military intelligence inside France, and one of the special commandos sent from Germany by the Gestapo had for its mission the destruction of this spy ring. They called it the Rote Kapell, the Red Chapel. The local French Party intelligence service was called FANA.

Their propaganda machinery, although damaged by the intensive French police drive against it, was still in existence. It simply changed its tune. It altered its tone somewhat, too, so as not to estrange the considerable number of moderates and even right-wingers drawn into the National Liberation Front. Special resistance papers for lawyers, doctors, screen actors, bus drivers, and workers in individual industries were not long in making their appearance.

Their first action groups, for sabotage and attacks on German Army personnel, were small shock units called OS (Special Organizations). Some of the independent groups founded earlier by Communists who had ignored the do-nothing Party line, put themselves under Party orders when the turnabout came. Others who had joined non-Party Resistance groups stayed where they were, ready to take over for the Party if the opportunity came. (And it did come for many when, just before liberation, a number of curiously coincidental deaths and arrests of non-Communist leaders made vacancies in command in non-Party organizations.)

The chief Communist apparatus was the National Liberation Front, operating in both zones. Its fighting wing (which in 1942 absorbed most of the OS) was the Franc-Tireurs et Partisans Français (FTP). The FTP recruited anybody useful, no matter what his politics. In fact, they preferred to reach into as many social, financial, and industrial groups as possible, to have a representatively French membership. The nonorganized of other political beliefs could not prevail against the Party core which controlled the units. This typical Communist-front tactic worked extremely well.

The Front National was less subject to mass losses than the other large movements because its construction, while clumsy, followed the airtight cell construction traditional — for reasons of survival — with the Party. Its chiefs had good schooling and long experience in clandestine activity. What the other organizations had to learn through bitter experience was already second nature to the Party men.

Their practice of violence was expert, the discipline severe. The techniques of underground warfare and existence (false identities, secret abodes, forged papers, street demonstrations, leaflet production, message centers, homemade bombs) had been learned in practice in assignments around the world. The Spanish Civil War had served as an invaluable practical military academy.

The Communists knew the value of de Gaulle as a symbol to the rank and file, and they piously exhibited his ikon. They made sure to win places in the "provisional government," yet until the last moment they held aloof. Except where FTP local commanders ignored Party directives, or where political expediency indicated it, the FTP avoided Gaullist control.

The way the Communists entered into action opened a question of resistance tactics which is still open.

The question: To attack or to wait?

The Communists maintained (and still maintain) that violence was the only way, especially in cities, to rip open the Nazi shroud of fear enveloping the populace, to demonstrate unequivocally that the conquerors were vulnerable, that armed resistance and eventual victory were possible. This demonstration was the basis for the eventual mass uprising against the foe.

Their second argument in favor of killing and destroying was that the enemy would never again feel secure in occupied territory. Further, as each fallen enemy was stripped of his weapons, the Resistance would arm itself.

The Gaullists contended that the Nazis were sure to take reprisals. Was a dead German or an armload of grenades worth the lives of a dozen or two dozen Frenchmen every time they struck?

It was worth it, said the Communists. Since repression affects all groups of society, it must eventually provoke a reaction which would permeate the entire population. It would push the nation as a whole to resist. Guerilla fighting in a city means to attack constantly by every means, make every street a potential death trap for the occupier.

To this day the Communists take satisfaction in the fact that de Gaulle's October 1941 cease-fire order came twenty-four hours after an "anti-terrorist" statement by Pétain: "We have laid down our arms. We do not have the right to take them up again to strike the Germans in the back." The Communists went right on killing. To them the order from de Gaulle "betrayed the whole concept of resistance." Because of the lack of liaison, and in reaction to German reprisals, and also in self-defense, some non-Communist action forces did not heed the order, either.

Hundreds of hostages (some of them Communist leaders jailed by the Third Republic) were executed by the Germans in the first six months the Communists entered into the Resistance. The members of the principal Party killer groups were caught — almost every one of them — within a year. These sacrifices, both the voluntary and the involuntary, paid off, the Party feels. Charles Tillon, commander in chief of the FTP, wrote in 1962, "The assembling of the Front National . . . was going to bring to General de Gaulle a support he lacked, in the laboring masses, and which he had not yet done anything to encourage."

The sabotage (most certainly not exclusively a Party activity, and which began virtually on the day of the French defeat) "immobilized by thousands the German soldiers required to guard all the 'nerve centers' of French transport," Tillon wrote.

In France the Communists have successfully implanted the legend that it was they who first began killing Germans. Even historians are apt to credit them with the first acts of violence against occupation troops. This is simply not true. An extreme example to the contrary of the legend is the execution of German spies by Vichy. For another there was Joseph, the one-man army of Rouen, who strangled German officers with the bicycle chain he wore as a belt. There were the stranded Senegalese soldiers who lived in the forest in enlarged fox dens and came out at night to slit German throats.

As to which plan is the proper one, to strike while feeble and risk the reprisals or to assemble strength underground and coordinate with outside help, the answer is the antique military answer: it all depends on the situation.

The "strike now" policy didn't work in Poland in 1945 and it didn't work more than a decade later in Hungary. Whether it worked in France in 1941-1942 is answered affirmatively or negatively by partisans of both points of view. One sure conclusion can be drawn from it – it did the Communist Party a lot of good.

The Communist aim was to make the Party the postwar party of the Resistance, with the officials, heroes and martyrs to substantiate the claim. They wanted the final upsurge of the Resistance to be a mass uprising of an armed population, and they wanted it to be controlled and directed by the Communist Party.

Their plans were excellent and well carried out. They did not prevail because they were blocked by one man: Charles de Gaulle.

SEARCHING FOR UNITY

The deputy de Gaulle dispatched to the Resistance on January 1, 1942 to form it into a unified command (commanded from London) was not a military man, and he was given no military rank. He was given the title of general delegate from General de Gaulle and he was the highest Free French authority inside France. To coordinate the Resistance movements, he had to find them, then persuade the chiefs to obey the General's instructions, and then devise machinery for carrying out the instructions.

His name is one of the three which remain illustrious among the veterans of the Resistance. He was Jean Moulin. The other two were Comte d'Estienne d'Orves and Pierre Brossolette. The count was shot as a spy. Brossolette jumped to his death from the window of Gestapo headquarters on the avenue Foch. Jean Moulin was tortured to death and buried secretly by the Gestapo. Moulin and d'Estienne d'Orves were both betrayed by Frenchmen.

The three had a great deal in common. They had a natural air of authority. They inspired confidence and admiration in wildly various kinds of people. They were men of extraordinarily high principle and high courage.

Naval Lieutenant d'Estienne d'Orves was a pious man with an aura of saintliness which affected most of the people with whom he came in contact, including the Nazis. He was sentenced to death along with two other men sent with him from London on a secret mission, and three members of the French reception group. The German court-martial's sentence, passed on May 25, 1941, said:

The tribunal finds itself faced with a heavy task. It must judge men and women who have shown themselves to be persons of merit, of great firmness of character, and who have acted only out of love of country. But even as they believed themselves obliged to fulfill their duty toward their country, we are obliged to fulfill our duty toward our own country, and to judge the accused according to the laws. . . .

Adolf Hitler pardoned the three reception group members, but not the three "spies"; the Germans were still being correct. The three condemned men were held in prison without being unduly abused. When the Communists gunned the German naval officer at the Barbès subway station, the three prisoners were taken out and shot.

Henri Louis Honoré, Comte d'Estienne d'Orves, Free French Navy; Maurice Charles Emile Barlier, commercial agent, and Jan Louis-Guilleaume Doornik, storekeeper, sang in the bus on their way to Mont-Valérian. They refused the blindfold and stood in front of the execution stakes without being tied.

By the time Moulin and Brossolette arrived on their Resistance-coordinating missions, the formality of public trials had been dispensed with, save for exceptional propaganda purposes, and capture meant torture and death, or the Nazi variant, the concentration camp.

Pierre Brossolette was political editor of the Socialist newspaper *Populaire* before the war, and gave political analysis over the radio. He worked with the réseau called the Committee for Public Safety, and after the Germans dismantled the group, he fell in with the BCRA réseau, La Confrérie de Notre Dame. He was taken to London aboard a Lysander aircraft in April of 1942. He worked with Passy of the BCRA, gave BBC broadcasts, and made several trips back to France to work on coordination of the northern zone Resistance and to maintain contact with leaders of political parties.

The magic of the Moulin and Brossolette personalities and logic, so instantly effective on others, mutually failed. They had very different ideas about how to organize the underground and they did not get along at all well. The divergence of opinion and the prickliness of relations between these two illustrates the gigantic difficulties of unification. Both were envoys from headquarters, both selflessly engaged in fighting the Germans, both personally instructed by General de Gaulle and Colonel Passy, both engaged on the same mission. Brossolette was a Resistance man who had come to persuade his brothers. Moulin was an executive introduced to transmit orders. Although Moulin's viewpoint was considerably altered after living with the Resistance, he could always keep in sight the broader concepts which guided London decisions.

Hunted by the Gestapo, Brossolette was ordered out of France at the end of 1943. Weather canceled the first pick-up mission. The second Lysander was shot down by anti-aircraft fire before reaching the landing strip, and the third failed to spot the signal flares. An attempt to get away by sea was thwarted by motor failure in a storm. The party got back to land only by chance. Brossolette, stopped at a roadblock, did not have the special sea-frontier pass requisite in the area.

Routine questioning and check led into a mesh of coincidence, and he was identified. During interrogation, the badly beaten suspect, the only man in France to know all the secrets of the Resistance, was left alone for a moment. He jumped out of the window. The date was March 22, 1944.

Jean Moulin was the youngest prefect in France when the German Army overran the cathedral city of Chartres in June of 1940. Unlike other provincial authorities, he stayed at his post in the bombarded city, trying to feed the flood of refugees, trying to extinguish fires, trying to organize medical aid. When the German commandant arrived, Moulin met him to arrange for aid to the population. He was arrested and told to sign a convention which blamed French soldiers for atrocities committed by the Germans.

Moulin refused. He was tortured, and eventually cut his throat rather than fail in his duty. The Germans sent him to a hospital and abandoned the idea of getting his signature on their paper. He recovered and was dropped from the civil service by Vichy. It took him more than a year, without underground connections, to reach London. Three months later, on New Year's Day 1942, he was back in France as délégué général de Général de Gaulle. He spoke hoarsely and covered his scarred throat with a scarf.

Jean Moulin was an experienced boss. He had tact, charm, and firmness. On this mission, he also had the authority of de Gaulle, a powerful name to conjure with in the underground. And he had money.

He was faced with a remarkable subterranean labyrinth with secret doors and secret corridors and with blind alleys and deadfalls. This secret maze was the Resistance, and the Germans and their Vichy cohorts were continually mining, infiltrating, tunneling in the same terrain to learn the key to the secret.

The strength of the various réseaux changed from day to day with deaths and disappearances. It was a rare leader who could tell at any moment exactly how large his organization was or exactly what all its branches were doing at any given moment.

There were groups whose chiefs had been captured, or whose liaison with London had been broken off, or never systematically established. Some members of these splinter groups were attaching themselves to other organizations, some were searching to re-establish the broken connection and some were simply stranded.

The northern zone was especially disjointed. Resistance there directly under the German boot was more dangerous and more difficult. Groups were smaller and more isolated one from the other. They were not as thoroughly organized into various services as were the southern organizations. Their main work was military information, although they were active in all the fields of resistance.

Moulin found nine major groups in the north, two of which disappeared before his eyes. The Comité National de Salut Public reached from Paris throughout the occupied zone, to Brittany, where it was especially active, and far to the south around Bordeaux. Almost destroyed twice in 1941, the organization was rebuilt each time, but it did not survive the crushing arrests, executions and deportations of November 1942. The remnants joined either Résistance or Ceux de la Résistance.

Ceux de la Résistance grew out of the ruins of the Normandy group set up by Robert Guédon, who had been detached for this purpose by the Vichy Army intelligence. The group was first called the Organisation Nationale de la Résistance and was the northern affiliate of Combat. CDLR was formed in Normandy and around Reims. As it grew, it took in the Lorraine movement, Défense de la Patrie, and established fighting and sabotage units in Paris and its suburbs. Its London link was through the SOE.

In the forbidden frontier zone, the department of Nord, militant Socialists built an organization around their newspaper, *La Voix du Nord*. This group fused with Libération of the northern zone in 1943, although its newspaper remained autonomous. Its intelligence service linked up with the réseau Cohors-Austuries.

Défense de la France was a student-faculty group which started by producing a newspaper in the cellars of the Sorbonne. It ran escape routes across the demarcation line and evolved a false papers service for escapees. Its newspaper attained the huge circulation of one hundred thousand.

Ceux de la Libération was one of the oldest movements, working as an intelligence net for the Vichy Air Force. Its main recruitment was among officers and ex-officers of the Air Force, and as it spread into both zones, it picked up a lot of disenchanted right-wingers who had belonged to La Rocque's prewar Parti Social Français. The founder, Ripoche, was arrested in March of 1943, succeeded by Lenormand, who was arrested and was succeeded by Médéric, who was arrested and took poison, and was succeeded by Colonel Ginas, who was also arrested, at the eleventh hour in 1944. It had members inside the police, the Gardes Mobiles (government riot troops) and the Paris Fire Department.

The initials OCM stood for Organisation Civile et Militaire, founded in December 1940. It was large and strong and spread through almost every *département* of the occupied zone. Its fighting wing was considerable, but its greatest worth to the Resistance was the widespread enrollment of highly placed civil servants, especially in the public works, agriculture, labor, post-telephone-telegraph and interior ministries. This was of great importance in restoring the civil administration after liberation. Its losses, through treason, were markedly high.

Faced with this, what was Moulin to do? His first contact was with Henri Frenay, leader of Combat, the oldest and best organized of the south zone groups. Combat had grown from the fusion of Vérités and Liberté, and was in process of discussing further amalgamation with Libération-Sud.

De Gaulle's first order was not for fusion, but for coordination of the movements under the central authority of Moulin's Délégation Générale. His second order was to separate the action wing from the "political" wing which performed the propaganda, false papers, intelligence and escape services.

This met with flat refusal by the Resistance. A chief is a chief, and much of every organization's success lay in his leadership, in the loyal response of sub-chiefs to his orders and his personal affection. Besides, they said, the organizations were really rather small, and the best men of every group took part in all kinds of activity. Many of the best intelligence men were obliged to take part in action, because they were on the scene.

The dispute was one constantly renewed and never really concluded. Frenay and Moulin failed to appreciate one another's sterling qualities. Frenay, to plead for his concept of the Resistance, went to London himself. The organizer of Libération-Sud, Emmanuel d'Astier de la Vigerie, left at almost the same time, but through the courtesy of SOE, which got him a sub-marine ride.

After long talks with de Gaulle and other Free French officials, the two leaders returned together on a BCRA-organized flight. This was just a few days after the Germans had occupied all of France, November 1942. Soon after, Libération, Combat, and another major southern organization, Franc-Tireur, united under the new name of MUR, which means "wall" in French, and stood for Mouvements Unis de la Résistance.

All three had shock troops, saboteurs, military intelligence units, and clandestine newspapers. Combat had sought to build an organization of professionals, intellectuals and career officers to form a framework around which a unified resistance could be fashioned. Libé-Sud (no organic connection with Libé-Nord) drew most of its leaders from among trade union executives, and wanted to build a movement based on the working masses. Franc-Tireur had no special philosophical base to begin with, and was socially and economically a widely diverse group. All were pioneers of the Resistance, dating from 1940.

The new MUR agreed to put its military reserves — the Armée Secrète — under a single command. The commander, a career officer, was named by General de Gaulle. He was General Charles Delestraint, known as Vidal, and he formed his own general staff from among other career officers, although his two deputy commanders were taken from MUR.

Some of the other Resistance groups which accepted Delestraint's overall command of troops included France d'Abord, which also published two papers in Lyon and had an intelligence group; Dupleix, working for the Americans; Libérer et Fédérer, which had started in Toulon and spread its réseaux north to Lyon, "capital of the Resistance." Its membership included Vincent Auriol and Jules Moch, future President of France and minister of the interior, respectively. L&F published a newspaper, reported military intelligence to the

British, operated shock groups, and was organizing its first maquis. Socialist Gaston Deferre was one of the leaders of France au Combat, based in Marseille.

The Front National agreed to "close collaboration" with General Delestraint, but said it wanted to wait to see how many parachute deliveries of arms the anti-Red BCRA would actually send before actually joining.

The ORA did not join the Armée Secrète at all. This group, L'Organisation de Résistance de l'Armée, was the underground version of Vichy's Armistice Army. After the Army was dissolved by Pétain on German orders in November 1942, all its carefully hidden armaments — cannon, machine guns, rifles, mortars, grenades, communications instruments, even armored cars — were discovered by, or reported to, the Germans. Its first action was to slip officers and noncoms to the American-sponsored Free French (Giraudist) Army in North Africa. Those who stayed behind organized an independent Resistance force, including some remarkable *corps francs*. They also detailed officers and noncommissioned officers to train maquis which were forming in the southern zone.

In April 1943, the northern zone groups — Front National absenting itself on the grounds that the other groups should join FN, the largest, most active, with the widest political spectrum — were brought together by Brossolette. Each of the major outfits took over the leadership of the territory in which it was strongest. Each organization adopted the same structural plan, with three separate services, military forces, military intelligence and civilian activity. It was a loose and awkward system.

The general, if not complete, separation of the "civilian" Resistance from the "military" was a relief to London, which did not want a vast army set up, itching for action. One reason for not wanting such an organization was security. A big group could be easily detected and obliterated. Another reason, far more pressing, was the fear that the fighting groups could easily become the troops of conflicting ideologies. This would mean Allied intervention and the destruction of all hopes for the "New France" so devoutly wished by de Gaulle and by the Resistance.

The Resistance was becoming political. The French, submerged in a sea of propaganda of all sorts, bereft of the familiar party framework of the Third Republic, were thinking out political philosophy instead of merely arguing over ready-made platforms.

De Gaulle really spoke for the main body of the Resistance when in June 1942 he castigated the old France and looked forward to the new. "While the people of France unite for victory, they are assembling for a Revolution," he declared in a radio address.

Claude Bourdet summed up the de Gaulle and the Resistance feeling in an editorial in the clandestine paper *Combat*. He said, "The men of the Resistance understand that they are fighting for more than the liberation of territory. No point in getting your skin shot full of holes if it's for an anarchic Europe, a talkative and sterile France, Stavisky (a reference to government corruption), the all-powerful trusts and starvation wages. . . . The wish for a new society, for a vigorous and just regime, animates all our combatants."

The program envisaged included a certain amount of nationalization, a planned economy with state controls "but without the slavery of statism," the rationalization of agricultural production, a "vigorous and fraternal foreign policy," and a colonial policy of association with peoples of the Empire and of collaboration with Europe."

The first step: liquidation of the trusts. "Trusts" is a word the French acquired at the time the United States passed anti-trust legislation, before World War I.

He derided the renaissant political parties, of which there

were thirty-six before the war. He said their word to the Resistance was, "To you the prisons and the cemeteries, to us the legislative seats!" He warned that "the same old causes, the same old names, the same old principles will produce the same old results."

Bourdet called for a new political party to "renovate French political life and construct the Fourth Republic."

"It will group all those who want to make, with us of the Resistance, a France young and beautiful, pure and strong."

There was to be no postwar Parti de la Résistance, although de Gaulle and a large part of the movement saw it as the main force for the re-creation of France. And it was de Gaulle himself who took the decision which made such a new party impossible. His decision was to call back to life the old parties by giving them places in the National Council of the Résistance.

Despite his castigation of the old political parties as the partners of social injustice and the architects of defeat, he decided he needed them to demonstrate that he was indeed the leader of the French people. Without such a demonstration, he could not survive. America and Britain had in their minds already replaced him with someone they considered more capable and, for their purposes, more realistic, General Henri Giraud, lately escaped from a German military prison. They realized the territorial and psychological worth of de Gaulle's organization, and they wanted him to toss his chips into the Giraud pot.

Roosevelt and Churchill insisted that de Gaulle come to North Africa at the time of their Casablanca Conference and accept Giraud as co-leader (and, with the support he would have, eventual chief) of Free France. The Gaullist underground in North Africa was obliged to stay underground. The Americans and British dealt only with Giraud, and gave him the prestigious title of Military and Civil Commander of Algiers. Among those who tried to persuade de Gaulle to accept the "inevitable'" was the British minister at Algiers, Harold Macmillan.

In their very brief meeting, Giraud told de Gaulle that he was "not interested in politics," and he saw no reason he should condemn the Vichy regime.

There was only one way to reverse the Allied choice, and that was to demonstrate that the French people had made a different choice, that they had chosen Charles de Gaulle as their leader. And this the National Council of the Resistance (CNR) did. In May 1943, at its first session (48 rue du Four, in the St. Germain-des-Prés quarter of Paris) the CNR acclaimed him as chief of Free France, accepting Giraud as military commander.

The National Council was composed of sixteen delegates. They represented the two trade union organizations, the eight principal Resistance movements, and the six leading political parties. In sum, they spoke for the disenfranchised voters and for the fighters inside France. Unanimously, they called for establishment of "a provisional government under the presidency of General de Gaulle."

This, the General wrote later, "produced a decisive effect." Edouard Herriot, last president of the Chamber of Deputies, sent word from inside France that he would be "ready at any moment to take a post in a government presided over by General de Gaulle." The municipal councils of the Algerian cities of Algiers, Constantine and Oran opened their sessions with honors for de Gaulle. Giraud troops and political supporters rallied to de Gaulle.

The first meeting of the CNR was, for security reasons, the last until after the liberation. A five-man committee took over the work, under Council President Jean Moulin.

Under the same impulsion toward unity, several organizations designed to serve all the Resistance movements were conceived. The Bureau d'Opérations Aériennes in the north and the Service d'Atterrissage et de Parachutages had a team in each of the military regions for Lysander aircraft pickups and for parachute drops. They also scouted for landing strips and drop zones. In some areas there were réseaux established to devote themselves exclusively to receptions, transportation and safe shelter.

The BCRA sent Mission Electre to establish radio transmission réseaux for groups which had no radio operators attached to them. Thus Thuya served the Limoges area, Cactus operated at Clermont, and Bouleau at Lyon. Much earlier, Combat had installed its own "Central" in Geneva, which was expanded to handle all the military intelligence emanating from MUR. As time went on, the Central was open to virtually all the organizations. This was not much liked by BCRA, because it meant direct contact between Gaullist resistants and the British and American intelligence services.

The eight principal organizations, pushed by MUR, formed a Central Committee of the Resistance, which formulated services common to all the movements, but which never worked with the efficacy hoped for. Some of these unified services included food supply, counter-deportation action, resistance seeding of state administrative services, and aid to families of arrested and deported resistants.

Moulin appointed two groups to work as part of his Délégation Générale, the General Committee of Studies and the Press and Information Bureau.

The Committee members were Primus, Secondus, Tertius and Quartus, and the secretary general was Tristan. In order, they were Paul Bastid, law professor and Radical Party ex-deputé, president of the group of sixty parliament members who voted no when the rest of the legislature voted an end to the Third Republic in favor of Marshal Pétain; Robert Lacoste, Socialist trade unionist; François de Menthon, Chris-

tian Democrat, law professor and one of the founders of
Liberté, one of the two groups which merged to form Combat;
Alexandre Parodi, *maître des requêtes* at the Conseil d'Etat
(one of the most august of governmental organisms, in the
nature of a court of constitutional law and procedure). Tristan
was Pierre-Henri Teitgen, a co-founder of Liberté. René
Courtin, Michel Debré, and Coste-Floret later joined this group.
All would hold high positions in postwar France.

The Committee studied the problems of how France was to
be run, once liberated, and prepared reports on such matters
as a new constitution, finances, food distribution, press. It published, starting in the spring of 1943, a review, *Cahiers Poli-
tiques.*

Georges Bidault resigned the editorship of *Combat* to direct
the Press and Information Bureau, which began issuing a
monthly bulletin. Its appearance, with news of all the movements and of the Free French organization, was a fine psychological bulwark to the two hundred underground leaders
who received it. It diluted the terrible sense of isolation and,
by showing the Resistance as a giant insurrection against
tyranny, it minimized somewhat the local and personal frustra-
tions. Bidault's commentary was trenchant, illuminating and
comforting. By popular demand, the bulletin was issued every
two weeks, then every week, then twice, sometimes three
times a week.

When "Max," as Jean Moulin was known (he had half a
dozen aliases besides, and maintained a small farm and a Nice
art gallery under his true identity, as cover) — when Max was
betrayed, Georges Bidault was elected to head the CNR.

Max was not the only leader who was lost. It was a terrible
year for the men who lived underground. The losses in their
ranks were frightful, even though the Compulsory Labor Service (service in Germany, to be sure) drove thousands more

young men and women into the Resistance. The blows the Resistance struck were harder and harder, but the blows the Gestapo and their Vichy cohorts struck were harder and harder, too.

A Street in Paris

*The Germans occupied Paris
from June 14, 1940 until August 25, 1944*

DECEMBER 1942

ORDINARILY, the Germans don't bother patrolling this street. It forms part of a nest of small twisty byways which they can check by looking down from the quais and the boulevards that pass along the outer edges. Besides, the whole neighborhood is patrolled by the French police in the ordinary way, and they haven't given up their habit of arresting people.

But night before last, the Boches were up and down the street, in every room of every house and down in the cellars and up on the roofs. They checked papers, asked a million questions. Naturally, they took some people away with them, because after all, everybody must have something to hide: an undeclared radio set, a Resistance pamphlet, a forged ration card, even a letter that says something unflattering about the Germans. Or it might be a matter of not being able to explain the absence of somebody who lives in the apartment.

They combed the area because on the rue Singer, the street behind this one, somebody shot a Gestapo officer. He was in plain clothes, they say, so whoever killed him must have done it very carefully and deliberately. They know the chances are slim that the Resistance man would loiter in the district after doing a thing like that. They probably figure, though, that if the Gestapo man was walking down a lost little lane like the rue Singer at all, it must have been for a good reason.

Most of its old houses have been made into a warehouse for a publishing firm, with huge iron shutters across the lower windows. There aren't many streetlights, and these are dimmed down to virtually nothing by the blackout. It's not the spot one would ordinarily choose for an early evening ramble. Well, he chose it.

At least it didn't happen right here in the rue du Bossu. God knows what would have happened to the residents. This is not what you'd call an ordinary street, though in its way it is typical. There are some very grand apartments here for the sort of person who prefers beautiful proportion and historic associations to modern comfort. In the same buildings there are young families stuck away in attic rooms for which they pay almost nothing. It runs just about the whole social scale.

The rue du Bossu is either two blocks long or five, depending which side of the road you take. The curbs are high and sidewalks little more than two feet wide. The cobbled roadway is perhaps fourteen feet across, five short paces.

There isn't a house here less than a century old, and the oldest have been standing here — some of them have a tendency to sag — for more than three hundred years. At least four of them are classified as historical monuments by the City of Paris. The street pushes its way among the houses like a stream at the bottom of a gorge. The sunshine gets very discouraged on the way down, especially these gray, gritty winter days.

Long ago this was an important thoroughfare, during an earlier occupation of Paris. The enemy garrison then was British. At that time too, the University authorities accepted the occupation, although the students and some of the faculty were refractory, as they are now. The Archbishop of Paris assumed the correct attitude as well back in those days. He

participated in the coronation of the boy King of England as
the King of conquered France. There were religious rebels
then, too. Joan of Arc was one.

This time the garrison is German. Der Kommandant von
Gross-Paris. Greater Paris. Greater Hell, really.

It is a pagan, glacial hell, a frozen and deserted landscape.
Not burning and bubbling, but numbing and silent, with slow,
icy devastation.

It always seems to be winter under the occupation. Last
winter was filthy, colder than it had been in years. This winter
is worse. In the dark, in the cold, the winters seem to go on
forever. Daylight comes so late. Of course, they have turned the
clocks to Berlin time. That sounds like a figure of speech, but
it's the truth. The time here has been adjusted to match the
clocks of the Greater Reich. This is against all logic, but then
so is everything these days.

Perhaps the winters seem longer because people feel hungrier
in the winter, especially when there isn't enough to eat, and
there never is now. Also, there is the discomfort, psychological
as well as physical, of being dirty. No hot water. One has the
awareness, always, of being not quite clean. And, my God,
it is cold.

Last winter at least, you could sit in one of the richer
churches by the hot-air register and get warm. They soon
ran out of coal, though. The banks are still heated, but they
soon caught on. They check over the waiting people at regular
intervals now, to see whether you've got one of those numbered
brass checks that indicates you're waiting for the cashier to
call you. Post offices aren't very well heated, but they are
warmer than one's apartment. Unfortunately, they don't have
any place for you to sit down, most of them. Some people sit
in the subway stations, but it isn't really warm enough to com-
pensate for that wet-dog smell. Besides, they've just closed another twelve stations.

M. Langlois goes to the government tax office every day.

He says they have stoves there, and that even if he had business to transact, he wouldn't be able to attract the attention of any of the surly bastards who work there.

When the wind blows the frozen dust along the street, not a scrap of paper blows along with it. Even German propaganda handbills are picked up, because they are paper and they will burn.

You wet the paper and squeeze it into balls, and when they dry you have briquettes, sort of. Enough of them and you can boil water for coffee. Not real coffee, of course. They call it National Coffee. Some people say you should make the paper balls first and then damp them down. Other people say you should burn the coffee and boil the paper and you get a better-flavored drink that way.

Being close to the Seine here probably makes it seem colder because of the dampness. Those people right on the river, with those big beautiful windows, they really suffer when the wind blows. Over on the Ile de la Cité, the Quai de l'Horloge was originally called Le Quai des Morfondus, the quai of the frostbitten. You could call the whole town La Ville des Morfondus now. Except for those who are playing the German game, and getting a fuel supply along with their extra rations.

The Germans will be putting up fresh posters tomorrow, about this rue Singer affair.

The yellow posters with the black borders are for executions of spies, the black and white are for executions of hostages, the blood-red with black borders are to announce the liquidation of "terrorists." Sometimes they change colors arbitrarily. It varies. But whatever the color and whatever the crime, the news is the same: death.

Sometimes the orders are signed by Der Kommandant von Gross-Paris, and sometimes by Der Militärbefehlshaber in Frankreich. No matter whose authority is invoked, it's going to be bad news. If it isn't actually announcement of executions,

BEKANNTMACHUNG	AVIS
1) Roger-Henry NOGAREDE aus Paris.	1) Roger-Henry NOGAREDE de Paris.
2) Alfred OTTINO aus Saint-Ouen.	2) Alfred OTTINO de Saint-Ouen.
3) André SIGONNEY aus Drancy.	3) André SIGONNEY de Drancy.
4) Raymond JUSTICE aus Drancy.	4) Raymond JUSTICE de Drancy.
5) Jean-Louis RAPINAT aus Pavillons-sous-Bois	5) Jean-Louis RAPINAT de Pavillons-sous-Bois
sind wegen Feindbegünstigung, begangen durch Teilnahme an kommunistischen Kundgebungen gegen die deutsche Wehrmacht, vom Kriegsgericht zum Tode verurteilt und erschossen worden.	ont été condamnés à mort par la cour martiale pour aide à l'ennemi, ayant pris part à une manifestation communiste dirigée contre l'armée allemande. Ils ont été fusillés.
.... August 1941	Paris, le 27 Août 1941

then it's threat of death for doing this or that, or else a punishment for the whole city — a fine to be paid by the municipal government, or locking up the town with an early curfew.

They have a new place to paste their posters, now that The Golden Cockerel is boarded up. Very handy, on the corner of four streets. The restaurant is there, intact, ready to go, behind the boards. Nobody knows what happened to poor Michel. They just came and got him — some say it was the French police and others say it was French members of the Gestapo — and nothing further was heard. He was probably deported, because his wife didn't receive any notice to come and pick up his things. That's what they do when someone's been executed: they send around a notice to come and pick up his belongings.

His wife, Léontine, the thin, dark one who ran the cash desk, just couldn't stand the waiting. It was too much for her, so she had the place boarded up and she went to his mother's in the country. They say Michel's place was a "letter box" for some Resistance bunch, where they dropped off and picked up messages. Nobody knows. You can't tell a Resistance man by looking at him any more than you can tell a traitor.

That makes the seventh store on this one street to close, not counting the three that didn't open again after the exodus of '40.

There was Jollivet, the butcher. It was the Ministry of Food that closed his shop. For black marketeering, if you please. He paid a big fine and went to prison. It's ridiculous; people couldn't live without the black market.

Cardinal Suhard himself said that the average family's black marketing was justified — that was the word he used, "justified" — because the transactions weren't financially important and because they were necessary to stay alive.

That they are. The official ration's twelve hundred calories per day, and you can't always get your full ration because the store doesn't always have it. They announce a ration of, say, dried prunes for September, and they honor the tickets in November. Anyhow, twelve hundred calories is exactly one-half the amount you need to stay alive and moderately healthy. The difference between what you can get with your ration tickets and what you need can be made up on the black market, if you have the price and the stamina.

At first, getting food was a matter of standing in queue for hours before the shop opened to be sure to be there before the merchant was cleaned out. Then, if you were an old customer, you'd give the wink to the butcher or the grocer for the extras. That didn't last long. Those who didn't get anything didn't hesitate to drop a line to the Food Ministry.

A lot of people around here think that old Jollivet the butcher was denounced by Benedetti, the other butcher. Not denounced, exactly, more like framed. Benedetti is an Italian, everybody knows. Nobody would hold that against him, even though they stabbed us in the back, but he used to have pictures of Mussolini hanging in the back room, and up front he put up posters for the Italian propaganda movies. And he was always a member of some rightist party or other.

He snoots the whole neighborhood now. He's away from his

shop a lot, and he wears new clothes. Not that stuff made of wood shavings they sell for cloth nowadays, but real prewar stuff. His clientele comes from other neighborhoods. Every now and then an automobile parks in front of his place and some overdressed hussy gets out to do the shopping while he scrapes and bows. An automobile. You know what that means. Only the Boches and their new French friends have automobiles running around Paris now.

The Boches are pretty sly. They run the biggest black market operations of all. They're in the market for everything. And their soldiers re-sell the food and soap and textiles that are requisitioned from France. And they're sly, too, the way they let the French authorities hold the bag.

After all, it is the local authorities who issue the ration cards and the Ministry which decrees what will be on sale and when. The Boches shrewdly allow the controlled press to report freely on how disgusted the French are with French bumbling. The papers are full of cute feature stories about troubles with rationing, nastiness of civil servants, stupidities of administrators, and the drop-dead attitude of shopkeepers.

Mme. Lebel from No. 40 had her views aired in the press on Wednesday. Her name wasn't printed, but she made sure everyone in the block knew she was the one quoted in *La Gerbe*. In answer to the question what would she do when the war was over, she said, "Personally, I shall set fire to my grocer's store."

It is the Germans who have turned the economy upside down, with their "war indemnity" payments from the national economy, with their incredible black market buying. They buy on the regular market too, but their occupation marks are over-valued by 100 per cent. The farmers can't get labor, or fertilizer, or spare parts or new machines.

However, if they can prompt the French to blame the French, or the British, or the Jews or the Communists, blame anyone but the Germans, then they are doing very nicely.

At five o'clock in the morning, when the Métro starts running and the curfew is lifted, housewives muffled beyond recognition clump out along the street, to be first in line when the stores open. Their wooden-soled shoes with the cardboard tops make a tremendous clatter in the dark.

Most of the women from the rue du Bossu know the two bakers and are registered with one or the other for their bread, so they can leave that until last. Even though the sign "No more bread" may go up at noon, they know their ration will be saved for them.

For vegetables, meat, butter and fats, most of them just go up to the far end of the street to the rue de Buci, near St. Germain-des-Prés. Last summer most of them stayed away from there for a while, after the "revolt" of May 31.

"About 10:30 this morning," reported *Paris-Soir*, "several individuals made their way into the premises of the 'Eco' grocery store, at the corner of the rue de Buci and the rue de Seine, and busied themselves in throwing, to the housewives massed before the doors, canned goods and other food products from the store's shelves."

Several policemen showed up within minutes, and collared one of the ringleaders. They were taking him off, on foot, to the station house, two short streets away. They got no more than a dozen steps when someone began shooting. A sergeant and a patrolman fell dead. Two more patrolmen and a chief inspector were wounded, but three men were arrested nevertheless.

Mme. Théo, from No. 29, looking rather disheveled, brought home a can of peas. Mme. Callard, her neighbor from across the landing, also had a sack full of goodies. They walked right down the middle of the street, passing out the inflammatory handbills they had collected: "Housewives, it is your war, too!"

That night at No. 29 they had a party for about twenty persons. Since no one was asked to bring any ration tickets, as is customary these days, and no one had to leave the build-

ing to go home after curfew, it was a great success and lasted
till one o'clock in the morning.

Within two weeks, twenty people went on trial before the
State Tribunal. Frenchmen arresting French men and women,
prosecuting them, trying them. The charge was "pillage." Nobody at the trial was allowed to bring up the matter of handbills which the Resistance had passed out to the women.

The patriotic aspects of the "revolt" were completely
suppressed at the trial and, naturally, in the press. Five death
sentences for pillage were handed down. One of these de-
fendants was a woman, Madeleine Mazarin. Marshal Pétain
made a big thing of commuting her sentence not long ago.
They actually acquitted three, and a dozen got long sentences
at hard labor.

Nobody from the rue du Bossu was arrested. This must
mean that nobody informed about the party at No. 29, or the
indiscreet redistribution of rue de Buci handbills. Which is
surprising, since this street is no different than any other. There
are informers and traitors here as everywhere.

Probably as part of the general demoralization campaign, the
Boches have allowed one of the daily papers, *Aujourd'hui*, to
print:

In Paris, there is a group of poor wretches determined to take
it out on their fellow citizens. Formerly, they threatened you with
the courts, or the Prefect of Police. These nice folk now summon
up the Kommandantur . . .

The appalling tide of anonymous letters and denunciations rises
daily. What has become of the kindly old France of yesterday?
You'd swear every Frenchman regards his neighbor as an enemy
to be destroyed.

As soon as the feeling of danger subsided, the rue du Bossu
ladies resumed queueing in the rue de Buci. The store counters
in most cases open right onto the street, as they have for

several hundred years, and there are dozens of shops in which to try your luck.

Luck isn't very apt to be good in the winter. There are rutabagas and turnips and sometimes parsnips or carrots, either spoiled or wood-hard. And as for meat, well, the butchers are open only on Wednesday, Thursday and Friday. Which doesn't mean there'll be anything for you. However, the queue is sometimes a good place to pick up good tips about where something might be had.

"There's a seamstress over behind the Gare du Maine who gets fish from the country, but you have to give her textile ration points. She uses the points to buy goods to make dresses she sells at black market prices."

Every housewife has her lines of communication for tips. Mme. Barrotte always goes to the Place St. Michel and takes a velo-taxi over to the Ile St. Louis, to her cousin's. They shop together. The taxi costs a lot of money, and she says she doesn't like the idea of being trundled through the public streets in a wheeled basket attached to a bike. She always takes the one named L'Eclair or else the Maillot Jaune, because the drivers always have a tip on some place for her to pick up something she needs. She pays the regular 5 francs-plus-9 francs the kilometer, but it must be worth it because she still does it.

When the war broke out, Parisians on the average — it was a depression year, remember — ate a quarter of a pound of meat a day per head. Now the ration runs at something less than a fifth of that.

There are something like eight hundred residents on the rue du Bossu — No, that's how many there were to start with. Now, with arrests and people working in Germany, and prisoners of war, and people not back from the exodus, there are about five hundred. At least one hundred are trying to provide their own supplementary meat ration. They raise rabbits under the kitchen stove, and chickens in cages on window ledges. They have the devil's own time trying to find food for the animals. And they are all experts on poultry and rabbit diseases. Lately there's been a big push on guinea pigs. M. Garbeau, who is lame and who is some sort of janitor at the Institut Pasteur, brought home the first pair.

Jeannot Castelot, who gets vitaminized biscuits free at school, finds they are good pigeon bait. Before he discovered this he used to swap them for other things. One boy in his class cornered just about all the biscuits one week, sold them on the black market, set himself up in the cigarette business and is getting rich, Jeannot says. Jeannot now uses the biscuits and an old fishing net up there under the eaves to catch pigeons.

A lot of people are wearing cat-fur gloves and waistcoats lately (fur isn't rationed), but they probably buy them — they don't look capable of killing and skinning cats on their own. There was this notice in the papers:

CAT EATERS, ATTENTION!

In these times of restrictions, certain hungry persons haven't hesitated to capture cats to make a nice "rabbit stew." These persons don't know the danger that threatens them. In fact, cats, having as their useful mission the killing and eating of rats, which are carriers of the most dangerous bacilli, can be for this reason particularly harmful. . . .

In the warm months, MM. Planteu, Morain and Barleaux, all of No. 20, formed a little garden club and planted seeds they got from the country. But the earth they were able to scrape up by the river must have been sour, because none of their window boxes produced any vegetables.

M. Barleaux, the only one of the group with any previous agricultural experience, blamed the city air. It was pointed out to him that the groundskeepers at the Louvre, which is just over the river, did very well last season. They planted the flower beds with vegetables instead of flowers, and raised a good crop of leeks, carrots, lettuce, cabbage and tomatoes, which they gave to the Secours National for its soup kitchens.

M. Barleaux believed the story about vegetables growing at the Louvre — he had seen them himself, he admitted — but he stopped there.

"Those fellows in their heated offices look pretty well-fed to me," he said. "If the Secours National saw any of those vegetables, they didn't see many."

Always distrust, these days. And talk about the cold. And food. The other night the movie house on the Place St. Michel showed an old film with a banquet scene. When the audience saw all that food, they stood up and cheered.

After several of the neighbors had gone to the country by train and succeeded in buying food from the farmers only to have it confiscated by the cops at the Gare Montparnasse, M. Laval founded Le Club des Bricoleurs (Handymen's Club).

He and M. Joseph and the men from No. 20 went out on their bicycles into the country. On the map they expressly picked a region served by bus, rather than rail, because bus service is so bad that not too many Parisians would head out that way.

Then the five of them went out there. By bicycle. It was a long trip, about forty miles, and they could hardly pedal any more by the time they got back, long after dark. But they came back with food. And it didn't cost them a cent. They couldn't afford the high prices, so they offered services. They fixed clocks, watches, electric motors, plumbing, music boxes, phonographs and radios. In return they got eggs and butter and meat.

Then M. Laval and M. Joseph were arrested, for being Jews. The others haven't gone out since then. They say it is too cold.

The one truly poor family on the street didn't want to face

another winter as miserable as last winter and the winter before. The father, Prosper, hasn't had a steady job since 1939. Nevertheless, they keep on having children. They live in a sort of metal shed in the courtyard of No. 29, which used to be, a long time ago, a blacksmith shop. Times are hard for everybody else, but they are impossible for this family.

After the armistice he was demobilized in the South and wanted his wife and kids to join him there, but he couldn't get them across the demarcation line separating the occupied and the Vichy zones. So he came home.

When he arrived, in September 1940, the German propaganda addressed to the unemployed was in full orchestration. *Germany Offers You Work,* said enormous posters. Employment offices opened all around town. The radio, the newspapers, brightly colored brochures on slick paper. Salaries in Germany are higher. Rations in Germany are higher. Paid two weeks' vacation back in France every ten months. Warm, spacious quarters.

This year the concert continued, only with added touches of "patriotism." One of the posters was dominated by the outline of a noble head in a German helmet. Below, two lines of cheerful, determined workers converged on a group of factories. *They Give Their Blood,* said the headline, and underneath the illustration, *Give Your Work to Save Europe from Bolshevism.*

They didn't forget hunger and poverty as a prod, however. Another poster, covered over now, showed a grinning Frenchman saluting from his workbench. In the foreground, a mother and daughter, heads touching sweetly, smiled. *No More Hard Times!* it read, *Papa Is Making Money in Germany!*

Finally, this autumn Prosper took the bait. But it wasn't bait dangled by the Germans. It was offered by Prime Minister Pierre Laval himself.

The press and the radio had been running items such as "From all over France, special trains of volunteers leave for

German factories, and applications for jobs flood the hiring halls," but it didn't fool anybody, because it was obvious very few men were leaving.*

Then up spoke Pierre Laval. The Germans had offered to release one French prisoner of war for every three skilled workers volunteering to work in Germany. In June of 1942, he announced, "This is the start of the Relief." He made the serious error of adding, "I wish for German victory." Although he added that he wished it because, "without it, tomorrow Bolshevism will implant itself everywhere," what people heard was the first phrase. And even so . . .

The reaction to "la Relève" along the rue du Bossu was bad. One of the jumbo posters, which showed a French worker and soldier arm in arm, had a big white panel with a message addressed to French workers. In the white space around the text passersby scrawled a host of editorial comment. A silly thing to get shot for — and you could well be shot, or at least tortured, for it — but people were that enraged.

A later poster showed cheering, waving "relieved" prisoners leaning out of train windows. More man-to-man text from Laval:

Workers, who leave freely for Germany, look at these men whom you pass on your way. They owe you their liberty; they will never forget you. The gratitude of the entire Nation lifts to you. . . . Brotherhood — which has so often been merely a big word — is translated here into a moving reality.

It was that sort of thing which reached poor Prosper, and when the Germans offered a 1000 franc ($26.70) cash donation for "equipment," that cinched it.

There were not enough poor Prospers. So Laval signed a

* Up until June 1942, German labor recruited about two thousand men a month instead of the thousand a day they sought.

decree in the beginning of September for the Service du
Travail Obligatoire (Compulsory Labor Service). "All Frenchmen between eighteen and fifty, all unmarried Frenchwomen
between twenty and twenty-five are liable to assignment to any
work the Government deems to be in the national interest."

In the twenty mairies of Paris, special offices were installed
for a census of everyone living in the arrondissement. This
way, house by house they could tell how many people of working age lived in each quarter, and whether they had any
special status, such as essential war worker or returned war
prisoner or wounded veteran.

At the same time, all employers were supposed to deliver
a complete rundown on their employees, classified according
to special skills, number of dependents, war service, salary.
Obviously, from what came over the air and what appeared in
the press — who knows what went on behind the scenes? — the
employers stalled. Civil authorities stalled. The fonctionnaires
in the Prefecture stalled.

The Germans have accepted delay after delay. Even Der
Kommandant von Gross-Paris has issued communiqués, saying
that all the fellows who were delayed by personal matters from
reporting as ordered last week will be given until next week
to show up.

The Kerougen brothers from No. 12 reported, had all their
papers stamped, and were told to go to a special waiting room.
They simply walked out of the station, and nobody's bothered
to come looking for them. Not yet. The brothers have been
tipped off that random raids will take place soon, and they'd
better get false papers or else get out of here.

The Nazis, as everyone has seen for two and a half years, are
"reasonable" and "correct" as long as that will get them what
they want. Then, if they don't get it, the mask comes off, and
the fangs show.

Everyone here bets that it came off on November 11 in the

South. With the Allied landings in North Africa, the Germans and Italians pushed into all of France. (The Italians got only the Alpine regions and the Riviera.) The billboards carried the text of a letter to Marshal Pétain ("believe me your wholly devoted, ADOLF HITLER"), and a letter to "FRENCHMEN!" and "Officers and soldiers of the French Army!" (signed, ADOLF HITLER).

The German Army was guaranteeing the integrity of French frontiers against Anglo-American aggression, Hitler said. He offered assurances that the freedom of action of the Vichy government was in no way impaired.

There would be no violence, the Führer said, unless the German troops were opposed "through blind fanaticism or by hirelings of England."

Read on street corners of a prison city, by a people who were dirty, hungry and cold, his closing paragraph was classic:

On the other hand, many French certainly manifest the understandable desire to be freed of the occupation, but let them be convinced that the German soldier, he also, would prefer to be able to live and work peaceably in his own country near to his wife and children or in his paternal home.

There has been one reaction that would probably please the Germans (it probably has come to their attention). Around here, the general reaction to the occupation of all France is roughly, "At last those bastards down there will get a taste of what it's like."

"Those bastards" are of course those Frenchmen who live south of the demarcation line. For two and a half years now, through three everlasting winters, the other side of that demarcation line has seemed like the Promised Land.

No ordinary gray-green uniforms, no élite black uniforms,

no oversized swastika flags, no 100-per-cent all-leather jack boots, no announcements from Der Höhere SS und Polizei-führer, may his soul roast forever in the blackest pit of hell.

Down there, more or less minding his own business, which is what most people up here have been trying to do, a man has been fairly free (*"Vive le Maréchal!"*).

But Parisians haven't rejoiced to know that at least the southern third of their nation was relatively free. They have envied it, begrudged it. The suspicion, the envy that flickers up and down the rue du Bossu exempts nobody.

In defense of the people on this street, it may be said that they are tired. And frightened. Their suspicion and their greedi-ness arise from fear. Nobody knows where anyone else stands, and everyone is as much afraid to ask as to speak out. There are so many sides to be on. What are you? Pro-Allied? Pro-Vichy? Pro-Nazi? Gaullist? Communist? Black Market? Col-laborator? Informer? Resistance?

What did you eat last and where did you get it? Do you have any money, and where did you get *that?* If the Gestapo — either German or French, it's all the same — questions you, what will you say about me? About my friends? About my brother?

And what about my brother? He had some funny ideas there for a while. Is he still my brother? Is he immune to temptation?

Nobody is frank and free. Everyone has something to regret, something to feel guilty about. Everyone has something to be angry about, something to be afraid of. Most people are hungry, most people are cold. Laughter is rare. Winter seems to last forever.

The news from North Africa? Everybody waits to get the nine-thirty broadcast on the English radio. Nobody believes what's in the paper. The paper gave another recipe for homemade soap last week. Burns your skin, but doesn't seem to get the dirt off. Today, one of the sheets gave instructions for making a warm waistcoat out of guess what — the newspaper itself. Isn't it cold, though? Isn't it cold?

Et Vous, Que Faites-Vous Pour Votre Délivrance?

"And You, What Are You Doing for Your Deliverance?" was the headline of an editorial in *Franc-Tireur*, one of the newspapers of the Mouvements Unis de la Résistance late in 1943. The opening sentence was: "There is a mass, still too great, of Frenchmen who remain inert and passive in the face of everything that is happening, as if alien to its own destiny forged by Fighting and Resistant France."

At the same moment, Philippe Henriot, a resoundingly pro-Nazi radio orator, wrote in *Je Suis Partout*, a legal (i.e., collaborating) Paris paper: "I state with regret, but without surprise, that a part of France, apparently its majority, is refractory toward the Government policy."

Both of these statements were true as 1944 began, with D-Day 175 days away: most were against collaboration, but few were for the Resistance. Despite the BBC, the American station in Algiers, the posters on the walls, the shootings in the street, the fires and explosions, the anti-occupation tracts in circulation, the Resistance press, despite the daily denunciations by Germans and collaborators of "Gaullist bandits" and "Communist-Jewish criminals," there were millions of Frenchmen who were learning only now that there was a Resistance. They were learning that there were men and women who were not just waiting for liberation, but who were "doing something for their own deliverance."

As the Nazis and their French cohorts bashed with increased fury at the movements, more and more Frenchmen were drawn into Resistance work. As each "safe house" fell, another had to be found. As each letter drop was discovered, another had to be established. As a réseau was dismantled, it had to be replaced.

As the Russians annihilated German armies, as the Allies crunched up the Italian peninsula, the bleak day-by-endless-day feeling that the war would never end, that the occupation would last forever, began to abate. Although the Germans were everywhere in France and their exactions against the French grew ever more cruel, it was clear that the invincibles were going to lose the war. Hope for liberation had flared with the British commando raids on the ports of Dieppe and St. Nazaire, with the Allied landings in North Africa, with the Italian capitulation, with the liberation of Corsica, and afterwards had each time guttered lower and almost gone out. For Frenchmen not directly active in the Resistance or in the collaboration (i.e., for 95 per cent of the population) daily life was daily more ragged, more hungry, more dreary. People were more haggard, more irritable, more skeptical.

As the police raids, the restrictions, the hardships increased, people became more withdrawn and suspicious. Any feeler from the Resistance could easily be a German trap. Any anti-occupation activity, from chalking a "V" on a wall to listening to the BBC, could be the first step to the concentration camp. The days of the "correct" occupation were centuries behind now, as time was counted out for the Thousand-Year Reich.

The V and the double-barred Gaullist Cross of Lorraine really irritated the Germans, the V more than the cross, because the V was universal. No sooner had the BBC begun broadcasting the Morse Code-Beethoven "V" than it began appearing on the walls of all the occupied cities. Ubiquitous, ineradicable, it haunted the myth-minded Germans. They had made a fetish of the swastika, and they loathed this counter-charm. It was the handwriting on the wall.

Since they could not obliterate it, they resolved to adopt it and pervert it, as they had done with the word "socialist" and with the revolutionary color red. This accomplished, when people tore their Métro tickets into V shapes and let them drop so the subway draughts carried hundreds of green or buff victory symbols dancing through the corridors, they would be spreading German, not French, propaganda. Forthwith, the *Propaganda Staffel* said, the V would stand, not for the French *Victoire* nor the English *Victory*, but for the German . . . the German what? The German word for victory is *Sieg*. All right, then, V for the Germano-Latin *Victoria!*

In June 1941, posters in Reich red appeared in the occupied zone, bearing a white V with a swastika under the point, like a medal hanging from a ribbon. The text said, *Victoria! The Triumph of Germany Which Fights for the New Europe.* Handbills were sown through the streets, bearing the inscription "VH," under which was printed *Vive Hitler.* The V was painted on German vehicles.

The master strokes of the propaganda plan were reserved for the Eiffel Tower and the Chambre des Deputés at the end of the Pont de la Concorde. On these two structures appeared huge V's, forty feet high, under which were enormous banners reading *Deutschland Siegt An Allen Fronten,* "Germany victorious on all fronts."

By the end of summer, the campaign was concluded. It was not renewed. The banners and the gigantic V's were taken down. No new posters appeared. When the Germans retreated from Paris in 1944, some of their trucks still bore weatherworn German-painted V's. By this time the V had been assigned to the flying bombs and the rockets hurled at London. This V stood not for *Victoria,* but for *Vergeltung,* vengeance.

The underground press was the target of similar stratagems

from time to time. Every now and then, the Germans would counterfeit a Resistance newspaper, and the entire underground press would denounce the false issue. Had the Germans put out their own carefully poisoned counterfeits on a regular basis, they might well have impaired, if not nullified, the impact of the true Resistance press. But this they did not do, and the regular issues of newspapers from the movements passed two million copies a month as 1944 ripened.

By this time, virtually all of them were printed on regular presses (some of them built out of spare parts). Paper and ink were virtually impossible to obtain, but the one hundred major publications (plus four hundred to five hundred regional and local) managed every month to get enough for their needs. *Combat*, for example, needed more than ten tons of paper a year for its printing plants in Lyon, Annemasse, Nice, Tarbes and Villefranche-sur-Saône. Not a scrap of it could be bought openly, of course. Writing, printing, distributing, procuring supplies were all criminal acts. The Vichy police alone in 1943 jailed 1700 people for illegal press activities.

One virtually painless method of finding newsprint was through the Vichy Government Office of Paper Distribution, which overordered from sources of supply when it could and gave the Resistance the difference between what was on hand and what was distributed to the legal press.

Another source of supplies was the Germans themselves, through the black market, although this cost too much for the slim resources of the movements. On one occasion, one of the organizations learned that a printing firm was going bankrupt, and that the owners, having milked it dry, had taken flight. A big order of paper was on its way, and so the Resistance simply signed for it with the absconders' signatures and took delivery. Railroad yard pilferage supplied some paper, but it was difficult to make off undetected with such bulky loot.

One of the more incredible operations of the underground press was the Groupe de la rue de Lille, incredible because it was never discovered, and because it would have been one of the biggest plums the Gestapo could have picked. From the very first days of the Resistance, leaders gathered at "the General Advertising Office," 37 rue de Lille, Paris VII. The owner was a broad-shouldered man with the face of a boxer, Emilien Amaury. His self-appointed task: to keep the Resistance press operating. He found printing plants, pressmen, typographers willing to risk their lives printing illegal periodicals. When one was seized, he found another.

When the plant for a paper was suddenly raided, Resistance men could appeal to Amaury to bail them out, to get the paper printed somewhere, somehow. His group took over transportation and distribution as well. In this way he was concerned in the publication of the *Cahiers* of both the Organisation Civile et Militaire and the Comité Général d'Etudes, as well as some of the twenty-five splendid volumes published secretly by Les Editions de Minuit. The movement newspapers aided by Le Groupe de la Rue de Lille included *Témoignage Chrétien, Résistance, Libération* (both *Nord* and *Sud*), *Lettres Françaises, Eternelle Revue* and *Défense de la France.*

This meant that Amaury knew leaders of most of the movements, as well as knowing the location of dozens of printing plants working for them. Resistance chiefs dropped in often to talk and sometimes held meetings in his office. Yet somehow, through four years, the Gestapo and the police picked up no thread which led back to the rue de Lille.

FALSE PAPERS

Everyone in France must have papers. Each significant event in every life is marked by a knot in the red tape which tethers the Frenchman from cradle to grave. At any moment he may be summoned by authority to show his papers. These are issued by the Government, and there is no aspect of French life in which the Government does not have some power, regulatory, licensing, recording or punitive. To obtain certain papers he must first present certain other papers. As he builds his life, he also builds a pyramid of papers.

The war added a sheaf of papers to those essential for survival. The occupation added even more, for if there is any bureaucrat more devoted to *paperasserie* than the French fonctionnaire, it is the German.

For those with false identities, all the proper papers had to be provided to sustain the reality of the fictional personage. Some chiefs needed several sets, one for Monsieur X at the cover job and address, one for Monsieur Y at his real address, Monsieur W in Lyon, Monsieur Q at Nice.

These were some of the essential papers: identity card, draft card, labor card, and seven kinds of ration cards (meat, wine, butter, bread, conserves, textiles, tobacco). Under certain circumstances, he would need a marriage certificate. If crossing any of the lines (the demarcation line between north and south was not lifted until 1943), he needed special passes, which meant that he needed other papers to obtain or sustain the passes.

If the man with the identity card happened to be circumcized, and happened to be caught in one of those strip-to-the-skin examinations, he would need evidence that he was not a Jew. This evidence would probably be in the form of a baptismal certificate which, if checked, would have to correspond to the parish registry. Thus, to serve as effective protection, the certificate would always have to be "genuine," even if the entry in the registry was false, which it often was, since both the Protestant and Catholic clergy in general had a lively animosity toward Nazi racial laws.

The identity card would have to correspond to a genuine registered identity, the Resistance soon learned. It was too easy for the suspicious policeman, either French or German, to make a phone call or send a telegram. Many "genuine" fakes were issued by friendly mayors. But more often they were simply stolen true identities inscribed on false cards.

Resistance men in Gardes Mobiles uniform would block a
street and copy the particulars on the identity cards of passersby.
In a city where the Resistance thronged, such as Lyon, they
risked copying off completely false identities carried by other
Resistance members.

All buyers and sellers of gold and jewelry had to surrender
their cards at the jeweler's, and everyone registering at a hotel
had to do the same. Both of these sources furnished details of
authentic identities for the Resistance. The Vichy National Sta-
tistical Service (whose director died in deportation) furnished
the movement a completely catalogued selection of five-
thousand true identities, male and female, twenty to sixty years
old.

Men of military age had to have papers showing they had
not been taken prisoner of war, but had been legally demobilized. Or that they had been prisoners of war and had been
repatriated. Once the Compulsory Labor Service was introduced, men and single women of the proper age group had to
show they were already working for the Germans, or that they
were medical students or seriously ill.

An ideal source of legitimate cards was a company engaged
in construction work for the Germans. It was an equitable arrangement — the resistant never collected his pay, but then, he
never reported for work. The boss of such a firm would do the
worst possible job for his clients, the Germans, using materials
sure to disintegrate under impact, slowing down the job, having
a record number of work accidents. It was often difficult, and
on some occasions impossible, to save such false collaborators
from punishment by post-liberation vigilantes.

Other "legitimate" work cards showed that the employee was
engaged in essential German war production — in the French
plant of a totally false company. One such fictitious company
was the Omnium Français des Produits de Synthèse, brainchild
of the Marco Polo Réseau. It was duly registered and licensed
by all the proper governing bodies, and it had thousands of

employees. Yet it never existed at all. Similarly, Lieutenant Colonel Xavier de la Borde-Noguès founded a company producing incredible amounts of charcoal in the Landes, all fictional. His employees reported for work for the first time at liberation, and marched on Bordeaux as an army of three-thousand men.

Every single one of these papers issued, from local authorities, Vichy ministries, prefectures, and a host of German military and zonal commands, had to bear authentic stamps and signatures. Some were copies, some were stolen. To copy the stamps, the false papers services of the various organizations had to learn how to make molds, how to vulcanize rubber, how to make perfect forgeries.

The Comité Contre la Déportation, which was set up to serve all this organization late in 1943, had fourteen-thousand molds for stamps and printed half a million false work cards. The services had to keep up to date on all the cards and stamps in use, since the organization of the occupation changed from time to time, and some of the cards themselves were changed from time to time by the issuing authority, as a security measure.

Fabricators of cards even had to know how individual issuing offices filled out the blanks in standard forms. There were municipalities which wrote the bearer's name in capital letters, and there were others which put the name in larger letters than the rest, but not in capitals. The counterfeiters had to know that the small "1" of the French Government Printing Office had an almost invisible cross stroke through the middle, and that a genuine préfet de police (Paris) heading had the "o" upside down.

It was hard work, pitilessly detailed. Any carelessness by the false papers people could cost the card-bearer his life, and might even lead to the destruction of the réseau. Those who worked in hidden rooms perfecting the forger's skills never engaged in cloak-and-dagger dealings or hit-and-run raids, but they gave essential services, and, when they were discovered, their lives.

DOCTORS

One of the groups which issued genuine papers with false information was the medical profession. The issuance of certificates which showed the bearer to be suffering from tuberculosis, or leukemia or angina pectoris (and therefore unable to serve the Germans) was only a small part of what the doctors of France did for the Resistance.

Since they were allowed to operate motor cars and travel after curfew in most parts of France, they often carried illegal passengers and messages. They took Resistance wounded into their hospitals and private clinics. They made room for Jewish physicians, forbidden by Nazi and Vichy law to practice. Some went out into the field as army surgeons to the maquis. In 1943, they formed a national organization, the Medical Service of the Resistance.

From the very beginning of the occupation, physicians were active in every phase of resistance. Some of them edited Resistance newspapers (Dr. Marcel Renet started the third *Résistance*). Some of them were chiefs of organizations (Dr. Henri Ingrand, of Ceux de la Résistance). Some of them opened their houses as meeting places and as reception centers for new agents (Dr. Recordier in Marseille).

When Paris Resistance was desperate for reinforcement, twenty missions set off to try to reach Allied headquarters. The one which bore fruit was that of Commandant Gallois, led out of Paris by Prospère (Dr. Robert Monod), chief of the Paris section of the Medical Service. Through his network of colleagues, Prospère was in contact with the Allies on the other side of the German lines. Gallois was passed along a chain of doctors to the Resistance combatants in liaison with the Americans.

Because so many doctors responded so quickly, and because,

perhaps, the public accepts the self-sacrifice of physicians as "natural," as part of their job, the extraordinary role of doctors in the Resistance has been almost taken for granted. As medical practitioners working under conditions of extreme hazard, they were exemplary. As patriots and warriors their services have not been adequately recognized.

POSTMEN

As a network of networks, the Post, Telegraph and Telephone Ministry was prefabricated Resistance apparatus — if the Resistance could capture it. Neither the Ministry's civil servants nor the humblest rural letter carrier waited to be captured. From the first, they began volunteering, and in the end the whole system was functioning as part of the uprising against the enemy. Vichy zealots and Nazi security officials did their best to impede the Resistance work of the PTT, using under-cover men and offering the usual compound of bribery and terror to induce treason: "their best" included the lives of five-hundred employees and officials, and the deportation of fifteen-hundred others.

There were more than ten thousand survivors to share the honor of a corporative Medaille de la Résistance and Croix de la Guerre. In an Order of the Day, General de Gaulle called their group "a magnificent movement."

As soon as mail cars were allowed to cross the demarcation line, in the days of the thirteen-line "family post cards," the mail cars were full of strange cargo. Fugitives were carried disguised as guards and letter-sorters, and illegal correspondence was hidden under the official government mail pouches.

This simple service in time became a complete secret postal system, picking up and distributing Resistance messages and packages. There was a regular daily service between Paris and nineteen other cities in the four corners of France, and starting in 1943, there was a Resistance man assigned to each mail car to give special handling to this special consignment. Messages and plans for London went to Britanny, where they were smuggled to a fishing boat which made rendezvous at sea with the Royal Navy. Starting in 1944, the Armée Secrète sent "orders, plans of attack, and funds" serenely by post, using other forms of delivery only in cases of derailment, bombing of the lines, or suspected enemy infiltration.

The PTT maintained a warning service for the maquis by telephone. Alerted by men of the NAP (Noyautage des Administrations Publiques, which recruited and organized resistants in civil services) or by Resistance infiltrators of impending anti-maquis action by the police, gendarmerie, Gardes Mobiles, Milice or the Germans, the PTT would phone the message from country post office to country post office until the word reached all the maquis on the route. The same system worked to let maquis on the move know whether there were enemy forces on the road ahead of them.

With its own printing plants and its superior knowledge of rubber stamps, the PTT was able to furnish every kind of false card needed, and with the proper stamps. In addition, it could supply invaluable documents showing the bearer to be an inspector of the service, obliged by his duties to travel constantly and to pass into every corner of the country. This sort of card would be accompanied by a German *Ausweis*, and special passes for the special zones.

Valuable though its services were to the Resistance, from a military point of view the PTT's services to the Allies were very possibly of more importance: military information and sabotage planning and execution.

The postal workers copied all official telegrams from Germany, from the German and Italian embassies at Paris, and to and from Vichy. All letters that might contain useful information were opened and copied. The code used by Joseph Darnand, head of the Milice and later head of all French police forces, was broken by PTT teams. In this way, the PTT frequently warned of surveillance or arrest orders, and warning was sent out to the Resistance. The location of forty V-1 launching sites was discovered in this way in a two-month period. The subterranean storage depot for V-2 fuel at Chartres was revealed by the same means.

A good deal of the military intelligence was broadcast to London directly by PTT radios. To foil the direction-finders, the messages were split up between several sending stations, each one broadcasting its portion for one minute only, in relay.

Executives of the ministry put together Plan Violet, the master plan for D-Day sabotage of the subsurface long-distance cables of the PTT. The sabotages were worked out to insure stoppage at the proper time, and to insure as well that post-liberation repairs would be rapid and easy. The cables put down by the Germans for their own use were to be destroyed entirely.

"Bloc planning" at the Free French headquarters in London, working in conjunction with the SOE to avoid duplication of D-Day behind-the-lines action, assigned execution of Plan Violet to no element of the FFI, but left it entirely in the hands of the PTT. The cuts would be directed by the men who had planned them, and carried out by regular wire crews. The BBC signal would be *"Je n'entends plus ta voix"* — I no longer hear your voice.

In addition to the PTT, other public administrations were infiltrated by the Resistance, at first through friendships and later through the "seeding" operations of the NAP. With the armistice, many a civil service official wisely kept his post and volunteered to serve the Resistance from within the permanent public administrations which had passed under the titular control of Vichy ministers.

Through the protection of such officials, Fred Scamaroni, a BCRA agent, was employed by the Ministry of Food. Henri Frenay, founder of Combat, was with Vichy Army intelligence. When, in January 1941, Frenay turned in his resignation to go underground, the assistant chief of the General Staff, General Picquendart, told him that if he hated the city of Vichy, he

could have his pick of Army posts anywhere. Frenay replied
— and it is now a classic of Resistance literature — "I am in the
position of a priest who has lost his faith and whose bishop sug-
gests a change of parish."

Although some prefects were ardent Vichyites, and others
stuck to their posts simply to do their best for their populations,
there were some who cooperated handsomely with the Resistance, and some of these paid for it with their lives.

The Ministry of Roads and Bridges helped the maquis of
several regions by bringing warnings from the PTT, by not co-
operating with the enemy. This ministry helped with the Plan
Tortue, which made assignments to the Resistance action groups
for cutting roads and blowing bridges to slow German reinforcements on the way to the Allied invasion front.

In the final days, when liberation and victory seemed im-
minent, even the members of Laval's personal bodyguard were
found to be enrolled in the Resistance. Before those days, the
civil servant who worked with the organizations did so at the
risk of his life. There were thousands upon thousands who took
that risk.

RAILROAD MEN

All the main organizations of the Resistance had their own
action groups. Besides these, there were the "private armies,"
the *groupes* and *corps francs*, and the many sections of the
maquis. All of these engaged in sabotage of canals, ports, factories, power installations and railroads, especially railroads. But
no group was more enthusiastic in thwarting the occupation use
of railways than the railroad men themselves, an army of experts, given to espionage and sabotage.

Since railroaders are traditionally independent-minded union
men, the Germans expected trouble from them. Under Army
command, German railroad men were installed on all super-
visory levels. It was announced that French employees were

subject to German military law and courts-martial. To empha-
size this point during the occupation, three hundred French rail
workers (*cheminots*) were shot and three thousand deported
in the northern zone alone. In 1944 some twenty-five thousand
trainmen were brought in from Germany to "stiffen" the doubt-
ful French crews.

When the occupation began, many railroad men began isolated spontaneous acts of resistance. Soon after, they were
formed into action groups by organizers from Combat, OCM,
and SOE. When the Socialist and Communist parties and the
two unions got back into action, they extended the Resistance
activity of the *cheminots*. The NAP lined up foremen, stationmasters, supervisors and executives.

Before parachute drops provided explosives, the men used
dynamite and homemade bombs. They set fire to shipments of
gasoline, oil, hay, wood, cloth. They greased the rails on sharp
curves, put sand and emery in axle lubricants, loosened cou-
plings, tampered with brakes, unbolted rails, jammed switches,
changed signals, "lost" cars, multiplied loading and unloading
damage.

The cables anchoring cannon and armored vehicles to flat
cars were partially cut or loosened so that the load eventually
ripped loose on a curve. The heavy armament would spill off
the cars and, with luck, fall onto the tracks and derail whole
trains.

A mechanical engineer named Ledoux worked for Combat's
(later MUR's) *Résistance-Fer* as a roving instructor in sabotage
techniques. He started on his own at the Hispano-Suiza works,
picking three hundred men out of the seven thousand employees. After members of the group made slight alterations in
the working drawings and readjusted a few machine tools and
provided for an endless series of small delays which disrupted
schedules, there was a notable drop in the plant's production.

Although collaborationist suppliers furnished materials for

1200 motors, the factory turned out only 614, and only one out of three would function for more than a few hours.

Ledoux was arrested by the Vichy police and turned over to the Germans but was broken out of jail by a Combat action group. After this, he turned his attention to railroads as well as factories to teach the use of explosives, time detonators and incendiary pencils as well as the art of the planned accident. He traveled all over France on his educational mission.

One artful achievement in sabotage was the destruction of turntables in roundhouses, which immobilized a terminus for weeks. This was accompanied, when possible, by the destruction of all the locomotives in the roundhouse, sometimes as many as fifty in a major terminal. Where explosives were not available or their use not advisable because of guards and reprisals, turntables were destroyed by simply ignoring all standard safety precautions and letting steam engines blow themselves to pieces. Faulty maintenance was a slow but effective sabotage technique.

Administrative mistakes about routes, and timetables, and pettyfogging application of all the regulations that had silted up since 1835 produced costly delays. Misrouting and accidental damage to wrecking cranes made it impossible to clear wrecks from the tracks, into which other trains could then be directed to make the tangle inextricable.

Resistance leaders were smuggled across the demarcation line in Laval's private train. The men lay on planks above the waterline in the engine's tank. Others were smuggled past searchers by outfitting them as crew members. Baggage men and stationmasters took care of valises full of explosives, arms, and illegal newspapers.

And they spied ceaselessly, reporting every German displacement by rail. (A sixty-train divisional convoy made a superb target for Allied dive bombers.) When the time came to put Plan Vert into execution, the French railroad men were magnificent, and the plan functioned beautifully.

LES BEAUX COUPS DE MAIN

Sabotage of inestimable usefulness was carried out all over the country. Sometimes instead of destroying factories or anti-invasion defensive works, steps were taken to insure that the products were fatally flawed. This led the enemy, until the time came to put the materials to use, into a false sense of security, replaced by a real sense of insecurity when the materials failed.

Thus, gun ports did not provide the proper field of fire after blueprints had been re-drawn; shells proved to be duds; chemicals were inert; electrical circuits burned out. This sort of built-in panic for the critical moment was installed not in French factories alone. French volunteers, whose heroism has almost never been cited, went to Germany to work and to carry out sabotage inside the Third Reich.

The Resistance was persuaded that sabotage is, in most cases, better than bombing inside a nation where the population is friendly. After an effective sabotage the object may remain standing, but it will be useless. This achieves the military objective without leaving civilians dead or wounded or homeless. Also, it's a lot cheaper, in lives of the attacking force and in training time and in money.

In September 1942, five Resistance men struck a blow inside France to aid Allied convoys out in the Atlantic. They got through the fences at Ste. Assise, dodged across the heavily and constantly patrolled road surrounding the huge steel broadcasting towers of the Kreigsmarine. They squirmed across the bare ground to the shadow of the towers. They had almost no time, and discovery was almost certain. Affixing the charges was physically and technically of the greatest difficulty: it's hard to bring down a set of enormous steel pylons with only the materials you can carry on your back. But they did it, and the Submarine Command was suddenly cut off from its U-boats.

A similar group was able to destroy a power station in Central France, paralyzing a whole complex of factories producing for the Germans. The action groups of the Resistance carried on their war of destruction, aided later by the maquis. They had a great many targets other than transportation and industry, however. They seized arms, ammunition, clothing, cars, trucks, fuel, and medical supplies for the Resistance. They broke into jails and hospitals to rescue Allied airmen, agents and Resistance men. They killed, kidnapped and raided.

In 1943, the *groupe franc* organized in Toulouse had eight joyous weeks which lifted them out of what might be called the "ordinary." This little army started with a dozen men and grew to forty. It struck night after night, running through the whole catalogue of underground violence. The Gestapo was unable to infiltrate, unable to catch one raider, or to find one traitor to serve them. Doubling, tripling patrols did no good, house-to-house search yielded nothing, nor did street search or drag nets. Even a 50-million-franc reward brought no claimants.

To trap the leader of the Phantom Squad — they got around to calling it that without the aid of headline writers — the Toulouse Gestapo chief took on a French counterespionage expert, a thirty-year-old former member of the Armistice Army. They couldn't tell him much more than that the leader of the group was called Riccardo. (They didn't know he was also called Morhange and Tabarre. This multiplicity of noms-de-guerre, employed for security reasons, often made the Resistance seem rather bigger than it was at the time.)

The newcomer was given one sole assignment, to capture his fellow countryman. He almost succeeded, but Riccardo always managed to elude the traps, although he was forced to leave behind some battered trucks or useless rifles every time.

The new man built up a little squad of his own, all French. They circulated day and night, stopping to check with patrols and roadblocks, coursing the region in their fast black cars. After two months the Gestapo, probably through the normal process of checking, found that their new demon detective, their Riccardo-catcher, was in fact Riccardo himself. He was Marcel Taillandier, owner of the Café Frascati, which had been raided on a tip from an informer. The Gestapo had picked up a nice netful of Resistance men there, deporting five and executing one, but Taillandier had got away. Not long after that, the Phantom Squad had made its first appearance.

They were livid with rage, the Gestapo. They had thousands of posters printed, using the photo from Taillandier's official Gestapo papers. They placarded fences, trees, barns, stores, telegraph poles with it. But the *groupe franc* continued its coups de main, and Taillandier was as free as ever.

Eventually, the photograph bore fruit, and the leader was recognized at a roadblock. He got away under gunfire, but was finally trapped in a courtyard. But the pursuers couldn't find him. The courtyard was empty. He was a phantom, all right. The Feldgendarmes were about to start a room-by-room search of the houses which faced the court, when a tile fell from a roof. They fired, and Taillandier fell too.

Of all the coups de main brought off before the liberation, the most spectacular was Operation Jericho. It was devised by Dominique Ponchardier of Sosies, the military intelligence réseau whose two leaders could not resist killing Germans, blowing up locomotives and staging raids.

Most of the réseau's big sabotage operations were carried out by a *groupe franc* recruited and directed by a Spanish war veteran named Pépé. Although Communist, and a part of the FTP after 1942, Pépé had started working with Dominique in 1940 and never stopped. His outfit served Sosies on a freelance basis all through the war, contrary to Party directives.

Pépé's ace train-stopper, Jean Baurin, was in Amiens prison, along with his brother and his mother, who had sacrificed herself in a vain effort to lead the Gestapo away from her boys. Jean had been caught after one of his best coups, derailment of a troop train on the Abbeville-Tréport line, with two hundred German dead, four hundred wounded.

Also in the prison were ten other men of Baurin's team, and at least five hundred other "political" prisoners. Like Baurin, many of them were under sentence of death. This was at the end of 1943, an awful year for the Resistance. Dominique and Pépé decided to attack the jail and rescue their men. They got hold of the plans of the prison, made their reconnaissance, and were now preparing the action.

The whole scheme was blown from the start. The Sosies contact man, carrying one-half of the prison map as identification, was arrested at the rendezvous. Pépé's contact man had just managed to avoid the trap, but he was picked up that night on suspicion of involvement in the theft of ration cards from the town hall. So now the Germans would be expecting a raid on the prison.

The only way to get their men out, said Dominique, and he was the sort of man who said such things at such times, was to march around the prison blowing a ram's horn till the walls came tumbling down.

Walls came tumbling down? Walls came tumbling down! He'd have the RAF come and tumble them for him. He was in his twenties and he had seen even more impossible things happen in his three and one-half years of doing the impossible. Pépé was older and knew more about the military mind. He helped to work out the details, but he nevertheless left Amiens after that and went up to Rouen. He thought that if the RAF felt disinclined to blow open the prison, perhaps a simultaneous Resistance strike at both the Amiens and Rouen jails would confuse the Germans and thin out the opposition.

To answer any question that anyone in London might have, Dominique dispatched every scrap of information he could find. By Lysander pickup in mid-January he sent the original blueprints of the prison, taken from the town archives. He sent details of anti-aircraft installations, the names, strengths and dispositions of the German Amiens garrison and of a Panzer battalion stationed nearby, together with the officers' roster for each. He sent the names, ages, work schedules and personal routines of the prison wardens, the times of day for guard changes and meals, a list of the prisoners and their war records.

This done, he inflamed his two hundred-man réseau to outstrip its former achievements, and inundated London with gems of military information on installations and plans all the way from Toulouse to Normandy. January passed and there was no reply. Dominique sent an eloquent sketch of the work of the Resistance and its current losses, urging the Amiens operation as an unparalleled morale booster for the French and a nasty blow to German morale as well. This brought a reply: "No."

Nevertheless, one day the Amiens anti-aircraft began popping away at a lone plane buzzing about in the prison area. Somebody in London had ordered reconnaissance pictures. The head of the SOE intelligence réseau Alibi, named Zloti, alias Chaubière, returned to France from London. Dominique found him and explained matters, and soon Alibi was earnestly giving London reasons why Operation Jericho should be launched.

London finally replied that Group Captain P. C. Pickard, commander of Mosquito Wing 140, had asked to see the photographs. If Pickard wanted to try, the RAF would let him, for Pickard was one of those heroes (three DSO's) who impress even the RAF. He had led a squadron of Czech daredevils on one hundred missions, survived a week on a raft in the North Sea, been H.M. the King's personal pilot, and his last assignment had been flying Lysanders, the tiny planes used to land and pick up agents and messages behind enemy lines. Pickard had been doing this inside Germany.

While Pickard was studying the project, two British agents parachuted right into German hands, and on February 12 were committed to Amiens prison. Dominique also learned the date set for Baurin's execution: February 19. This news was radioed at once to London. It evoked an immediate reply.

IN RETURN EXCEPTIONAL SERVICES RENDERED RAF CONSENTS TO
PUT AT YOUR DISPOSITION SQUADRON MOSQUITOES WHICH
ATTACK REFER YOUR PLAN BEGINNING FIFTEENTH AT NOON
GOOD LUCK.

London could also have added LOVE, because this message
arrived on St. Valentine's Day, the fourteenth. This left little
possibility of security breach, and it also left less than twenty-
four hours to arrange the ground action for the jail delivery.

Pépé was still in Rouen, but Dominique persuaded the FTP
to honor the plan. Next day just before noon they showed up
with one hundred men and a dozen trucks. The planes did not
come. Snow fell instead of bombs. The FTP very prudently
got away from there. Nor could they be lured back. Dominique,
with twenty-two men and three antique charcoal-burning
trucks, kept vigil the next day. And on the seventeenth. And
on the eighteenth.

As the last peal of the noon bells died away (Baurin, alerted
and waiting in his death cell, counted the bell strokes), there
was a tremendous explosion.

The cruciform three-story prison, with arms pointing north
and south, had common criminals in the central building, politicals in the wings. The structure was surrounded by a wall
twenty-five feet high and three feet thick.

This wall was the target of Wave A, six planes. The first
500-pound bomb (they had tested a variety of charges against
brick walls in England) struck at the perfect angle, five feet
from the ground, and blew a breach three yards wide.

Wave B, six more planes, was to strike the walls of the two
wings and smash the guard's mess hall. Its mission went off
exactly as planned. All the planes, including reserve Wing C,
scooted off to blast the secondary target, the railroad yards.
Their British Typhoon fighter cover engaged the Focke-Wolffs
bearing down from the north. One Mosquito was hit, and

Pickard's plane circled to be sure the crew bailed out safely. Pickard was then shot down and died.

At the prison, although all had gone according to plan, it was evident that there had been a mistake in the planning. The bombs should have been 200-pounders, because the old bricks were held in only by crumbling mortar. Many prisoners were trapped as portions of the building collapsed. The wooden timbers burned and blood streamed down the stone stairways. There was a good deal of screaming. Surviving guards began firing from the rubble. The rescue party fired back, and kept them from shooting at the fleeing prisoners. By twelve-fifteen the firing ceased (twenty Germans dead, eighty wounded).

It was past the time to get out of there. Still, the FTP did not come, though they must have seen the smoke and heard the noise. Some prisoners stayed to help the trapped and wounded. Others, believing that the Germans would still let them go when they'd served out their terms, chose to stay at the prison. One hundred and eighty, fearing reprisals against their families, came back within a day or two. In the bombing and the shooting eighty-seven prisoners died and eighty were wounded. One of the wounded was Mme. Baurin, and she was rescued from the hospital later.

About 250 got away, including the two British agents, Dominique's contact man, and Baurin. Within the Resistance, there was an energetic cleaning out of Gestapo infiltrators and Resistance traitors, identified by the ex-prisoners. At escape time, only two of Dominique's trucks would start, but he got away. He worked with Pépé and Baurin on the Rouen jail delivery in June.

SPIES

The Germans had three great secrets. The Resistance pierced them all and reported them to the Allies: there were the strengths and dispositions of troops; there were the secret

weapons, the V-1 flying bomb and the V-2 supersonic rocket
with warhead; and there were the details of the Atlantic Wall
of Festung Europa.

German officers made prisoner in the first phase of the Allied
invasion were stunned to see that field commanders had complete maps of fortifications, tank traps, minefields. Keyed to
the map was a chart of every unit on service and in reserve
along the invasion front, including the names of the officers.

In *Sie Kommen,* a book describing the Allied campaign from
the German viewpoint, Paul Carell wrote:

Richly provisioned by the talkative, the slow-witted, or by traitors,
an army of secret agents had collected this information in Occupied France. The combatants of the Résistance had done the rest.
As dishwashers in the mess, or as "volunteer auxiliaries," they
succeeded in spying, discovering, picking up, and everything they
got was carefully noted, recorded by them and transmitted. Sabotage
was equally organized on a grand scale. It spread over the whole
of France and comprised thousands of members. . . .

Spying had not stopped when the Germans conquered
France. Polish and Czech intelligence officers working for the
British inside France remained where they were. British spies,
some of whom had been implanted years before in France in
impeccable cover jobs, remained at their posts. The tradition
of spying on one's friends thus paid unexpected dividends,
because the friendly nation had suddenly become enemy territory.

In the world which the spy inhabits, there is no such thing
as a friendly nation. In the main, the world of nations is a
pagan world, expressing no ethic except that of individual
survival. It is dark and cold out there, and nothing grows
save suspicion and fear. "War is the continuation of politics
by other means." This is the world in which the spy lives,
alone and concealed. If he is discovered, he is supposed to re-

main an unidentified, unclean body, unconnected with the ethical societies which prevail back inside the pale.

A voluntary exile from the organized body of society, the spy is supposed to divest himself of every tenet of the ethic except loyalty. This loyalty is not really an expression of any moral obligation, however; it is merely, like expendability, one of the terms of employment.

What would be a foul, heartless deed for anyone else could be a matter for congratulation in a spy. Unfair, indecent, immoral? These are words for propagandists, for people inside a society. In the frozen void, the dark side of international politics, they are not words with meaning, words such as *gun* or *document* or *orders*.

"The work of an intelligence service . . . is an obscure, ungrateful work; it is composed of the sum of tasks which have about them nothing of the romantic, the amusing or the comfortable . . . It demands an effacement of personality, a modesty and a spirit of sacrifice of which few men are capable, and of which even fewer men are capable for very long."*

In the intelligence réseaux of the Resistance, the majority were untrained in the work, unschooled in the disciplines of solitude, anonymity and immorality. They worked, not out of icy devotion to the lethal game, but out of hot-blooded patriotism. They were in general guided by a purity of heart rather than a knowledge of the rules. Out of innocence, they died in appalling numbers.

The numbers are hard to come by, because the spy is officially a fictional character. Although they cannot possibly cover the full number of men and women involved, these are the official figures: dead, 8230; jailed, but missing, 2578; returned alive from concentration camps, 7381. In proportion to the number of people involved, the intelligence réseaux had the heaviest losses of the whole Resistance.

* Colonel Georges Groussard, Resistance-British Intelligence spymaster, in his 1964 book, *Service Secret*, Paris.

There were perhaps a hundred réseaux, but so many of them were smashed and rebuilt that the statistics are not really statistics at all. The réseaux varied in membership from fifty to nine hundred. The réseaux Marco Polo had nine hundred members when it was successfully assaulted by the Abwehr. A good many of the nine hundred went into hiding and survived. Some of these remade the old Lyon headquarters organization into Promontoire, and the former branches in Marseille, Paris and other cities gave birth to Béarn, Surcouf, Marceau and other independent units.

There were two kinds of intelligence operations conducted by the normal réseaux: "subscription" and "mission." The first was the essential diet of routine information from a fixed area. When sifted and collated, it gave a complete running account of German activity in France. It revealed strong and weak points in the occupation web and indicated targets for attack by saboteurs, aircraft or naval units.

"Subscription" sometimes exposed infiltrators or double agents, gave news of arrests and gave warning of contemplated operations against the Resistance. It charted patterns useful in possible future strikes by action groups — times of patrols, regular departures and arrivals of high officials, payroll deliveries, and such. Weekly, or even daily, each operative noted whatever was assigned to him: port movements, troop movements, rail and road traffic, the progress of military works or modifications of existing organizations. There were periodical questionnaires from the "Central" which received all the reports, asking for specific information. These reports were filed by agents resident in the area.

Here too there was divergence of opinion between réseau chiefs. Some believed in the "thousand eyes" technique which employed as many neighborhood people as possible to be volunteer spies, reporting every scrap of information or overheard conversation, no matter how trivial-seeming. With this system a considerable security risk and a workload generally too big for the Central were balanced against a valuable mass of minute detail.

The opponents of this system believed in the "expert eye" technique. These recruited men whose regular employment gave them access to critical information, such as the captain or chief pilot of a port. The number of operatives was kept to a minimum, security was reinforced, a great deal of time was gained in laying hands on the information, and the chances were greatly improved that the information would be reliable.

The "mission" operation was just that. Special missions, either individuals or teams or relays of teams, were assigned to carry out special tasks.

Although the rule was "Intelligence does not undertake action," at times the mission was a hair-raising blend of both. After all, what if you had to kill someone or blow a safe to get what you'd been sent after?

Assignments made to two of Spymaster Colonel Groussard's officers can be considered as typical of "action" missions. One had himself lowered down the baronial chimney of a chateau to eavesdrop on a meeting of the Abwehr (German intelligence) and the Vichy police. The meeting went on all day and into the night as the réseau operative hung just out of sight in the chimney. After almost twenty-four hours, he was hauled out, a sooty human pretzel. None of the thousand tiny accidents that might have happened to betray his presence had happened.

Another was sent to frustrate a dragnet operation by the Italian secret police, the OVRA, at Nice. The operative was Lieutenant André Devigny, who later made an historic unaided escape from Montluc prison outside Lyon (footnote page 145). The dragnet would have scooped up a key intelligence agent, destroying an important part of the Groussard network. The mission was to delay the action until the intended victims could turn their work over to others and disappear. There was only one way to do it: kill the OVRA man in charge. This was done.

Even the ordinary functions of intelligence were extremely dangerous. The nature of the work exposed those engaged in it to every risk the enemy could impose. It required an iron discipline and a strict security system which basically meant isolating operatives from one another and chiefs from subordinates, so that even if torture produced confessions, there was not much any one person could tell. This essential requirement was often ignored through the amateur zeal for service, and even the most professional groups lost as many as 10 per cent of their effectives, while the poorest run had up to 90 per cent casualties.

Once material had been gathered by the field operative, at the risk of death, it was, again at the risk of death, transported to a letter drop. From each drop it was taken — at the risk of death — to the Central. Here the information was examined by the chief of the group. He matched it against similar reports, spliced together bits which were parts of a whole. He verified it from his own knowledge, or sent out to have it verified if that seemed needful. He assessed the value of what he had assembled, and then boiled the valid material down to message form. The messages were then encoded and sent to the radio operator for transmission, or else dispatched by hand to a Lysander or sea pick-up point or across the frontier to Switzerland, sometimes to Spain. Every step of the way was a gamble against capture and torture.

Several French réseaux were involved in reporting the existence of the German V-weapons, identifying as launching ramps the "ski sites" which so puzzled Allied Headquarters, and in pinpointing Peenemünde as the lair of the rocket scientists. Some réseaux reached inside Germany. Several acted as liaison for the Italian underground, too.

After the war, a July 1943 report on the V-weapons from the Churchill top-secret files was ceremoniously returned to "Marie-Madeleine" Fourcade of the réseau Alliance-Druide.

One of the most sensational exposures of secret plans was made by réseau Promontoire. This was the revelation of the German "Operation Easter Egg," to drive the Allies out of France by Easter 1945. As described by Jacques Bergier of Promontoire, the plan had four elements: (1) assassination of Allied generals, starting with Supreme Commander D. D. Eisenhower. The killings were to be carried out by men selected and directed by Otto Skorzeny, the most audacious and capable coup de main expert of the war; (2) operation of a pro-German maquis in the South of France; (3) the von Rundstedt counterattack through Ardennes, and (4) launching of V-weapons from the Pyrenees, perhaps from Spain.

The first three operations were launched at the end of 1944, even though the starting signal — Eisenhower's death — could not be given: an American counterintelligence officer had seen a GI puzzling over a package of cigarettes, obviously ignorant of how to get the cellophane wrapper open. The soldier had been picked up and quickly identified as an English-speaking German in American uniform. His fellow infiltrators were winnowed out by Operation Tarzan, in which sentries challenged unfamiliar U.S. soldiers with, "Who is Tarzan's mate?"; "Who is Superman?"; "Who is Betty Grable's husband?"

The German-trained maquisards and saboteurs, all French, were either left in place as the Germans retreated, or were landed on the southern coast by kayak. When they headed for their secret stores of arms, they found the French police waiting. Bergier says there were eight hundred caches of weapons in France, and fifteen hundred agents, two hundred of them found with genuine identity cards from the Sûreté Nationale.

As for the Atlantic Wall, the Allies received detailed drawings of every emplacement. Literally day by day, each change, each addition gave London a progress report as detailed as that received by the Todt Organization which was building it. When Rommel inspected the wall, he had a lot of military fault to find with it, and this useful expert critique was also delivered to SHAEF. In fact, there was one thing London knew about the wall that its builders did not: at what points and in what way the structures had been sabotaged.

The Forces of the Interior

In the year of 1943 more than forty thousand French men and women were arrested for Resistance activity, German Ambassador Otto Abetz reported to Berlin. At least a thousand more were killed outright, rather than lingeringly. These were killed in gun battles on the streets or in the maquis, killed while trying to escape arrest, killed while sneaking across borders, killed by guards at the scene of sabotage, or, as in the case of one parachute reception group, simply surrounded, killed and left where they lay.

The Resistance man is a hunted man. The people who are hunting for you are not like the cop on the corner; you slip past him and you're home free. The men who are hunting for you are from the Abwehr (German armed forces intelligence–counterintelligence), from the Gestapo and from the specialized brigades of French collaborationists.

They are looking first for "suspicious persons." They know what that means, and after a month in the field you know what that means, too. It's a matter of constant exposure to the subject, of repetitions of the lesson, so that recognizing something not quite right or something too quite right becomes a conditioned reflex. The reflex becomes so automatic you start thinking you can smell the suspicion on a suspicious person.

They are looking next for weapons, messages, clandestine newspapers, large sums of money, false papers, any of which you might be carrying.

If it involves a roadblock or a dragnet, they are looking for confusion, guilt, flaws in the story of where you are going and why.

If they have seen you before in other ticklish places or with other suspicious characters, they may recognize you as you innocently wander into a café for a cool drink on a hot afternoon.

If they have cracked your true identity, then they are looking for you, specifically for you. They have "physiognomists" at work now, fellows who work the gambling casinos all over Europe. Their profession is looking at faces and recognizing them. They are posted, in normal times, at the entrances to the casinos, and if they spot a face from the "undesirables" file, they press the buzzer.

Now they walk around town. Each has an assignment of five faces. The photos are pasted inside the sweat band of his hat, so he can make a double check. Paris has become especially dangerous since the middle of 1943. Thirty-two thousand Gestapo agents comb the town.

Of course, the first lesson in the underground is *never write anything down,* always memorize it. Whole réseaux have been destroyed because some incompetent messenger wrote down the name and address where he was to go. Of course, reports must be written down to be coded, and then someone has to carry them to the radio operator or the pick-up point. Stolen papers, maps, photos, they all must be delivered somehow. Since they must be transmitted, the rule must be broken, and if the rule is broken, sooner or later somebody . . .

The second lesson is *never go about armed.* But, of course, it may be your mission to kill somebody tonight, or to protect a meeting. So the rule is broken . . .

There are a lot of small footnotes to the rules, normal, simple security regulations. Which often turn out not to be simple after all. Never let anyone know what your base address is: fine, you always make dates elsewhere, receive messages elsewhere; you have a cover job where you will be seen most days of the month. But still, one or two people will have to know, for emergencies. And they may be followed there. Or they may, also in an emergency, give the address to someone else, somebody who might write it down . . .

When you say goodbye on the street corner to a pal, never tell him where you're bound, and hope that he doesn't tell you where he's headed: one of you might be arrested five minutes later and asked in a manner difficult not to answer. And after you have shaken hands and smiled, you make off and turn the corner, walking purposefully and in the opposite direction from the one you intend to take, eventually.

Never loiter at a rendezvous. Your organization should have standing shifts in signals. If you miss at 9:15 on Tuesday at No. 40, you try again at 15:09 on Thursday across the street at No. 39. All you have to do to be picked up is stand staring at a store window or sitting too long on a park bench or obviously waiting on a street corner. Some nervous informer will decide he'd better tell the Germans.

Never keep regular hours, except at your cover job. If your daily life has a pattern, somebody will either notice the pattern or notice departures from the pattern when work interferes.

The third rule is *keep your head.* It isn't just a matter of saving your neck. It's a bit more superstitious than that. Réseaux have a tendency, when they go, to go all at once, or lose all the leadership at once. It won't all be on the same night, very likely, but it spreads like a horrible, swift rot. So, as they say, "The duration of each contributes to the duration of all."

The work itself, even if it were magically stripped of all danger, is hard work. It must be done meticulously and yet at high speed. It is full of frustration, because you can pull off a minor miracle, such as getting detailed information on every aspect of a shipyard, and send it off. And wait and wait for bombers that don't seem to come.

And if you are involved in quick strikes against fixed objectives, or in planting bombs, or in straight assassination, especially in straight assassination, you have to watch yourself. You have to be a killer without developing the sort of drugged killer mentality. Not very many healthy persons really relish murder, even when fueled by a general hatred. It adds to the wear and tear.

The work stretches your nerves, the fatigue stretches them even further, but the constant peril which engenders constant fear, that damn near snaps them. You cannot let anything go by unnoted and unquestioned.

Say you are safe at home. The door is locked. The concierge is persuaded you are M. Buffau, under-conservator at the Museum of Art (which you are, as often as you can get there). You have changed your hat twice during the day (brim up, brim down, feather, no feather). You have worn your scarf on the gray side part of the day, on the blue side part of the day, not at all part of the day. You carried an umbrella, you discarded the umbrella. You wore a folded piece of picture canvas in the heel of your right sock to change your walk before you left the café. And you are safe at home. Early, in time to warm up yesterday's meatless cassoulet.

You look out the window. Who are those fellows lounging along the street down there? Is that a car you hear? A gasoline motor? Only the Germans and their associates have gasoline-driven cars now. The rare other vehicles run on a charcoal-burning arrangement. Is that somebody running up the stairs? One, or more than one?

It could be any minute now. They could come any time. Of course, you aren't thinking about it. You're thinking about not burning the beans and about what a real meal tastes like. You are thinking about Charlot and when you'll get the signal from Switzerland. You are thinking that you'd better have another look at the construction reports from the North: something didn't seem to fit.

But subconsciously you're thinking about it. Your intuition is flung out and vibrating like a spider web. No minute goes by when you aren't listening for the doorbell (or will they hammer with their pistol butts?), or the hurried, heavy tread on the stair, or the chink of metal down in the street, or the unfamiliar head silhouetted against the window across the way.

So you are in a constant state of fear, you run a low scare, like a low fever. And it works to keep you alive, it keeps your instinct for self-preservation fully charged, even when you're sleeping.

It's always there, the way a bellyache would always be there if you had chronic indigestion. But some days suddenly you are sick with it, and it rushes up and overwhelms you, as if you suddenly had to vomit. And you ask yourself just what in hell is the use of it all anyhow? It would be doing you a favor if they would come right this minute and blow your head off. All the gimmicks you use to kid yourself into relative normality don't work. The big ho-ho for the comrades sounds so hollow, just as hollow as their big ho-ho for you.

You are all in there pitching and keeping each other alive and not letting your common fears pool into panic, and for what? The nerves scream, and then all at once — the mind protecting itself from collapse probably — there is an illumination. You have touched bottom. You realize that man is no bigger than a flea and that life is nothing, not individual life, not when measured by the life of the universe. It's nothing, but it's all we have, and since it's all we have, it is our everything.

At the time, this makes sense and requites you for your agony. You cannot feel sorry for yourself. You cannot feel ashamed. This would not only interfere with your efficiency, but it might lead to a real nervous breakdown. Man, you could get everybody killed if you went on like this.

The nervous breakdown does come, a form of combat fatigue peculiar to underground fighting, though it is said that pursuit pilots get the same thing. It's euphoria. It's delusions of invincibility. Or if you don't really entirely believe yourself invincible, your instincts stop telling you that death might come any minute in any of a thousand disguises. You stop thinking about what can happen to you. You are enfolded in your good luck. You're still alive, and you'll live forever. Hurrah and here I come, ready or not.

If you don't catch yourself right there, if you don't recognize the symptoms of euphoria, then you have had it. You will go on and you will make mistakes, and your mistakes will be the death of you.

If somehow your luck holds you alive through this period of thinking your name is so-and-so and you can lick anybody in the house, then you are in for a real breakdown.

You will get the shakes and the sobs and you'll have just about all the destructive withdrawal symptoms you can imagine, now that you've broken your psychological opium pipe. You'll know your name is so-and-so and anybody in the house can lick you.

When you see yourself starting on a euphoria jag, or one of the bunch spots it, force yourself to take some time off, at once, far away. Go over the border if you have to. If you find, once you are really safe, you haven't the guts to come back, you'll be saving a lot of lives if you stay away.

It is easy to get confused in this business. There are no landmarks. Nothing is permanent. Nothing is the way you have spent a lifetime expecting it to be. You need a touchstone beyond all this shifting world, because everybody in it is as out of touch with real realities as you are. You need religion or love, some sort of faith. It's amazing, with all the cynicism this underground existence of murder and treason breeds in its members, how rock-real patriotism becomes. At another time, in another place, that might seem funny.

As one of the Resistance people has noted, "Only men who have been through it can really understand. That's why war veterans are such a pain in the ass."

If you follow all the rules and you are not directly betrayed, you still need luck to stay alive. A lot of luck. And if your luck is good, you'll develop a sixth sense. Premonition has saved many men in this business. And they have ignored it to their extreme disadvantage.

Wing Commander Yeo-Thomas, working out of London with the réseaux Confrérie de Notre Dame, had a feeling he really ought to go and see his father, who persisted in living in Paris. But his British sense of duty overcame his psychic sense and he made another trip up the stairs at the Passy Métro station, where the tracks are elevated, and where he had a Resistance rendezvous. And that's where they grabbed him, on the stairs.

Major Philippe de Vomécourt, one of the chiefs of the resistance organized by British intelligence, was on his way to a rendezvous by car not long before D-Day. He ordered the driver to turn back to the Bologne village they had just left.

"We've got to get to Salbris — Michele is in trouble."

When they got back to their secret headquarters in Salbris, they found that Michele (Muriel Byck), de Vomécourt's radio operator, had been spotted at work and was preparing for flight. Her chief rushed her out of danger. He said that although there was no explanation for it, he had *known* she was in danger.

Henri Frenay, founder of the Combat organization, told one of his réseau leaders, "Premonition is the breath of the rising tempest that is about to break. Arriving through mysterious ways, it sometimes warns its intended victim."

Frenay's dearest friend and closest collaborator from the beginning was a girl named Berthy Albrecht. In 1943 she was going to the Hôtel de France in the town of Mâcon, when witnesses saw her stop suddenly, turn, and hurry away. From all evidence, there was no signal warning her away from the trap the Gestapo had set in the hotel. (They caught up with her that same day, transferred her to Paris, where she was tortured — she didn't tell them anything — and then killed.)

Dominique Ponchardier (also known as Elizabeth, Beaujard, Prévert, le Docteur) directed, with his brother, the Sosies organization. He had a dream that he and a new recruit, Martineau, were bound hand and foot and stretched out side by side on a floor.

Two German officers stood over them, speaking in low voices. The thinner one pointed to Martineau. "This one will give us the leader because he is half mad; he's a morphine addict, and by withholding the drug we'll have what we want."

Though the dream woke him early, Ponchardier was late starting for his rendezvous with Martineau at a bistro near the Gare d'Austerlitz. As he went down into the Métro, another premonition hit him. "It was as violent as a blast of cold air when a window abruptly blows open."

He sat on a bench and let train after train pass by. He made himself get aboard, finally (After all . . . a dream. How silly!). But then he rode past his station. He went back toward Austerlitz on foot. As he approached, he saw ostentatiously harmless little knots of loiterers on the street. Across the way from the café, a big, black Citröen *traction avant*, the Gestapo's favorite make of car. Two men stood on the curb right before the bistro door. One of them wore a green fedora, the favorite hat of the Gestapo plainclothesman.

Ponchardier walked on, crossing the Austerlitz bridge, away from the ambush. Martineau had been arrested two hours before, half an hour after the bad dream.

The métier obliges a sensitive man to bury his sensitivity so that he will not crack under the daily blows. While his mind is occupied with the details of work, his intuition takes over the job of watching to duck the suddenly looming peril.

You live constantly brushing up against death, isolated and forcing your psychic antennae farther and farther to pick up vibrations of danger.

Fatigue and fear remove most of the ordinary blocks we impose on the subconscious. You live more and more not upon immediate resources, but upon psychic reserves. You are beamed in on those you hate as acutely as on those you love. By staying alive you may yet kill the enemy and save the comrade.

You force and force your reach into the unknown. And sometimes you break through.

Ravens O'er the Plain . . . *

LOSSES — 1943

Toward the end of 1942, a Gestapo-Abwehr special commando of two hundred experts in clandestine radio techniques spread out over the southern zone. They hunted and captured at least fifteen Resistance radio operators.

The detection vans, although disguised as ambulances and delivery wagons, were easy to spot because they emitted a singular electronic squeal, and because they were obliged to operate in areas where their appearance would not pass unremarked. When closing in on their quarry, the vans crept along, keeping pace with the fine-tuning operators who went on foot, their work jumpers or raincoats curiously distended around the chest, their hats pulled down to disguise earphones. As they plodded along, these technicians had to keep glancing down inside their coats to check the dials on the machines strapped to their chests.

In spite of this clumsy approach, the commando was able to pounce on posts serving Resistance organizations in and around Marseille, Pau, Toulouse and Lyon by the beginning of 1943. Then the Funkspiel, the radio game, began. To play it, the Nazis had to capture the operator's codes and learn

* From the first line of "The Song of the French Partisans," "Friend, do you hear the heavy wings of the ravens o'er the plain?" The last line says, "*Ami, if you fall, a friend comes out of the shadows in your place.*"

how to use them. Then they either had to persuade the operator to work for them or else send messages on his set themselves, imitating as closely as they could his "fist," his touch
on the sending key.

Clandestine radio men were protected against serving their
captors by a number of extremely simple and undetectable
devices. They could use a dated code on the wrong dates, they
could make tiny, preconvened variations in the standard "all's
well" security signature. They could misspell agreed-upon key
words to signal that the Funkspiel was on or, simplest of all,
they could omit the agreed-upon words from the agreed-upon
sequence to let headquarters know they were prisoners. Any
one of these changes should alert the radio security officers
at the receiving end.

Unfortunately, almost every message sent out of France had
a certain amount of garble in it by the time it was received
in England. Also the influx of messages was heavy and the
reception from the portable sets often weak. Whatever the explanation, the British did not realize for months that messages
were coming from captured sets. (They had a similar and far
more drastic failure in Holland.)

According to German files, the RAF parachuted twenty
thousand weapons with ammunition, explosives, thousands of
dollars worth of francs, and many precious documents to German reception committees — or to legitimate reception committees which were then rounded up by the Boches. British
agents parachuted into German hands.

In this way several réseaux of the SOE were rolled up, in
Normandy, Orléans, Angers and Paris. It was only late in 1943
that the British penetrated the Funkspiel and began feeding
false replies to the false stations.

Though not caught in the radio trap, the BCRA lost its key
réseau, Remy's Confrérie Notre-Dame, whose members had
created and trained intelligence groups inside France, effected
liaison to London for groups who wanted to be part of the

Free French movement, and supplied money and arms to other Resistance organizations. The Centrale de Parsifal and Marco Polo, both invaluable intelligence réseaux, were scattered into isolated groups after their leaders were captured.

The execution of hostages was intensified. For two grenade attacks (one in a sports arena, one at a cinema) on German soldiers in Paris, two hundred and four hostages were shot.

SS General Oberg had agreed with the Vichy secretary general of police to take as hostages only those Frenchmen directly involved in attacks against the German Army. Once made, the agreement was ignored by the Germans, who took hostages out of French prisons whenever they wished. At the end of 1943, the Gestapo succeeded in having Secretary General of Police Bousquet removed and replaced by Joseph Darnand, who was head of the recently formed Milice.

Vichy gave Darnand the title of secretary general for the maintenance of order, giving him power over not just the police, but over all law enforcement agencies under French control. For their part, Himmler's men had Darnand made honorary Obersturmführer of the French contingent of the Waffen SS. Thus, the forces of repression were distributed through every corner of France, and there was not a single city without its Gestapo installation, backed by French cohorts.

Across France, the entire population was suspect. The lights would suddenly go up in a theater, the exists from subway stations would be blocked, trams would be halted, a street would suddenly fill with police or Milice, and everyone in sight would be searched, papers examined, packages opened. Sometimes innocents whose papers were quite in order were taken to the police station, just to frighten them, to spread the terror a little more thickly.

The Germans and the collaborators were aided beyond measure, fantastically out of proportion to their numbers, by traitors. The traitors were of two sorts: they were Resistance people who talked when captured and sometimes were permitted to live as long as they worked for the Gestapo, or else they were Frenchmen on the German payroll who entered the Resistance for the specific purpose of betraying the patriots.

Jean Multon ("Lunel" in the Resistance), was of the first species. His odyssey of infamy led fatally across the paths of many Resistance leaders. Where Multon, *l'âme damnée,* wandered the losses to the movement were appalling. The Marseille headquarters of MUR was taken; the head of the Armée Secrète, General Delestraint, was captured along with his chief of staff; Jean Moulin, de Gaulle's delegate and president of the National Council of the Resistance, was caught, along with other chiefs. Multon's baleful presence also affected the first mysterious turn in the harrowing, perplexing story of René Hardy.

Multon was picked up in May 1943 by chance. It was an ordinary street blockade, but he promptly revealed himself as second in command of the MUR Marseille region, and turned in his chief, Maurice Bertin ("Chevance"). Wounded, Bertin escaped from his apartment under gunfire and was sheltered by the Marseille police. Eventually he returned to the Resistance and became a general in the French Forces of the Interior.

As soon as he was able, Bertin sent a warning all through France: "Watch out for 'Lunel,' traitor." Like a dog on a leash, "Lunel" was perambulated around France by the Gestapo. Starting in Marseille, he led his keepers to cafés and restaurants where Resistance members sometimes met. He haunted the railway stations of Toulon, Cannes, Nice, Montélimar, Lyon, looking for faces he could recognize and point out to the men with him.

On the night of June 8, 1943, "Lunel" was seen aboard the Paris express as it waited to leave Lyon. René Hardy, by one of those incredible wartime coincidences, had time to pass the word to a man on the platform, a British agent Hardy should not really have known under the security compartmentalization in force. Then, in a sort of reverse panic, Hardy got aboard, in complete disregard of primary security precautions and simple common sense.

When the train arrived in Paris next morning, Hardy did not appear. A few hours later, waiting for Hardy near the Muette station of the Métro, General Delestraint was picked up. Thinking himself escorted by the Resistance rather than captured by the Gestapo, Delestraint led the enemy to his chief of staff, Gastaldo, and thus within ten minutes L'Armée Secrète was decapitated.

When Hardy did reappear in Lyon ten days later, he was a wreck. Dirty and rumbled, sleepless, unshaven and begrimed, he looked ready to drop. A bony blond, he seemed more frail than ever. He couldn't stand waiting for "Lunel" to point him out to the Gestapo on the Paris express, he explained, and he finally jumped off as the train slowed for a station. Since then he had been riding trains, any train that came along, to cover his trail.

His superiors had no reason to doubt Hardy's story. He had made escapes before, as they all had. His past services to France and to the Resistance were exemplary.

He had studied for a career in railway administration and had well embarked on it when the war broke. Refusing military service deferment, he went into the Army. Twenty-eight years old and anxious to taste combat, he found himself stuck in a Corsican garrison until the collapse of France. The day after de Gaulle's radio appeal, he began gathering fellow officers to make a group sally to North Africa and from there to England. The expedition failed to materialize.

He went back to Paris and worked with the Regularisation des Grandes Lignes out of the Gare Montparnasse. Through chance, he made connections with a British agent, to whom he supplied railroad information. Warned by someone in his office that the Germans were suspicious and had him marked for questioning, he set out again for London.

He couldn't make the right connections to cross the Pyrenees, and groped his way from town to town until he found a sea escape being arranged in Toulon. But somebody talked, and Hardy was thrown into Toulon Naval Prison, where the term "Gaullist" was a synonym for "rebel," and he was given a hard time. His sentence ran for fifteen rotten months.

When he emerged he was, thanks to ex-prison mates, at last in touch with the elusive Resistance. Eventually, he went back to railroading, where he could best serve. For Combat he constructed Service-Fer, which had two sections. One was for "action," i.e., sabotage of rolling stock, rails, equipment and the destruction of trains used by the Germans. The other section supplied train-movement information and gave cover to the "action" group.

During one twelve-month period, he was credited officially with reporting 1091 German military trains to London (useful RAF targets, base material on troop disposition), and with "directing or controlling" 567 sabotage actions, 126 of them direct attacks on trains. Because of his work that year, 101 trains, 289 locomotives, 51,000 tons of ammunition and 1257 Germans were destroyed. He had also perfected a system for sending supplies of explosives by train, to be handled at destination by railroad workers who were members of the réseau, and who passed along the explosives to saboteurs.

Hardy's major work was the master plan of nationwide rail sabotage for D-Day. When he had finished all his calculations, with different patterns of sabotage related to three possible invasion points, Channel, Atlantic, Mediterranean, it took eight days to write it up. Twenty draughtsmen worked in round-the-clock relays to produce the necessary maps and drawings. Instructions were drawn up for 12,000 railway stations, including 850 prime missions planned in detail. The entire plan was keyed to the accompanying blueprints and maps. In final form, the coded instructions appeared as 2500 groups of three numbers. Because the original was typed on green paper, it was called the Plan Vert.

There was no doubt that on his record Hardy was brave, tough and dedicated. But he was hardly back in Lyon when the Caluire affair occurred, and his life and the lives of a number of others were never the same after.

Caluire, a suburb on the heights over Lyon, is a black name in the history of the Resistance. It was there that "Max," Jean Moulin, the head of the entire underground movement, was betrayed and captured.

"Max" called a secret meeting of Resistance leaders and military advisers to make organizational reforms and to strengthen security measures in the wake of the Delestraint disaster. It promised to be a stormy session, for Max, as de Gaulle's delegate, and the other men from London headquarters would probably propose further separation of the Armée Secrète from the parent Resistance movements.

The meeting was hermetically secret. Nevertheless Hardy, as the railroad and sabotage expert on Delestraint's staff, persuaded Aubry, an old Combat comrade, to take him along. Arrangements for the meeting place were to be made by a Lyon anchor man, André Lassagne, who at the last minute would pass the word to the delegation members through the BCRA liaison men, and would tell the organization members himself.

Lassagne had arranged the meeting at the home of Dr. Dougoujon in Caluire. On Monday, June 21, he met Aubry and Hardy on the street and showed them the way without telling them exactly where they were going (Funicular to Croix-Rousse, then tram 33 to Caluire, first turning on the left to Place Castellane). The others arrived singly, except for Max, who came with Aubrac of Libé-Sud. They were hardly settled when the Gestapo burst in and took them all, including the innocent doctor, who had told Lassagne it was all right to use his upstairs room during office hours for what had been described to him as "an important business meeting."

Manacled together, they were marched out to the Gestapo cars drawn up in the Place Castellane, guarded by a black-uniformed detachment of Sipo-SD men. The haul was bigger than the Nazis had expected, and there was one man left without handcuffs, his right wrist held by a chain gripped by the Gestapo agent who walked alongside him.

This last man bent over to get into the car, turned, whipping the chain from the agent's hand, butted another Gestapo man onto the pavement, and ran zigzagging through the black-clad cordon and across the square, out of sight. The stunned guard did not use its submachine guns, and only a couple of the arresting agents drew their pistols and fired. The escaping man — Hardy — pulled his revolver from the secret pocket inside his left sleeve and fired back as he ran.

Shot in the arm, he managed to reach a friendly house down in Lyon, but the French police, hearing reports of a "bleeding man running into a house," found him there. Hardy gambled that they would not be collaborators and told them who he was.

He won that gamble. The police brought him Leblond, his assistant in running Service-Fer, the railroad sabotage and intelligence group. He gave Leblond instructions, and then the police moved him to a hospital. After he had been patched up, they moved him to another. But the Gestapo found him the next night. Very curiously, since they care nothing about prisoners' wounds, they left him there in the hospital under guard.

Lucie Aubrac had rounded up some of the boys as soon as she learned that her husband had been arrested. She and they took Aubrac out of a Gestapo car at gunpoint and got him safely away. Aubrac accused Hardy of having led the Germans to the meeting. Claudius Petit convened a council of other MUR leaders, and Hardy was condemned to death.

They believed Lunel must have turned Hardy in to the

Gestapo on that Paris train, and that Hardy had agreed to
deliver Max as the price of his freedom. Lucie Aubrac was
given a jar of poisoned jam to take to the hospital, an extremely
delicate and dangerous undertaking. She waited for a day
in order to work out everything in detail, and she waited too
because it was so hard to believe Hardy a traitor, although
really it wasn't hard in those days to think of anybody as a
traitor, really. As she delayed, and within twenty-four hours
of his condemnation by the Resistance, Hardy escaped from
the hospital.

The Resistance tracked him down to a farm — it was one of
the MUR's safe houses — near Limoges. They sent a detective from the Sûreté, who was a dear friend of Jean Moulin,
to interrogate Hardy. The detective found him extremely nervous, almost hysterical, but was satisfied that Hardy was telling
the truth. Some double agent who knew Hardy by sight must
have followed him to the rendezvous and reported to the
Gestapo.

Hardy got out of France and into North Africa, where he was
detained by Free French counterespionage. They wanted to
know day by day and night by night what he had done from
the night of June 8 on that train until he returned to Lyon.
And minute by minute what he had been doing during the
two days before the fatal meeting of June 21. They wanted
to know centimeter by centimeter about his unusual escape on
the night of the arrests at Caluire, and his even odder escape
from the hospital later. He told them, and they let him go.

His old chief, Henri Frenay, founder of Combat, gave him
a job. Frenay was now — April 1944 — minister for deportees
and prisoners of war in the Algiers Government. Hardy, as
expected, did a good job at the ministry. Frenay was not shaken
in his belief in the man. After all, nothing had happened to
any part of MUR with which Hardy was familiar. If he had
talked, the whole structure could have been dismantled. True,
there had been losses, but they had nothing to do with Hardy.

The intelligence Central, which had been moved to Paris, had been "burned," with a great deal of damage to the service and the loss of several esteemed comrades. But they knew how this had happened. A convalescent tuberculosis patient, a youthful Resistance veteran, had grown lonesome in his Alpine hideout. When a courier arrived with supplies and messages for the patient, he — against all regulations — undertook to mail a letter to one of the Central ladies who had looked after him. The courier was caught at Annemasse, and the unmailed letter was found. After that it was a simple matter of routine police work to uncover and destroy this Resistance nerve center.

Although Hardy's old chiefs never doubted his loyalty, the cloud of suspicion was never totally dissipated. He would eventually have to undergo two trials. Many important people believed that Hardy had sold Max to the Germans; after the liberation he was re-arrested.

Lunel, the traitor, had turned himself in. He claimed that he had denounced Hardy on the Paris train, and that Hardy, after his arrest, had worked for the Germans.

The Marseille Gestapo file on Lunel had one line in it which said, "René Hardy allowed the dragnet at Caluire to function." It did not add any details, did not mention Hardy again. Lunel was quickly tried, condemned and executed, but, strangely, the Hardy matter was never brought up at his trial. Hardy's own trial, on charges of betraying the Caluire meeting, did not take place until 1947, when he was found innocent and released.

Two months later he was back in prison, arrested anew on new evidence: sleeping-car records showed that he had indeed been arrested by Lunel's Gestapo warders on the night of June 8, and taken to Gestapo headquarters in Lyon. At his second trial in 1950, Hardy admitted that he had been lying all these years about having been arrested on the train, but maintained he had not lied about anything else.

"Why did you lie?" That's how it was in the Resistance. If you were caught and released you were finished, unable to go on with the fight because you were suspect. So he had lied, he said.

The second trial formally charged him with having betrayed the Plan Vert to the enemy. The evidence: a file found after the war at the German Foreign Office. It was not very sturdy evidence, the statements being vague and largely inaccurate. Hardy pointed out that the plan had been used against the Germans and had worked. Besides, he said, it was so voluminous he could not possibly have given it to the enemy from memory.

It was really the Caluire matter which was being re-tried, although no longer within any court's competence. It came into the proceedings because if it could be shown that Hardy worked for the Gestapo at all, that would be relevant to the Plan Vert charges. The chief of the Lyon Gestapo, Klaus Barbier, though still alive and not in hiding, did not appear at the trial. American occupation authorities, using Barbier in their zone of Germany, decreed that it "was not in the national interests of the United States" that he cross the border into France. It has never been explained just how Barbier's trip could have militated against the interests of this sovereign nation. Barbier was permitted to transmit a deposition in which he swore that Hardy had indeed betrayed the Caluire meeting to him. Most of his key statements were easily disproven, however, and dates, names and places were wrong.

Mme. Delletraz, a French Resistance member who had become a Gestapo tool, but had never been arrested for it, was the next government witness. She testified that Hardy was the culprit. Mme. Delletraz spoke as an expert on how these things were done, having set the trap for Berthy Albrecht, a Combat founding member. She said Hardy had been at Gestapo headquarters the morning of June 21. However, on the morning of June 21, even if he had been there — and there was some evidence to the contrary — he could not have known where the meeting was to be held. Her story, too, had large inconsistencies and falsehoods. But it was damningly true that Hardy had lied to everyone for eight years about what had happened on the train. What else was he lying about? Henri Frenay, asked for testimony, said that his lie was "neither explicable nor excusable," and had nothing more to say. The lawyer's big argument for Hardy was: how can you let French justice condemn a Resistance hero on the word of a Nazi war criminal and a confessed traitor? There was applause from the court-room spectators. A split decision of the military tribunal found Hardy not guilty. He had spent five and a half post-liberation years in jail, officially innocent. He went on to become a prize-winning novelist.

There is no official answer to the question, "Who betrayed Jean Moulin?"

PETITE VISITE CHEZ LA GESTAPO

It was really stupid of Michel to run across the bridge that way when they spotted him. No cover, no escape. They just fired down the length of the bridge. So now Madeleine, who was known as Renée in the movement, was the group leader, the only one of her little band to know where the arms were hidden, to know the identity of her section leader.

So it was she who passed along the order, "Retaliation for the massacre of Oradour-sur-Glane: every member of the Paris regional organization will kill one German." Headquarters had picked out a special German for her, a Gestapo major. He strolled along the Seine every Sunday morning, as far as the Pont de Solférino. There he stopped for about twenty minutes and watched the fishermen dangling their long poles over the river.

She arrived on her bicycle at the bridge. Henri was sta-tioned up the road at the Pont de la Concorde and Clamart was down the road at the Pont Royal. They were to cover her getaway along the Quai des Tuileries, intercepting any pursuers. They didn't expect any trouble, as the major was never accompanied, and the quai, with the river on one side and the wall of the Tuileries Garden on the other, was normally deserted at this hour.

The major was leaning on the parapet, smoking, watching the anglers. Renée took her revolver out of her handbag and walked up to him. Hearing the clack-clack of her wooden soles, he stood erect and turned toward her. She raised the revolver to his face and pulled the trigger. He rocked back, but did not fall, and she fired again, into his chest.

She put the gun into her handbag, but instead of fleeing at once, she stopped to crouch down and pull the major's pistol out of its holster — the organization needed arms so badly. Then she ran to her bike and began pedaling furiously down the quai toward the Louvre. There were no cries, no sound of running feet. Nothing.

Except the noise of an automobile coming along the quai behind her. Then she realized that it was the sound of a gasoline engine, either German or German-employed. She pedaled harder. The car speeded up.

It was alongside her, it was on her, over her and then it stopped. The pocketbook had spilled open. The two pistols lay on the pavement. The bicycle wheels were twisted out of shape, but she felt all right. She scooped up her pistol and the handbag (they mustn't get the identity card, her real one, with her true name). The officer's pistol must be under the car. She rose to her knees to begin firing, but it was too late. The driver had grabbed her wrists and twisted it from her grasp, and now she was handcuffed.

It was one of those unlucky accidents. A suburban police chief out for a Sunday drive with his mistress. He had just happened to be driving along the quai, and here she was handcuffed, bruised, dizzy, in the back of the car while the policeman's girl friend nervously held a gun on her. Three minutes later they turned in at the back entrance to the Police Prefecture, across the square from the cathedral of Notre Dame.

Ordinarily the beating would have begun right there. This

was a special squad of super-collaborationist police. They weren't career police, but members of the PPF and the Bucardist parties. Many of them had been Gestapo-trained. But now the Allies had landed. They might break through any day now. They might be in Paris in a month. So the boys didn't torture their victims any more. They didn't even beat them. They had long interrogations and they were mean as hell. They gave the prisoners very little food, and that very bad, and the cells were filthy, with bare wooden boards to sleep on.

For a week, they tried all kinds of tricks on her. Assuming that the section leader must certainly be cuddling up to so young and so pretty a girl, they reported they had seen him embracing another girl up in Montmartre. Why hold out for a rat like that? Tell us his name. That's all we want, his name.

One of them, extremely tall and handsome, with a sympathetic face, came to her cell. He said she really ought to tell them what they wanted to know, because if they learned nothing, they would have to turn her over to the Gestapo. He had done his best to prevent the Gestapo from finding out, but after all, when one of their own officers is murdered in broad daylight, you can expect them to be sore. He actually brought her some hot soup.

One night he opened her door and beckoned her out into the corridor. He explained that the cells had listening devices, but no one could hear them out there. He revealed to her that he was an undercover man from the Resistance. He wanted to arrange a jailbreak. Any five men could pull it off. Just give the name of somebody, anybody on the outside, who could pass the word along. He'd fix everything on the inside. Please, he implored her, don't let herself get sent to the Gestapo. Nobody could keep secrets from them, and her whole section would be smashed.

She had told her story, and that was the only story she had to tell: "I was outraged at the atrocities in Oradour, and I decided to go out and kill a German. I saw the officer and I killed him. It was an act of individual resistance. I belong to no group, I know nothing about the Resistance."

Later she shortened the formula to "I don't know anything." Through everything that happened to her, that was the phrase she repeated. "*Je ne sais rien.*"

When the Gaullist policeman told her about himself, she decided to be cautious. She listened without saying anything. He kept insisting the guard would pass in three minutes, that she had no time, she had to tell him. Saying nothing, she walked back into her cell. That night he brought her some more hot soup.

When he told her a couple of nights later that she must give him some contact for rescue, he added, "You see, it's not just for you and for the Resistance. It's for me, too. I, I love you!"

She knew he was lying, although he lied beautifully, and it was apparent that women prisoners were his permanent assignment. She was taken to the Gestapo.

She had not forgotten what the orientation booklet said: "You are young, but you are brave and you fight for a just cause. If you are arrested, you will probably be tortured. Do not invent a story. The men who question you are professionals. They can detect any inconsistencies, and probably trap you into making inadvertent revelations. Tell them you know nothing and that you have nothing to say. No matter what they ask you or suggest to you, answer that you have nothing to say. This is the only way to resist torture and protect your comrades and your country."

The Gestapo came to pick her up in one of their big black cars. She was handcuffed, hands behind her back, and put into the rear seat between two burly, silent men in black uniforms. As they drove through the soft summer afternoon, she looked out at Paris. As they turned left off the bridge, leaving the Ile de la Cité, they slowed almost to a halt.

She wondered about jumping out, about calling for help. Just then, an old lady peered in through the window. She saw the girl sitting between the two Germans.

"Whore!" screeched the old lady. "Traitor! Consorting with the enemy!"

The two men remained impassive. Renée felt tears rolling down her cheeks. The car rolled on toward the rue des Saussaies.

Walking between her guards at the end of the ride, she held herself ready: she had heard they like to push you along brutally. If you fall, they kick you so hard and skillfully you can't get up, and then they scream at you to get to your feet, kicking and punching all the while. The lesson seems to be that no matter what, you are going to do what they tell you to do.

However, they simply led Renée along a corridor which was clean and airy and rather pleasant. From loudspeakers cascaded the music of Bach, the music of joy and clarity and logic.

She was led into an impressive office — rugs, bookshelves, chandelier, maps, photos, inlaid desk, drapes. Her handcuffs were removed. The man behind the desk was in civilian clothing. Slim, in his early thirties, eyeglasses, a rather mild face. His voice was light and his French not bad. He called her Mademoiselle. He asked her to be seated, and offered her one of those Turkish-flavored cigarettes.

Such a reception. They must think her somebody important who must know a lot. Perhaps the Gestapo fish she had hooked was a more important officer than she realized. This man explained that as the person in charge of the office, he was very sorry to see her there, since it meant she had refused to cooperate with the French police. He was sorry, because if she did not talk now, she would be shot. She would first be interrogated by whatever means seemed needful.

Perhaps she did not understand about the interrogations. He would arrange for her to see, and they could have a talk afterwards.

They took her upstairs, and when they opened the heavy doors to the third floor, she could hear the screams, the moans, the cursing and the roaring. From door to door they took her and they made her look. The men being questioned were torn, bleeding wrecks, but the torturers kept battering them. She felt sick. She began repeating under her breath, *"Je ne sais rien."*

Later that day when it was her turn, they battered her, too. They shoved her into a room so that she fell hard on the floor. They kicked her to her feet and took off her handcuffs. A man said, "Take off your clothes." She couldn't believe her ears. Two staggering slaps across the face. She believed.

She was eighteen years old. It was the first time she had ever been naked before a man. They put her hands behind her back and replaced the handcuffs. She felt them looking at her. Finally, she raised her eyes. A man was walking back and forth, swishing a riding crop. She almost smiled. It was something out of an old movie. It was too much. First they wanted to scare her, then shame her and now threaten her.

The man with the whip said, "You really want to go through with this? We don't really want a kid like you. You're just the patsy. We want the man who got you into all this. The man who is really responsible for your acts. He knew what he was doing, getting a girl, a child of eighteen to commit his murders for him. Why should you suffer because he tricked you? If not his name, tell us what he looked like. You can still save yourself."

"Je ne sais rien."

He hit her with the crop. "Liar!" He hit her again. "Murderer!" He hit her again. "Terrorist!" He hit her again. "Communist!" He hit her again. Shouting louder and faster, he struck her harder and faster. "Talk! Confess! Stubborn bitch! Talk! Talk! Killer!"

She screamed over and over. She was so scared. So alone. And it hurt so horribly and it got worse and worse. There was only one way to stop it, and that was to talk. She hung on, through the pain and the fear, to one thought, *"Je ne sais rien, je ne sais rien."* She stumbled back into a corner and turned her back to receive the blows. He beat her over the head with the weighted handle. The blood coursed over her face, into her eyes. She couldn't see. He drove the handle into her kidneys. She howled. Finally she passed out.

It had begun like almost all Gestapo interrogations. It went on like almost all of them. After the beating, the bathtub* and after the bathtub, the electrodes,** then dressed and back to the cell, to be yanked out by the hair in the middle of the night and dragged back to the interrogation room.

Sometimes there would be a day or two when she was left alone. When they started again, the old wounds would burst open to bleed or to drip pus. Always the hands manacled behind the back, even in the cell. She learned to sleep perched on the edge of the plank, leaning her shoulder into a corner of the wall. If she rolled back in her sleep, the handcuffs would click closed another notch and bite further into the flesh and it would take hours to learn to bear the new pain. When some fresh stab of pain woke her — there was not much difference

---

* Bathtub — an ordinary tub filled with ice water. The subject, hands secured behind back, is knocked into the tub face forward. He is held under until he begins to go limp. He is then pulled out, revived, and thrown into the tub again. It is hoped in the panic accompanying the sensation of drowning, he will talk to save himself.

** Electrodes — applied to any portion of the body. Current slams frightening, painful shock through victim and contacts make deep burns in skin.

Also — hot irons on soles of feet, hot irons brought slowly to eye, cigarette burns, attacks by police dogs, injection of ice water or drugs. Lieutenant André Devigny was subjected to all except the electrodes and the eye damage, but was in addition hung by his handcuffs (hands behind him) from a hook and also laid across an anvil in the machine shop and beaten with pick handles. He lived, and escaped.

between sleeping and waking, floating half-conscious as in a terrible, consuming fever — she would start and cry out, *"Je ne sais rien!"*

After a few days it became true. She knew nothing, nothing at all. To survive torture, there must be one unshakeable reality by which the blood-drowned brain can reassure itself, one undestroyable thought it can retain. For Renée this was the talisman, the repeated phrase, *"Je ne sais rien."*

Her hair, her face and dress were matted with blood. Her wrists were infected. Her eyes were puffed almost shut.

One night they threw somebody into her cell. The light was left on, probably so they could see each other and reflect on what they saw.

The new arrival was not handcuffed nor marked in any way. On one of her wrists was a bracelet of tiny Mediterranean sea shells, and around her neck a little collar of the same shells. She wore a brand new summer dress, white, with a flower design, and low cut. Her hair was blonde and short and shimmering. Her arms and neck were slender, her jaw delicate, her mouth and brow were wide.

The girl had been on a mission from the South. Her rendezvous was in the dress shop where she bought the clothing she wore. They had been waiting for her. All night long they talked. She at least had been in love. Renée thought it was a shame to die as she would, without having known love. For warmth in the chill cell and for a fleeting touch of humanity, they clung together.

In the morning the new girl was taken out first. Later Renée was marched out. At the door of 37, she was halted. Inside, the new girl, tied to a chair, lolled unconscious. Her pretty little delicate jaw hung open and grotesquely twisted. It had been broken already. Renée never saw her again.

For several days she was left alone. They even took off her handcuffs. An orderly poured some caustic liquid on her wrists. They gave her a little more food. Finally they took her out. She was confronted by a boy barely sixteen years old. He looked at her blankly. She looked at him and at the Gestapo men. She recognized the boy as the son of a Neuilly doctor. The boy had joined the subsection only a couple of days before her arrest. He didn't recognize her for the good reason that he had never seen her.

But how did they know he belonged to her group? How could they? Had she said something in her sleep? In delirium? Had she talked under torture without knowing it? Or had they picked the boy up and simply taken the chance they might know each other since they were both teen-agers? Or had someone else been arrested and talked?

They asked the boy, "Have you been mistreated since your arrest?" He said, "No, sir." (Damn these well-brought-up kids! Saying "sir" to a Boche.) "Have you been asked any questions?" "Only if I recognized this lady when she came in." ("This lady." My God. Two years her junior. Maybe her hair had turned white.)

"All right, son, just sit in this chair." It was a big chair, like an electric chair. In an instant, the boy was strapped in. If she talked, they said, they would do nothing to the boy. She kept silent. "Everything that happens to him is your fault. You can stop it any time."

They broke his fingers one by one. Every time they did so they asked if she had anything to say. When she remained silent, they asked her if she didn't like children. *Alors, vous n'aimez pas les enfants, Mademoiselle?*

The boy sobbed. He screamed. She sobbed, too. They broke his wrists. His arms. *"Alors, vous n'aimez pas les enfants, Mademoiselle?"* His feet. His ankles. His legs. *"Alors, vous n'aimez pas les enfants . . ."*

The boy was unconscious for all the last part. Finally, they shot him through the head. She fainted. But she hadn't talked.

When she revived, she was in a small room near the entrance. The loudspeakers played Bach. They said she had been sentenced to death and was being taken to Fresnes prison.

She cried, out of relief and gratitude.*

WINS – 1943

In spite of the crushing and repeated blows at the Resistance in 1943, the movements grew. A report prepared in October 1943 showed two hundred fifty thousand men enlisted in the Armée Secrète, the Communist FTP and the ORA, the ex-Armistice Army group. Of these, seventy thousand were organized for the Immediate Action program (although only sixteen thousand were armed). The vast majority were signed up for D-Day mobilization.

These figures did not include the maquis in process of formation, nor independent groups, nor the "civil and political" membership of the Resistance, which needed proportionately little manpower, but grew as the movements grew.

There were a dozen new clandestine publications launched during the year, some by newly founded organizations. Several new intelligence réseaux were founded. In the factories, on the railroads and on the canals, there were acts of sabotage every single day in widely separated parts of France.

Every day, in spite of the continued cease-fire orders from London, Germans were killed. More than three a day died inside France, and more than six a day were wounded in 1943.

---

* Twenty years later, Renée says that there is one thing she cannot forgive the Nazis for: the way they reduced their victims to their own level of animal hate and complete mistrust of other human beings. Liberated from prison by the Swedish consul (see chapter on liberation of Paris) she fought in the Resistance that historic week in August.

"I was probably out of my mind at the time, but under the circumstances, it wasn't visible. I didn't really break down until years after the war, when my baby was ill. The nurse said to me, 'You should have brought her here long ago. *Alors, vous n'aimez pas les enfants...*' That broke me. They said at the hospital I kept repeating, '*Je ne sais rien.*'"

The prize items of assassination during the year were General von Schaumburg, Kommandant von Gross-Paris, and Julius Ritter, the chief of the Nazi forced labor procurement in France.

As the Nazis slaughtered hostages, so the Resistance exterminated Gestapo officers and agents, collaborating French law officers, informers, spies.

Three thousand members of a maquis organization in the South of France were able to arm themselves when Italy signed a separate peace with the Allies. Italian Army deserters, some of whom live in the South of France to this day, handed over the weapons in exchange for civilian clothing and false papers.

The most ringing coup of all in 1943 was the liberation of the island of Corsica by the Resistance.

Corsica is a mountainous island of 3367 square miles, which lies 100 miles off the Mediterranean coast of France. A normal *département,* it is an integral part of "mainland" France.

The word "maquis" is a Corsican word for the dense brush of the hill country, to which Corsicans historically repair when they are in trouble. In the Resistance, the name is applied equally to the act of hiding out and to the bands of men who "took to the maquis." A member of the maquis is a "maquisard."

The first Resistance group in Corsica was formed by Corsican-born Fred Scamaroni, a Free French naval pilot who arrived by commercial boat at Ajaccio in 1941, under the ideal cover of a Vichy civil servant from the Ministry of Food (which in fact he was). He brought together isolated groups of would-be resistants, searched out terrain for parachute drops, finding almost none satisfactory, and located hidden bays for sea delivery of arms. Upon his return to Vichy, he was whisked back to London just a few steps ahead of capture. Other BCRA agents went into Corsica to carry on the work he had started, and after Italian occupation of the island following Allied North African landings (November 1942), Scamaroni returned. Through the disregard of security regulations by one of his men, he was captured, and died in March 1943. The Italian secret police, the OVRA, tried the Funkspiel with his radio but failed.

By the end of summer, MUR had only small sections in operation in Corsica. But the Front National had ten thousand FTP ready for action, and in the battle for liberation, they were joined by the others. The radio link was not with London, but with General Giraud in Algiers. His liaison officer, Commandant Colonna d'Istria, worked with the Front National.

Toward the end of August, the Italian capitulation was awaited, and the Resistance made a careful sounding of the sentiments of the thirty thousand Italian occupation troops. It proved almost unanimously anti-Fascist and anti-German.

The Resistance made plans therefore to rise up and take over the island whenever the surrender was announced. They would not engage the Italians, but concentrate their fire on the twelve thousand Nazi soldiers installed along the west coast from Bastia to Sartène.

The announcement came September 8, and there was an organized civilian demonstration in the streets of Ajaccio, the capital. The following day the Resistance occupied the Prefecture and proclaimed Corsica's adhesion to Free France. A general strike paralyzed Bastia, principal port and center of German strength.

Two days later, eighty-eight Nazis were killed fighting at Champlan, and truck convoys were destroyed at Folelli and Querciole. German naval forces took the Bastia port installations, but with the Italian garrison fighting alongside the patriots, the port was re-taken. Italian dead — five hundred. The eleventh and twelfth, all Bastia was in Corsican hands, but the expected Allied arms and men did not arrive, and they had to give up the port.

From Sardinia, thirty thousand German reinforcements arrived. Mountain guerilla fighting at Levie September 16–17

Musée Carnavalet, Paris

JUNE 1940. The outriders of the Greater Reich move into the silent, empty Quai d'Orsay in a silent, almost empty Paris.

OCCUPATION, THE "CORRECT" PHASE. From Paris on the Seine (*above*) to Bordeaux on the Gironde (*below*) the Germans take over their zone. In the early part of the occupation, every day at noon, like figures from some frightful folkloric clock, they emerged to parade.

Le Parisien Libéré, Paris

QUEUE FOR BREAD. Will there be enough? Will they put up the *Plus de pain* sign and pull down the shades before it is my turn? And after all this, the ration is so small and the bread so poor. The grocery queue will be just as long.

QUEUE FOR FREEDOM. This is Moulins, a favorite place for crossing the demarcation line which separated occupied France from Vichy France. Thousands of Frenchmen were arrested at check points such as these, and at the railroad stations where passengers' papers were examined. Yet, through ingenuity, daring and bluff, thousands of refugees and resistants slipped over this border.

Le Progrès de Lyon

FIGHTING BACK. Railroad sabotage maddened the Germans and cost them heavily. Eventually the maquis made these hills a death trap for the enemy. Trains became scarce, moved slowly and erratically, guarded by troops really needed elsewhere.

COUP DE MAIN. This is an extraordinary photograph, showing an attack group of the Maquis du Limousin jumping off to blow up a German munitions dump. Eight of the dozen raiders can be seen in the picture. The mission was a success.

Documentation Française

SABOTAGE. The man who took this picture was a demolition expert parachuted into France. Part of his mission was to train maquisards in the proper use of explosives to cut rail lines. This photograph is part of his report to London headquarters.

THE MAQUIS DEFIANT. In uniforms "liberated" from Vichy quartermaster stores, the maquisards of the Ain Department occupied the town of Oyonnax on Armistice Day, 1943. This was a period when Nazi blows against the Resistance had taken heavy toll, and this act of defiance was tonic for the morale of the whole movement. The soldiers of the maquis paraded through the town, placed wreaths at the war memorial, and marched out again.

Documentation Française

Tous aux Barricades! That was the Order of the Day as the people of Paris fought to liberate their city. This barricade was made of ripped-up paving stones; others were contrived of shop signs, household furnishings and felled trees.

SUMMARY EXECUTION. The two kneeling men are members of the Maquis de Lantilly in the "Golden Slope," the vineyard hills of Burgundy. Just captured, they are about to be shot by the smiling German "anti-terrorist" patrol behind them. But not before the souvenir snapshots are taken.

PARACHUTE DROP. Daylight drops were rare, but this (*above*) was the 1944 Bastille Day delivery of arms and supplies to the Free French Forces of the Interior assembled in strength on the isolated plateau of the Vercors, near Grenoble. *Below:* Delivery is taken by the reception committee, whose job was to signal for the drop, empty the parachuted containers, and take the supplies to assigned depots.

MASSACRE. While Resistance troops fought off attacking German divisions, airborne attackers landed behind the lines, among the villages of the Vercors. They slaughtered everyone they could find, civilian or FFI, as here in the hamlet of Vassieux-en-Vercors.

PERFECT MODEL. The identity card of this bearded schoolteacher from Clermont-Ferrand is false. It was supplied by the Resistance to General (later Marshal) de Lattre de Tassigny after he had been broken out of Riom prison, where he was being held by the Vichy government.

UNDERGROUND RAILWAY. German soldiers strolling along the terraces of the Palais de Chaillot above the Seine across from the Eiffel Tower. The four civilians strolling among them are escaped American pilots with their underground guides. The Réseau Bourgogne had the audacity, before putting their charges on the road to neutral Spain, to give them a tour of Paris in the spring — and to photograph the tour.

Le Parisien Libéré, Paris

TENEZ BON. "Hold fast," General Leclerc had signaled to the defenders in the Préfecture de Police. There were more men than weapons in the besieged building, so one of the defenders pointed his camera out of the window as the attackers moved in again, two tanks supporting infantry having a go at the rear door (Notre Dame behind them).

Le Parisien Libéré, Paris

PARIS LIBERATED. General de Gaulle marching down the Champs Elysées with the gesture of universal embrace later to become so familiar. Behind him are General Koenig, military governor of Paris, and General Leclerc, commander of the French 2nd Armored Division. Civilians in the front row, left to right: Joseph Laniel, National Council of Resistance (later Prime Minister); Yves le Trocquer, minister in the Provisional Government (later president of the National Assembly), Georges Bidault, president of the National Council of Resistance (later Prime Minister) and Alexandre Parodi, de Gaulle's delegate in occupied France and titular chief of all resistance (later United Nations delegate).

turned back a tank company, and an infantry battalion supported by artillery. There were heavy guerilla attacks at other mountain passes. German dead — 250. The city of Sartène was liberated.

The German forces began to fall back on Bastia, the best evacuation port, and the Resistance appealed for aid. The Allied High Command, whose forces were deeply engaged in the just-opened Italian campaign, refused. General de Gaulle, chief of the Free French, took no action. General Giraud, still officially commander-in-chief of French forces, did what he could. He sent out the lone vessel to have broken out of Toulon the year before rather than obey the scuttle order, the submarine *Casabianca*, into which were crammed 109 soldiers.

There followed two torpedo boats, *Fantasque* and *Terrible*, loaded to the gunwales with a battalion and its heavy armament. Without artillery, the island could not, in all likelihood, have been liberated.

On September 20, the Germans evacuated Porto Vecchio and Bonifacio. On the twenty-fifth, French artillery was bombarding Bastia. On October 4, a flight of U.S. planes bombed the city, twelve hours after the last German on the island had been captured.

The Normandy landings were eight months away. In one month of fighting, the Resistance had shown what it could do by routing forty-two thousand German troops.

Of this singular achievement not much has been written. This shining page of Resistance history seems to be turned with unseemly haste in most available histories. It was a Communist-led battle supported by a general who tried to supplant de Gaulle, failed, and retired in pique before D-Day.

Charles Tillon, the FTP commander-in-chief, comments on the lessons of Corsica in his book about the Communist share of the Resistance. He says, "One shouldn't make absurd comparisons with the situation on the continent. But Corsica did know how to seize the best circumstances for its victory, one worthy of the better general!"

The Maquis

THE maquis action on D-Day was alone enough to lift France from disgrace to glory.

Although their numbers swelled dramatically for the final assaults in the battle for France, there were those who had lived and fought in the forests and in the hills since 1940. Not many had come in 1940. A few more, on the run from the Gestapo and the Vichy police, came in 1941. A great many more in 1943, especially the young men coming of military age, escaping the dragnets of the STO, the German forced labor drive. And an even greater number came early in 1944. At the signal for general uprising, thousands more, who had enrolled over the years as reservists (especially the ORA, Resistance organization of the ex-Armistice Army; the Armée Secrète; and the FTP) dropped their daily tasks and took to the maquis.

They did receive some reinforcements by parachute, too. There were the Jedburghs, which were liaison and command teams of two officers, one French and one English-speaking Allied officer, plus a radio operator. Ninety of these teams were dropped into maquis combat areas. There were also the operational groups, thirty-two-man parachute-commandos which could function as independent eight-man armies. And there were individual officers of the American OSS, the British SOE and the French Special Services dropped to units as weapons instructors, demolition experts and auxiliary commanders. They often brought explosives, weapons and money, as well as orders for specific missions.

When the call to general attack sounded, most of the maquisards were not armed, and those arms that they did receive from the Allies were not adequate to the kind of fighting the maquis were obliged to do.

Units were scattered all over France, but their ideal ground was rough terrain, especially in the thinly populated regions where occupation troops would not be concentrated. In the northern zone, this meant Brittany and the mountains of the Jura and the Vosges. In the South there are great stretches of splendid guerilla country. The whole Massif Central is well adapted to this kind of fighting, easing off toward the Atlantic coastal plain in the west and the three major river valleys to the other three points of the compass — the Loire, the Garonne and the Rhône.

South of the Garonne, the Pyrenees rise and run from Atlantic to Mediterranean. East of the Rhône lie the Alps, which overflow the Swiss and Italian borders and shoulder down to the Mediterranean shelf.

In the maquis regions the civilians often suffered for the Germans, and the Milice slew hostages and burned villages as demonstration that it was unwise to help the guerillas.

The maquis were the special prey of the Milice and of Frenchmen spying for the Germans. Betrayal killed more men than actual combat in the years before the great battles.

The underground newspaper *Libération* reported a German sweep through the department of Corrèze with these details:

. . . Terror reigns. Arrests can be counted in the hundreds. Anyone suspected of patriotism is certain to be denounced and taken, if he does not escape in time. It is a field day for informers, and one can imagine the part that personal grudges play. Anyone suspected of having aided the maquisards or given them food or shelter is put up against the wall without any pretense of trial.

Jews who have taken refuge in this region . . . are being hunted down and shot on sight . . . All the houses where Jews had lodged were systematically burned, like the farms that had given shelter to the maquisards. The Boches have spread ruin through the once-prosperous villages of La Bachellerie, Le Lardin, Terrasson, Mansac, Larche and Varetz . . .

That was in the spring of 1944, and the Germans were smarting from their unsuccessful attempt to clear the Corrèze five months earlier, when they had been fought to a standstill by the maquis of the *département* in a series of battles which ran from the middle of September to the middle of November 1943. The departments of Ariège, on the Spanish border, and Gard, in the southern Rhône valley, were subject to similar sweeps.

The big drives against the maquis were started by the Italians in the Haute Savoie, just two months before the Italians capitulated to the Allies. Because the maquis in the region was ill-armed and had never been seriously hunted before, the groups were not prepared to defend against a heavy attack, nor even to disengage and melt away in good guerilla fashion. The units were too large and cumbersome. One maquis was annihilated, the other surrounded, surprised and captured.

From then on, no maquis unit was considered safe if it numbered more than sixty men (preferably fewer), and security measures were rigorously enforced. The PTT, the Roads and Bridges Department, the Forestry Service and the gendarmerie kept the maquis alerted when enemy forces were on the move.

The de Gaulle delegation called meetings of regional maquis chiefs in Lyon, one in October 1943, the other in January 1944. 1943 had been an especially costly one for all the services of the Resistance, the maquis included. Although there was an appalling poverty of armament, the maquis refused to sit still any longer and take it. The January meeting resolved, against orders, to start general guerilla war. In the South there were two thousand men (boys, really, most of them) in the maquis of the various Resistance organizations, and eight thousand "independents."

For the most part, they lived miserably. A recruiting leaflet, one of the starkest appeals to volunteers ever issued, described it honestly:

Men who come to the maquis to fight live badly, in precarious fashion, with food hard to find; they will be absolutely cut off from their families for the duration; the enemy does not apply the rules of war to them; they cannot be assured any pay; every effort will be made to help their families, but it is impossible to give any guarantee in this matter; all correspondence is forbidden.

Bring two shirts, two underpants, two pair wool socks, a light sweater, a scarf, a heavy sweater, a wool blanket, an extra pair of shoes, shoe laces, needles, thread, buttons, safety pins, soap, canteen, knife and fork, flashlight, compass, a weapon if possible, and also if possible a sleeping bag. Wear a warm suit, a beret, a raincoat, a good pair of hobnailed shoes.

You will need a complete set of identity papers, even false, but in order, with a work card to pass you through roadblocks. It is essential to have food ration tickets.

From which it is evident that the maquis had nothing. Nothing except the will to fight. It was sometimes dismayingly true that some recruits had only the will to hide, and these broke and ran at their baptism of fire.

"It is essential to have food ration tickets" indicates that the organization producing this notice intended to buy food for its men. Later, parent organizations supplied counterfeit tickets, and independents simply stole theirs from mairies.

There was never enough money. "Max," Jean Moulin, distributed more than $2 million to MUR in the first five months of 1943. By the end of that year, London was supplying the maquis of the southern zone over a million dollars a month. This would have meant less than $50 for each man in the maquis for food, clothing, shelter, medical supplies and pocket money. However, not all the London-supplied funds could be used for the direct support of the maquisards.

Some of it was used to buy prisoners out of jail when jail raids were impossible. Some of it never reached the maquis, but fell into the hands of the Germans when couriers were captured, or disappeared when couriers were killed or planes crashed.

Arms and money were the two things maquis chiefs were always demanding. They rarely got what they asked for.

For food, they generally depended on neighborhood farmers, who usually shared what they had out of patriotism. But when the active strength of the maquis grew much larger, scrounging expeditions spread out over the countryside, sometimes taking what they needed at gunpoint, leaving a "requisition receipt" ostensibly payable after the war. This sort of thing happened for the most part in the last weeks before and the first weeks after liberation, but left some bitter recollections of the maquis as "bandits."

To get money, some maquis eventually did turn bandit, but what they took (except for those bands which took up brigandage after the liberation) was money belonging to Vichy or to collaborationist corporations. Thus, in the Lot-et-Garonne Department in June 1944, 2 million francs was the booty from robberies of forty-four post offices and railway stations. There were payroll holdups that netted more than that in a single coup. The most sensational scores were made against the Banque de France.

The FFI of the department of Ain took 100 million francs from the Banque de France at St. Claude. Near Clermont-Ferrand, in the Auvergne, the FTP grabbed 1.5 billion from a Banque de France armored car in February 1944. The most fantastic sum, that of 3 billion francs, was taken in July 1944 in the most fantastic robbery of all. It was a train robbery, and it was phenomenal not only because of the sum involved, but because the Resistance robbers did not know that the whole coup had been arranged for them by Vichy officials.

Vichy Prefect Callard had been supplying money to the Dordogne maquisards through the simple process of embezzlement: he had his treasurer-paymaster draw more than was needed for pension and social security payments, and gave the difference to Lieutenant Colonel Martial (real name, Gaucher), chief of the Dordogne FFI.

The difference did not amount to very much, and a great deal was needed. Who had a great deal? The Banque de France! The main regional bank at Bordeaux had transferred huge supplies of banknotes to the branch in the city of Périgueux, where it would be safer from Allied bombings. When the German Navy needed banknotes for payrolls and such, Bordeaux sent to Périgueux, changing times, itineraries, means of transport each time, often at the last moment.

Callard kept a prefectoral ear open for the propitious moment, and it came when he was officially advised of the July shipment. One of his secretaries (long an active resistant) was sent to alert Gaucher, who detailed the groups Valmy and Roland to "intercept an armored train" when it stopped at 6 P.M. in the unoccupied town of Neuvic.

The men weren't told that it was a hoax, because it was necessary for them to work at top speed and to be on guard against any Germans who might stumble onto the scene.

An hour before train time, two hundred men occupied Neuvic, took over the railway station and installed roadblocks on all access routes. They mined the tracks and made all the troop dispositions possible with their limited force, to defend against possible attack and to assault the train.

Tooting from afar, the solid gold train was right on time (at creeping pace because of all the patched-up cuts in the sabotaged rail line). It pulled into the station and stopped. Far from being armored, it was an ordinary passenger train. Sensing a trap, the maquis showed themselves, ordering everyone on the train not to budge. Hands in the air, the conductor muttered, "Baggage car up front."

The maquisards threw themselves against the door, which promptly swung open to reveal four Banque de France guards waiting to help unload the money. The baggage car was uncoupled and levered out of sight into a shed. There the raiders grunted and sweated, shifting six tons of money bags into trucks.

Although he never robbed a train to do it, one of the most resourceful feeders and clothers of his men, and one of the gifted battle commanders, was chief of the Ain Department maquis, Colonel Romans (real name, Petit).

A reserve officer who took to the hills in 1941, he found groups of men in hiding as he went from farm to farm. They were not maquisards — the word was hardly known — but simply men hiding from the authorities. Romans went back down into the towns to search out officers to train the fugitives to be soldiers and form a small army. He found them.

He set up a training camp for his future chiefs higher in the mountains, where they were kept working from morning to night. The day started with stiff physical training in all weathers, followed by two study sessions, one on guerilla tactics, the other on the enemy's anti-guerilla tactics. The morning concluded with field exercises to put the lessons into practice. The afternoon brought studies of camp organization, military organization, and the special leadership techniques essential to maquis existence, a blend of discipline and comradeship.

Once the leaders had finished the course, Romans sent them to the farms at the forest edge where they found the recruits. The total armament for this fledgling maquis: two hunting rifles and two revolvers. They had no food supplies, no money, and they belonged to no Resistance organization.

Romans took care of all that. By the time he had three hundred men (split into ten maquis which lived separately), and twelve submachine guns and five trucks, he set out after uniforms for his people. The arms and trucks had been picked up in previous raids. This time they were going to hit one of the old Vichy Chantiers de Jeunesse which had once housed two thousand men, but was now watched over by thirty gendarmes. It was at Hartbur, between Ambérieu and Culoz.

Romans and two officers went out to reconnoiter. When they returned to HQ, the whole strike was rehearsed with charts and the timing perfected. Eight teams were to operate simultaneously, one cutting the phone wires and silencing the sentinels, a second isolating the officers from the men, a third rounding up and holding those not on guard duty, while a fourth disabled Chantier vehicles to prevent pursuit or premature alarm.

They arrived in their stolen trucks. The gendarmes on guard were taken without a shot. Some had to be slugged, but there was no killing — these men would prove useful allies some day. Those who were sleeping were encouraged to continue with doses of chloroform. The trucks were loaded with one thousand uniforms, one thousand pairs of shoes, knapsacks and cooking utensils. Total elapsed time: one hour and forty-three minutes, during which not one of the raiders spoke a single word. The Vichy papers said a thousand men had carried out the raid.

For the time being, that took care of the clothing problem. But what about food supplies? Especially when snow came, food would be hard to get and difficult to transport. The quartermaster depot at Bourg had lots. Of course, Bourg, being the departmental capital, was occupied by the Germans. Romans sent an officer into the city.

Entering the QM depot shortly before closing time, he succeeded in being locked in for the night. From the shadows, he looked over each of the night watchmen as they went to their posts. Taking one of those blind chances the Resistance sometimes required, he picked out the "fellow with the most likely face." He picked well. The man helped him draw a detailed plan of the installation and hid him for the few remaining hours. Next day, the maquis officer sauntered out of the depot and headed for camp.

Two nights later the watchman with the likely face unlocked the depot wicket for the advance patrol of the maquis. They bound and gagged all the guards. Again, absolute silence and no shooting. All was ready for the "liberation" of the supplies.

After curfew, Romans' trucks left their hidden base and rolled toward Bourg. The Germans let them pass ("A ninetruck convoy of armed men could only be official").

The advance patrol inside the depot opened the gates, and each member guided a truck to its assigned warehouse. In twenty minutes, two hundred men loaded forty-five tons of food. The bound guards were locked inside the stripped warehouses, and the laden trucks returned the twenty-five miles to their main base unchallenged.

When the depot day shift came on at 6:30 A.M., they gave the alarm. At the exits from Bourg and on the highways outside, roadblocks were established at 7 A.M., by which time the raiders had been home asleep for several hours. It was such a good stunt, they did the same thing all over again a few days later at Ambronay.

On November 11, 1943, Romans did something which endeared him to all of France, and which is still talked about. The Germans had forbidden all observance of this anniversary of their defeat in World War I. The French felt the prohibition keenly, for it is a day on which they honor the dead of all wars, a memorial day with personal significance for every family.

On that day, the Maquis de l'Ain took the town of Oyonnax.

It was a serious risk for the fifteen thousand inhabitants as well as for the maquis. Romans selected it for his demonstration because it was a friendly town. Also, it is near Nantua, where Gendarmerie Captain Verchier was a firm Resistance member. Verchier approved Romans's plan for the day. The first step was to plaster the region with provocative posters, announcing observance of Armistice Day in the city of Nantua. After they appeared Verchier would clamor for reinforcements, thus decoying the region's gendarmes into Nantua and away from Oyonnax.

The night before the parade (for they planned nothing less than a full-dress parade) Romans and his officers walked the whole line of march through the town, accompanied by the Oyonnax chief of police. The briefing went on until 3 A.M., with everyone knowing by heart what he was to do.

The morning of the eleventh, two truckloads of picked maquisards rolled toward the town. Combat teams guarded all the roads in and out. The town hall, post office-telephone central, the gendarmerie and police station were occupied. By way of alibi for them, the police chief and his men were disarmed and locked up (but they could watch the parade from the jail windows). Houses of collaborationists were occupied and their residents guarded.

Starting at nine o'clock, the first truckloads of maquisards entered Oyonnax. They came in by different routes at carefully spaced intervals. In front of the post office 280 men (in uniform!) assembled just before 11 A.M. They formed ranks at the trumpet call. Romans and his staff performed inspection. The townspeople, unbelieving, gathered. Romans faced his troops.

"Le Maquis de l'Ain, at my command, attention!"

The crowd howled with joy. So loud and prolonged were their cheers of *"Vive le maquis!"* and *"Vive de Gaulle!"* and *"Vive la France!"* that the order to parade couldn't be given.

When spectators were quieter, the tiny force moved off to trumpet and drum, flags flying, cadence smart. The color guard wore white gloves. All the officers wore all their medals.

They marched through the cheering throng to the black-draped Monument to the Dead. Romans laid a flowered cross of Lorraine at the monument. It was inscribed "To the victors of yesterday from those of tomorrow." All saluted. Bugles sounded "To the Fallen." All sang "La Marseillaise."

The crowd then fell on the soldiers, kissing them, pressing money on them. There was a good deal of happy weeping. The timetable was inexorable, however. Ranks re-formed. The Maquis de l'Ain marched off singing the national anthem. They got into their trucks, which left according to the ordered rotation. Romans was the last to go.

On the way back to the camp, he asked his driver to pull over and stop. The man who had put on this brave show, thrilling all France, was tired: he had not slept in several days. He had been worried about hostages, German reprisals. And now it was done. His boys had been perfect. He sat alone in the back of his car and he cried.

Some months later, when the chief of the Haute Savoie maquis was arrested, Romans took over command of that *département* as well. He was helped in the reorganization of these men by Lieutenant Tom Morel, who later became commander at Glières (see page 165).

In the end, he had seven thousand men, all armed, equipped and staffed. His Plan Vert operations included the destruction of 350 locomotives at their terminals. In July 1944, he was made a Companion of the Liberation.

Citation:
Magnificent officer, never having paused in the fight against the enemy, was one of the pioneers of the Maquis, where he lived from 1941 on.

By his example, by his courage and by the total gift of his person, was able to provoke and encourage the flame in all the lads of all the camps under his authority.

Has no other ambition than to liberate his country from oppression.

Is one of the purest figures of the French Resistance.

On D-Day, his men liberated six hundred square kilometers of their *département*. The Germans attacked in great strength on July 11, and the grossly outnumbered and outgunned maquis fought effectively for a day and a half, then disengaged and dispersed. They re-formed ten days later and resumed phantom guerilla strikes. In their territory there was absolutely no train traffic. Near the Swiss border, they took and held the fort and town of Les Rousses. On August 29 they made junction with an armored column of the French First Army, which had pushed north from Marseille. On September 2, they won, without help, the thirty-six-hour battle for the town of Meximieux. Against tanks and artillery, one thousand maquisards who had neither tanks nor artillery took the town. There was hand-to-hand combat and some positions changed hands twice before they were finally taken. One hundred maquisards died in the battle. On September 5, they took Bourg, and the Ain was free.

Five months before the Normandy landings, the Germans made a massive effort to clean out the maquis, when the snow in high places obliged the maquisards to live close to their holes, and when they were deprived of the cover afforded by trees and bushes in leaf. The enemy struck at the Ain with three divisions, suffered a thousand casualties, and took vengeance by torturing and murdering civilians and burning farms and villages.

They had more success at the mile-high plateau of Glières, which they assaulted toward the end of February with gendarmes, Gardes Mobiles, the Waffen SS (Frenchmen enrolled in the German forces), and members of the Milice. The seven hundred entrenched maquisards beat back this assault. Then regular German troops took over the operation. Supported by dive bombers, two groups of mountain artillery and ten armored cars, seven thousand German soldiers went to the attack. Outnumbered one hundred to one, the maquis fought back fiercely. A traitorous officer of the Gardes Mobiles shot the maquis leader, Tom Morel, and the fortunes of battle seemed to desert the maquis.

They held out under constant attack for two weeks, from March 18. The defender's losses in combat were far fewer than those of the assailants. But after they were obliged to surrender (some got away, joined other maquis, and fought in winning battles), they were shot or deported.

According to the report in *Franc-Tireur* the month after, more than 100 escaped (the actual figure was close to 200), 150 were killed and 160 captured. Germans killed, 350, wounded 350; Miliciens killed and wounded, 150.

The battles of Mont-Mouchet, near Clermont-Ferrand in the Massif Central, and the Vercors, near Grenoble in the Alps, took place because of the large concentrations of maquis in each spot. Although it violated the basic concepts of guerilla warfare — hit-and-run by "invisible" troops — the massing of men corresponded to a concept equally ancient, the notion of the national redoubt. This was an idea that had been enthusiastically planned and agreed upon by the French many times in the past, always to be canceled abruptly at the last minute. (For example, in 1940, plans had been projected for regrouping the shattered French forces in such a redoubt either in Brittany or the Massif Central.)

The Mont-Mouchet and the Vercors operations were planned around an amalgam of maquis troops and of regular troops with heavy armament and modern equipment. Success depended on the arrival of these regular troops, a French airborne force, Force C, which never arrived. It really existed. Or almost existed. According to General Guillain de Bénouville, "Several elite French regiments (in Algiers) were put under the orders of Colonel Billotte."

The general (one of three Resistance combatants to win this rank during the underground war) explains, "A detailed plan had been prepared by Special Services. A group composed of special units with an unusually high proportion of officers would be parachuted and glidered to the interior of the redoubt organized by Resistance combatants . . . I was to go back rapidly to France (from Algeria) with a staff, effect the concentration of Resistance troops and organize the first liberation operations."

That was in April 1944. In July, he noted: "The news came from London that the operation for Force C would not be realized." At Mont-Mouchet and at the Vercors, the Resistance believed to the end in Force C.

The Massif Central plan was brought to COMAC (Military Action Committee of the Resistance) at the beginning of 1944 by General Revers, chief of the ORA (Organisation de Résistance de l'Armée) and was forwarded to Free French headquarters in London and Algiers. A few months later, Revers offered another version, "Plan Caïman," which had Toulouse as its primary target, the Massif Central as an alternative. This was political more than military.

The original Revers plan had been to hack out an island of free territory and hold it with maquis and airborne troops while implanting the first elements of the Provisional Government, flown from Algiers. The Massif Central (Military District R-6) was dominated by non-Communist Resistance organizations, whereas the Toulouse area could quite possibly fall into the hands of the Communists. Thus, to assure Provisional Government control of the Toulouse area, the plan was shifted to cover District R-4, (seven *départements* with parts of four others, making a strip up the center of southwestern France). However, at the last minute, this plan too was dropped.

But the Resistance thought the first plan was still in force.

In April, all the departmental chiefs of District R-6 met in the Auvergne for a briefing by Colonel Gaspard, regional chief of the FFI. Three separate assembly points for troops and reserves were agreed upon, as well as a plan for simultaneous mobilization. This would concentrate ten thousand to fifteen thousand men in all, building on the 2700 maquisards already armed and organized.

Gaspard chose Mont-Mouchet, about a mile high, for his headquarters. By May 20, reception and training centers were ready, and a complete headquarters staff and services installed. A Jedburgh assigned to Colonel Gaspard dropped from the sky. The fact of its arrival confirmed the mistaken belief among the maquis leaders that the redoubt plan was still valid, and that Force C would arrive. The reserves, except the Communist FTP, which waited until June, responded to the mobilization call. Three thousand men reported to Mont-Mouchet, as planned, and accelerated parachute drops furnished weapons for them. Four days before Normandy D-Day, eight hundred Germans struck. They were stopped, pushed back and driven in retreat from the field.

After this battle, more reservists flowed into the area. La Truyère, the second redoubt, received fifteen hundred and the St. Genès strongpoint found its garrison swelling from two thousand to six thousand. The tenth of June, the Germans hit Mont-Mouchet again, but this time threw in more than eleven thousand troops, supported by tanks and armored cars, and artillery. The three thousand maquis started their incredible day with only their usual light arms, but ended it with two captured cannon and an armored car.

When darkness fell, the Germans drew back from the sorely pressed maquis. During the night, all maquis vehicles, all stocks of food and clothing were removed to La Truyère, in case the Mont-Mouchet defenders should be forced to pull out next day.

The expected attack came — two hundred truckloads of

Boches, up to five thousand men, were reported approaching at dawn. They came, they were slain, and more came. The three thousand maquis were ordered to pull out at dark, which they did in good order, undefeated by fifteen thousand troops with planes, heavy weapons and tanks. The French had lost 160 dead and 100 wounded, the Germans 1400 dead and 1700 wounded.

Into La Truyère swarmed still more reservists. Fortunately, the Allies were still delivering arms and munitions. Then, because the signals had been misunderstood, new recruits — not members of the reserve — suddenly began to arrive. The headquarters men sweated to sort out the newcomers, keeping those who might be useful, if there proved to be time to train them.

There was no time. En route to La Truyère, where four thousand defenders had only one day's ammunition, were twenty thousand Germans.

The Resistance newspaper *Mur d'Auvergne* reported the battle this way:

. . . More than a thousand vehicles, among them many tanks and armored cars, swept up the Truyère valley . . . Trench mortars, 75's and 105's backed up the infantry, while ten planes — what an honor! — strafed our machine-gun emplacements. . . .

All day long our boys defended their positions. They cut bridges and roads. Machine guns and submachine guns spit fire. The Germans called for still more reinforcements. But night was falling. The Boche casualties, in the frantic attempt to wipe us out, were much higher than ours. . . .

During the night, our forces withdrew to a new position. The next morning the Teutonic horde continued their attack on our now vacated positions. Yet, so great is their fear of our troops, it took them all day to reach their objectives. . . .

THE VERCORS

The Vercors is an Alpine plateau in the southeast quadrant of France. On the map it is shaped like a crude stone arrow-

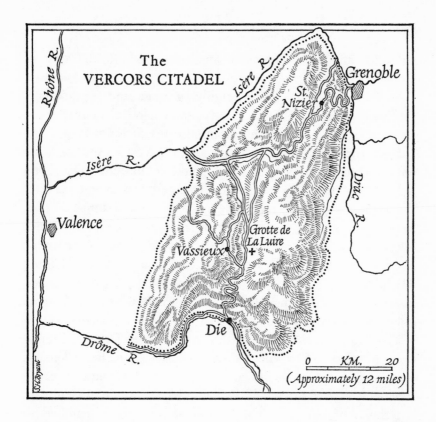

The
VERCORS CITADEL

(*Approximately 12 miles*)

head carved, even to a notch in the base, by three rivers, the Drôme, the Drac and the Isère.

From the air, the Vercors is seen as a series of plains and valleys, of peaks and cliffs, of mountain torrents and gorges. Narrow roads writhe past alpine farms and forests and a score of hamlets.

From the river flats below, the half-mile-high walls of the Vercors thrust abruptly up: a natural fortress thirty miles long and ten miles wide. There are fewer than two dozen mountaineers' trails leading in, and seven roads. The roads are local marvels of engineering, clambering across the cliff faces, leaping by bridge, burrowing by tunnel. There is only one weak spot in the natural defenses: by the village of St. Nizier near the tip of the arrowhead there is a break in the towering palisade, and here begins a long slope off to the city of Grenoble.

With food, water, shelter readily to hand, and seconded by the hardy, patriotic highland farmers, a handful of marksmen should be able to hold the mountain passes forever.

However, the first men who came to the Vercors were seeking not a citadel, but a sanctuary. They could hide there, and help on the farms in exchange for bread and cheese, and, if the enemy appeared, take refuge in the heavy forests. Soon, at the end of 1941, two strange warriors came among the hiding men to found an army. One was Mathieu, owner of a small café in Grenoble, and whose real name was Aimé Pupin. The other was a physician, Dr. Samuel Ravalec, called Ernest, himself a fugitive installed as a pharmacist in the Vercors village of Villars-de-Lans.

They enrolled their tiny forces in the Franc-Tireur organization. Another café owner, Eugène Chavant, called Clément, remained in Grenoble to act as the recruiting and security-screening officer for would-be maquisards (there was always the threat of treason). The people of the region searched in attics and old trunks and found arms for the maquisards: German pistols taken as war trophies in 1917, ancient hunting rifles and half-rusted carbines.

When Axis troops flooded into the "Free" Zone in November 1942, officers and men, but mostly officers, of the dissolved Armistice Army came into the Vercors. Many of them brought their weapons. All of them brought skills and knowledge for the training of the maquis.

It was the Italians who occupied the eight *départements* through which the Alps prevail. The maquis made them nervous and piqued their Mediterranean pride by raiding Italian Army gasoline stores, supply dumps and arsenals to supply their own needs. Time after time the Italians swarmed onto the plateau from Grenoble, and time after time the ill-armed maquis faded into the brush. It was good training and excellent morale building for the irregulars. It became almost a game.

In the north of the Vercors, almost at the tip of the arrow-head, near the village of Sassenage, lived an architect, Pierre Dalloz, who had withdrawn from the warring world. He knew the Vercors through his passion for mountaineering and had retired with his wife to an isolated farm. It was he who devised the detailed plan of Operation Montagnards, a plan since much criticized by those who do not know its provisions.

Again it was the redoubt idea, again the exploitation of a natural fortress which would be an island of freedom in a sea of tyranny, again the reliance on an airborne force from a regular army, with vehicles and heavy armament. But there was a proviso: the plan was to be put into operation only after Allied Armies invaded the South of France. The Vercors was to be filled with Resistance and regular troops, not as a bastion attempting to hold against overwhelming enemy forces, but as a deadly surprise, a bomb exploding in the ranks of an enemy already under attack and in disorder.

Dalloz envisaged a hard fight, but a short one if properly timed. After the regular troops had secured the southern beaches and broken the German lines, only then were the Resistance men to assemble on the Vercors, ready to swoop down on the enemy from the rear.

January 1943, Dalloz took his plan to Yves Farge, a Resistance chief in Lyon. Farge passed it along to Jean Moulin, president of the National Council of the Resistance. Moulin found it good, gave it all his support. Thus, Dalloz was taken to meet the commanding general of the new Armée Secrète. The general, Charles Delestraint, said he would present the plan, the maps and the photographs to de Gaulle's staff in London, where he was scheduled to be flown at the next moon (the little Lysander planes operated only in the light of the full moon).

At the beginning of March, the Vercors heard the BBC announce, "The Montagnards should continue to scale the heights." This meant that London had adopted the plan. By April General Delestraint was back in the Vercors to examine the terrain and advise on preparation for battle. For all anyone knew, June 1943 might bring the Allied landings.

What June brought was the death of Jean Moulin and the arrest of General Delestraint. Having survived two years of torture and German concentration camps, Delestraint was murdered by his Nazi jailers at the approach of Allied troops in 1945.

Suddenly the game the maquisards had been playing with the Italians for half a year turned ugly. Fourteen men who went down to Mens to raid a gasoline supply were captured. Tortured, some of them talked, and consequently some of their leaders, Aimé Pupin among them, were arrested and dragged off to Italy. Others, warned in time, fled.

After the hunt was ended, Dr. Ravalec, Pupin's deputy, found some surviving leaders and persuaded Eugène Chavant to leave Grenoble for the plateau. A new governing committee was formed. Pierre Dalloz was sent to London to work out further details of Operation Montagnards.

Separate military commands were established for the northern and southern halves of the plateau. The "actives" were strictly separated from the "reserves," and stationed in groups of thirty in new camps. The "reserves" took up arms only for training exercises or for specific missions, and then resumed their daily lives. They also managed recruiting, military information, construction of the security screen and reinforcement of the warning system through the foresters, Roads and Bridges Department, the gendarmerie and PTT.

The "actives" numbered about 350 men, and they continued their coups de main even after the Italian troops were replaced by Germans after the capitulation of Italy in September 1943.

They struck at the supplies of the Milice and the closed camps of the Chantiers de Jeunesse, and even went as far afield as Lyon, where they liberated Senegalese prisoners working as orderlies for German officers and took them back to the mountain fortress.

As the winter of 1943 closed in — and winter comes early to the windswept mountains — here and there some maquisards trickled away, seeking the less rigorous life of the plain. The number of *trentaines* (groups of thirty men) dwindled from thirteen down to eight.

Nevertheless, forays by the maquis continued. Joining with *corps franc* of Grenoble, they went into that city and blew up a munitions dump. Then not long after they captured three automobiles of the Feldgendarmerie and took several prisoners. Allied planes circled on the appointed nights to parachute arms and explosives.

By January, having ignored the Vercors for four months, the Germans came storming up from Grenoble. Because the snowfall had been much lighter than usual, their way was not even impeded by drifts.

One arm of the German force struck across the upper tip of the plateau, another turned and swept down the center. The defenders of the hamlet of Malleval found that their natural fortress of gorges and mountain trails — a Vercors in miniature — became a death trap when assailed by overwhelming numbers of men with proper weapons. The Germans burned the few houses in the village, and when they found eight maquisards and civilians in an isolated farmhouse, burned both house and humans.

The other column was held up for an hour by a *trentaine* which then melted successfully into the bush without a single casualty. A few miles further on, a second *trentaine* assailed them for forty minutes. When their ammunition was exhausted, the guerillas vanished. The Germans lost a total of eleven dead and thirteen wounded, and in revenge destroyed the village of Barraques-en-Vercors and part of the hamlet of Rousset. Then they went back to Grenoble.

There was another bloody blow in March, and still another, this by the Milice, in April. As spring slowly climbed the mountains, the maquis began preparations for the forthcoming battle, sure that this year must be the year of the Allied landings. They planted explosives to blow bridges, block tunnels and tear away cliffside roads.

Eugène Chavant, head of the Vercors governing committee, headed for Algiers. Scheduled to leave by submarine, he missed connections on the beach, and came back home, where he was finally taken out by Lysander.

Obviously Algiers was still interested in the Vercors, but once there the café owner–maquisard–Resistance chief was somewhat lost among the corridor commandos of headquarters. Theoretical objections to the plan he countered with facts. He was passed from one contending group to another, each in the end assuring him that the operation would go forward as presented in London by Delestraint and later refined by Dalloz. And in London, Dalloz was also caught in the office politics of power-seeking cliques.

However, "Montagnards" still held, although it was not clear who among the exterior forces would be responsible for its operation. Chavant went back to the Vercors and assembled the chiefs for a briefing. The meeting took place the night of June 5, 1944.

At the same moment in London, Pierre Dalloz was being urged to "explain what he knew about the alpine region of France." He said it was all set forth in his plans. Plans? What plans?

Operation Montagnards for the Vercors and its supporting plan for the nearby plateau of Oisans, he said. The papers have been in process for more than six months. . . .

That's very odd. They don't seem to be here . . .

Eventually they were found. Montagnards was planned for execution after the Allied landings in Southern France, landings still months away, and it was in the "pending" file at BCRA while attention was devoted to the Normandy operations. The Oisans papers were in the staff offices of General Koenig one floor above (and a world away). The BCRA was still in charge of parachutings and Lysander pickups and other special operations for the French; General Koenig, as recently appointed commander-in-chief of the FFI, was, in a way, more or less in charge of the same thing.

There had been a good deal of shuffling, and apparently the Vercors had been lost in the shuffle.

Although it was long before time for Operation Montagnards and the mobilization of the Vercors forces, the D-Day radio signals had been broadcast to all the underground all over France the night of the fifth. The purpose of the signals was to unleash action everywhere for assigned sabotage and limited guerilla strikes, thus confusing and inhibiting enemy action. However, the flood of messages and the subsequent appeals to arms by Eisenhower, de Gaulle and a host of inflamed French BBC orators gave the impression to those in the field that orders for general guerilla warfare had been issued. They had not.

The men in the Vercors were sure they heard the order they wanted so much to hear, that they had waited and suffered so long to hear. They marched.

By June 9, five reserve companies had reported for duty from the nearby cities of Grenoble, Royans and Romans and from the villages of the plateau. Many isolated groups reported to the headquarters of the northern and southern commands. The five hundred defenders overnight became fifteen hundred. There were, of course, not enough arms for all.

However, the maquis believed they could hold off attacks from any force under twenty thousand men. This was a correct application of the standard five-to-one odds in favor of a well-

mounted defense, but not correct given the ridiculous in-
equality of arms and armor of the two forces. The defense
was unruffled. After all, they did not have to hold out very
long. The airborne force would be there any hour, any day.

Defending St. Nizier, the first Vercors village of consequence
on the road from Grenoble, the Brissac and Goderville companies did not even dig in, since they would soon be backed up
by the cannon of the airborne troops.

"The weather is magnificent this June. The sky is a resplend-
ent blue. *Il fait délicieusement bon à mille mètres d'altitude . . .
on se sent libre.*" The mobilization was a sort of holiday, a
remarkable fusion of all the volunteers into a company of
Frenchmen with no other identity than that. It was a joyous
patriotism engulfing all in a free fellowship, a glorious moment
to have lived.

Two days later, the test. Thursday, June 13, 1944, fifteen
hundred Germans drove unmolested in their vehicles from
Grenoble to the village of Pariset. They disembarked, formed
up, and attacked St. Nizier. The 250 maquisards held them
off with fire from their light weapons, and the Germans sent
in fresh troops. As hand-to-hand encounter began, a section
of ex-Armistice Army mountain troops, Chasseurs Alpins,
lumbered up in a bus to reinforce the FFI line. The Germans
retreated under a rain of hand grenades. At nightfall, the
Germans collected their sixty dead and drove back to Grenoble.
The maquis had lost ten men.

That night, or rather at three o'clock the next morning, Allied
planes from Algiers dropped arms to a pick-up party directed
by the indefatigable Chavant. The weapons were degreased,
mounted, and passed directly to the combatants in the line,
who were either relieved or reinforced. Field kitchens near the
St. Nizier mairie kept the hot food coming.

Next day the Germans stayed in Grenoble, content to fire
forty heavy shells at the maquis lines without hitting anyone.

Colonel Henri Zeller, COMAC chief for the Southeast (Military Districts R-1 and R-2), from Provence to the Jura mountains, arrived to see how he could help. The announced parachute drop that night did not come off.

The morning of the fifteenth at five o'clock, another artillery barrage. Then the Germans struck, this time three thousand against three hundred. If only the Allies would drop some mortars as the Vercors command had been asking for a year! Light weapons could not hold off the field-gray wave forever. At 10 A.M., the order to disengage was given. Two men refused to obey.

One was Sergeant Itier of the Goderville company. He had fired twelve rounds from his bazooka from a good position and still had more ammunition. It takes two men, ordinarily, to fire a bazooka. No matter, said Itier, I am too badly wounded to move, get out of here and I will cover you. "He fights to his last breath, refusing to let himself be carried off. His dog licks his bleeding wounds."

Company Sergeant Chabal, commanding the Chasseurs Alpins, also refused. His section fought on past noon. Almost encircled, he and his men broke out and fell back. They lost only one man. The defenders in all lost thirteen others.

The maquis would have held out longer, perhaps even won again, but for the Milice. Dressed in worn clothing and unshaven to look like the ragged maquisards, the Milice infiltrated the defense, which took them for men of their own. Once inside, the Miliciens fired their automatic weapons point blank at their nearest neighbors. They killed perhaps only eight or nine this way before being cut down, but it worked hell with the defense.

In one of their paroxysms, by now hideously familiar, the Germans stormed into St. Nizier and burned it to the ground. They hauled the maquis dead out of the mortuary and threw the corpses into the flames.

Colonel Huet, the Vercors military commander, ordered all forces back into the southern half of the plateau, back beyond the gorges of the Bourne: the enemy was inside the redoubt.

The defense felt it would be even more effective along its new, shortened line, but it was still too feeble in numbers and arms to hold even these crests and gorges against a modern army, without help. But a few days later most of the German force withdrew to Grenoble. The maquis defense perimeter remained as it was.

When the Germans did not return to battle, there ensued the remarkable month of the "Republic of Vercors." Volunteers, some from as far away as Paris, flocked to the plateau. Air-drop followed airdrop, enabling the command to arm and instruct its troops.

Newspapers and radios around the free world rang with the praises of the heroic defenders who at that moment were defending only against time. Distinguished Resistance figures came to admire, to breathe the air of liberty, to help.

Yves Farge, already secretly named as post-liberation Commissaire de la République for Lyon and its region, was one of those helping Chavant run his tiny "republic." There was food distribution for the civil population, including daily "collaborationist" milk and butter deliveries for children in German-held localities. Pensions and family allowances were paid out, and all the normal civilian authority continued to function. There was even a police force assembled from gendarmes who had come to join up. On July 11, General Koenig's order of the day cited the Vercors — ". . . you fly the French colors over a corner of the French earth."

Huet, who had been dashing about on his motorcycle to watch over his contingents and give orders, found time to set up a normal staff, with quartermaster corps, medical service, transport, repair shops, military courts and a stockade for Milice and collaborationists at La Chapelle-en-Vercors. Minefields were laid, defense positions determined, roads and bridges readied for cutting.

Out of the sky soldiers came tumbling. It was not the awaited airborne force, but a twenty-man U.S. combat team; then an Allied mission of mixed nationalities (Mission Eucalyptus); and finally Mission Paquebot, a team of five French officers (one of them a girl). Paquebot's task was to clear and maintain the proper kind of landing ground for airborne troops at the village of Vassieux. You see! They are coming, they are!

By now there were four thousand fighting men on the plateau. On the fourteenth of July, deep in the Lente Forest, there was a traditional Bastille Day military review, and a military memorial mass for the St. Nizier dead. There was a holiday banquet at La Chapelle-en-Vercors. And there was an absolutely stunning aerial display in the middle of the afternoon by fourscore USAF bombers, dropping hundreds and hundreds of parachutes red, parachutes blue and parachutes white over Vassieux.

The Germans added a fireworks display. As soon as the American planes had gone, the swastika-blazoned bombers from a nearby (and unscathed) base in the Rhône valley dropped bombs on Vassieux and La Chapelle-en-Vercors. Their ground forces, however, did not attack.

Not until five days later, and then two divisions began the investment, the encirclement of the natural redoubt. Here were the twenty thousand men the Vercors hoped to hold off.

The Germans went at it as if it were a field exercise, as if the cliffs and mountain passes and the defenders were all chalk marks on a War College blackboard. Two red arrows streaked out of Valence to the west in the Rhône valley and two others flashed out of Grenoble to the northeast, and where the four arrows met, the circle around the plateau was closed. One column rammed up the St. Nizier road and toward the heart of the plateau. Seven other columns climbed the escarpment, forced the passes and crashed upon the defenders.

The encirclement took most of the day on the nineteenth. The assault began on the twentieth at six in the morning. At seven the rain began to fall, as it would fall through most of the battle, adding to the discomfort and fatigue of the poorly clad maquisards. At eight o'clock, first contact; at eight-thirty the first falling back by the maquis. The enemy columns trying to push through the passes farther south were stopped, at least for the moment.

And then suddenly the throbbing-thrumming of planes. Half past nine. Through the shredding clouds, the men on the plateau could make out the shapes: two planes — one-two-three — twenty of them, coming from the south, from Algiers! Each towed a glider. At a minimum of twenty men to a glider, that made four hundred, and with their mortars and heavy machine guns, they were as good as an army in these hills. The airborne force was here! Operation Montagnards was taking place as planned. Down through the mists the gliders swept onto the scarcely cleared field. Out jumped the soldiers, and . . .

. . . Out jumped the soldiers and they were German soldiers. It was the SS . . .

Most of the defenders froze in incredulity. They stood there, mouths agape, guns almost slipping from their fingers, telling themselves it could not be true. In a very few minutes, they were dead, more than one hundred of them.

Some of the more experienced reacted more swiftly. Aviation Corporal Victor Vermonil threw himself upon a heavy machine gun (one of the few the maquis owned, to be used for anti-aircraft defense) and kept up fire for a quarter of an hour. He wiped out two glidersful of SS. When a bullet broke his right shoulder he picked up a submachine gun and fired with his left hand until his wound put him out of action and he crawled away to safety.

Captain "Paquebot," who had been directing the work on the landing field, was wounded and hid for twenty-four hours in the water of a bramble-covered abandoned well, and got away the second night. Some few others fought valiantly and died at their posts. Very few got away.

Four hundred maquisards, including the twenty-man American unit, were ordered to encircle the invaders and wipe them out. But more gliders came, and on the unfinished landing strip, troop-carrying aircraft landed, unloaded and took off.

The FFI counterattacks were directed by Major Chabert, military chief of the Rhône Department, who had escaped Gestapo arrest a couple of days before and made his way to the Vercors. He launched three attacks in the next twenty-four hours, but each was driven back.

Within the German perimeter, all was death and devastation and horror. The sixty-four civilians at Vassieux — a few men, some elderly persons, women, children and babies — were slain. The Germans hated and feared the "terrorists" and they purged themselves with an orgy of torture and murder and arson.

Three children, Suzanne Berthet, 8 yrs., Alice Giraud, 10 yrs., Lucien Emery, 4 yrs., were hidden behind a rock. The Germans threw grenades at them. The first was wounded in the foot, the second in the back, the third had his left wrist almost torn off.

Mme. Marie Bonthoux, an old lady of about 70, came out of her hiding place to beg pity for these three little ones and for herself, whose son-in-law was a prisoner in Germany. She was shot point blank.

Later little Suzanne was being carried away by her mother and her father, who was mayor of Vassieux, when they saw a patrol coming. They hid in a cave, but their barking dog gave them away. The Germans, crying "Terrorist!" routed them out. While M. Berthet was fumbling through his pockets for papers to show who he was, they shot him. They said to little Suzanne and her mother, "If you cry, you'll get the same thing."

They worked the seesaw trick at Vassieux, too. After torture, hang a victim on each end of a suspended beam, toes not quite touching the ground. When one manages to get his feet on soil, the other strangles, and struggling, pulls the first man into the air where he in turn strangles, and thus it goes on for a long time until they are dead. And the big joke is that the Germans haven't killed them, but they have killed each other.

Here too they burned houses with people locked inside. Those who broke out of the flames were shot down.

On the twenty-seventh of July, after the fighting had stopped, the Abbé Gagnol found Arlette Blanc, twelve, trapped by her leg inside a ruined house, the only living thing in the hamlet of Château. She had been there for seven days with nothing to eat or drink.

"I saw some Germans and asked them for something to drink. They looked at me, but they didn't give me anything and they went away, making fun of me."

Her leg was trapped by the bodies of her grandmother and her aunt caught under burned timbers. ("My little sister Jacqueline is under them. Over there is Mama. She died a few days ago, begging me to get her a drink and I couldn't. And back in the ruins are my little brother Maurice and . . .")

They got her out, but she died of blood poisoning.

It went on like this over the whole plateau, but the grotto at La Luire was notable, even for Them. It is a cave sixty feet across, sixty feet from floor to roof, and twice as deep. This is where the Vercors headquarters hospital took refuge after evacuting the village of St. Martin. On the twenty-first they headed with their wounded down the plateau's central highway for the town of Die on the plain below the notch in the base of the Vercors arrowhead.

Before they could reach it, the Germans took Die. The hospital abandoned its vehicles and spent twenty-four hours carrying patients off the road, along a grassy dell, over a hill, and along a faint forest trail to the cave.

Those who could walk or hobble were told to take to the woods: the grotto was invisible from the road, but still, they were "terrorists," and if the Germans found them, they would be exterminated.

This left thirty-one wounded, including four German POW's and Second Lieutenant Chester Meyers, a member of the U.S. combat team and an appendicitis patient. In addition, there were Doctors Fischer, Ullmann and Ganimède, Dr. Ganimède's son, and his wife, who was one of the nine nurses. There were two civilian women who had been wounded in the bombing of Vassieux. Father de Montcheuil, SJ, professor of theology at the Catholic faculty of Paris, was chaplain.

They hung a Red Cross banner along the front of the grotto, and went on tending the patients for almost a week. Then a spotter plane saw the flag, and on the afternoon of Thursday, July 27, the SS found them. Those now capable of walking walked, and were locked up with the staff in a filthy pen in the hamlet of Rousset. The seriously wounded were man-handled to the top of the hillock, shot, and their corpses rolled down the slope into a pile.

Next day the American, the two women of Vassieux and the staff were driven to Grenoble. The remaining walking wounded were shot on the spot. A total of twenty-four patients was murdered.

The aged Dr. Ganimède and his family were released, as were the two civilians and a wounded nurse passing as a civilian. The remaining seven nurses were shipped to Ravensbrück. Doctors Fischer and Ullman and Father de Montcheuil were shot in a public square. "The first two," writes Major Pierre Tanant in his eyewitness history of the Vercors, "for being of Christ's race, the third for being His apostle."

The actual battle, the thirty-five hundred against the twenty thousand mechanized ground troops and thousand airborne troops, lasted two and one-half days. The mountain passes were forced and the defenders blasted off the main roads.

The story of the battle is replete with stories of heroism. Just two such incidents can stand for hundreds of similar actions: one at the Pas de l'Aiguille (Needle Pass), the other the story of "the last defender."

Seventeen men from the tiny force holding the Pas de l'Aiguille set out to help the handful fighting at the Pas de la Selle (Saddle Pass). They were caught by German gunfire on a stretch of bare rock. There was nowhere to dig in. So they slithered and slid down the incline to a cave where they could hold off the enemy. The Germans — one hundred of them — installed themselves on the bluff directly over the cave and on the high ground on the other side of the gulch.

Up the rainy slope toward the pass at this moment came a shepherd, walking under a big blue umbrella. Hearing the gunfire, he cut off at a tangent, loping with mountaineer's deliberate strides, his big blue umbrella rising and falling with the arc of each step. Just before he was out of range, the Germans cut him down, and the shepherd and his blue umbrella vanished.

When night fell, the maquisards in the cave tossed out a few pebbles to see if the Germans were alert: flares bloomed, tracers cut the air, grenades fell from overhead. It was no go.

Next morning, the Boches machine-gunned the entrance, harmlessly, the angle being wrong. Galland set up an automatic rifle at the mouth of the cave and a mortar shell blew him and his weapon to pieces. Lieutenant Blanc rushed to the spot, firing, and killed the German mortar man and knocked out the machine gun.

Later in the day, the Germans rushed the maquis with three grenade attacks. The defenders picked up the grenades and threw them out of the cave, killing the attackers with their own weapons. Boulard didn't throw fast enough, and the French lost a second man.

Then from the cliff overhead, the Germans lowered an explosive charge on a cord. It blew up just above the cave, but caused no casualties. The Germans tried again, with a longer fuse, but this time the charge was seized from inside the cave, the cord cut, and the package flung out into the ravine to explode harmlessly. The Germans were stubborn. They tried it again and again and again, always with the same result.

Then they lowered another charge, a bigger one, with an even longer fuse. When the defenders grabbed for it, the Germans yanked it up out of reach, then quickly dropped it again to explode directly at the mouth of the cave. Everybody was burned a little, and bruised, but no one was seriously hurt, although they had the sensation of having been blown out, like candles. The Germans failed to follow up with a clinching rush.

Another night. No food, little water, no sleep. Two of those injured by ricocheting bullets died. Better to die in the open, the thirteen remaining men decided. They waited. Then they bolted. The Germans heard them and fired flares. A mountain fog swallowed the flares. The blind, furious German fusillade failed to hit any of the maquisards as they galloped along the ravine, up the slope and back to freedom.

The "last defender" of the Vercors was Lieutenant Chabal. It was he who had refused a month earlier, when he had been Company Sergeant Chabal, to obey the order to retreat. As the Germans were breaking through the final defenses along the main road at noon on the twenty-third of July, he again refused to give up. In a niche high in the rocks covering the road to the interior of the plateau, he made a stand with his Chasseurs.

His position was being assaulted in mass. Smoking his pipe, standing behind a parapet of piled stones, he aimed his bazooka at the oncoming Germans and fired. He and his men were slaughtering the assailants, but for every man killed, two new men clambered toward the little outpost.

The fire against the niche grew more intense. Defenders were falling. The youngest, just turned seventeen, called out, "Tell

Mama that I died for France!" The survivors followed Chabal's storybook example, calmly loading and aiming and squeezing off the shots.

Chabal sent one of his men out with a message: "I am almost entirely surrounded . . . *Vive la France!*" He picked up a submachine gun, firing almost into the faces of the swarming Germans. And then he fell. He pulled himself erect once more and threw into the gorge the pocket notebook company roster, and the bullets knocked him down again. His men then pulled out, slowly, still firing.

Military commander Colonel Huet gave the order to disperse. Then he sent his final message to Algiers and London: "We are bitter at having been abandoned, alone and without support in the hour of combat."

And civilian chief Chavant sent his final message: "If you don't send help now, we will agree with the population in saying that you in London and Algiers have understood nothing of our situation here, and we will consider you criminals and cowards, repeat, criminals and cowards."

Huet went on to fight in the liberation of Grenoble and beyond, participating in the capture of the German 157th Mountain Infantry Division, which had forced the defenses of the Vercors. And Chavant, ten weeks later, stood at attention in Grenoble before General Charles de Gaulle who pinned on his chest the Cross of Liberation.

But during all the time from D-Day to July 23, hadn't anyone tried to do anything at all? Pierre Dalloz daily stormed the gates of military bureaucracy and was daily turned away with soft words of vague reassurance. He finally got to Algiers a month after D-Day and got the same reassurances, only in vaguer terms.

Colonel Henri Zeller, a career officer attached to the Military Action Committee (COMAC), sent some unvarnished messages from France to the General Staff to back up the beleaguered maquis of the Vercors and other spots, to "wake up to their responsibilities."

Communist Fernand Grenier, who held the portfolio for air in the de Gaulle cabinet, patched together a circus troupe of transport planes — too few, too old, too slow and too small for the job, but nonetheless twenty-four planes that could take off and land. He was following the gambler's example set by General Giraud almost a year earlier to reinforce the Resistance in Corsica. But General de Gaulle left Grenier's draft orders for the airborne relief of the Vercors on his desk, unsigned, from June to the end. "Force C," in process of completion, was abandoned, as were both plans Caïman and Montagnards.

On the night that the SS was shooting the wounded at the grotto, Fernand Grenier held a press conference. The Vercors had been lost (he thought all thirty-five hundred had perished), and he blamed the government. "For my part," he wrote de Gaulle, "I don't intend to be associated with the criminal policy which consists of having at our disposal means of action and not using them when our brothers in France call for help."

At next day's cabinet meeting de Gaulle said anyone who felt this way should certainly quit, or else retract the whole thing. Grenier called Communist Party headquarters and asked what to do. He was told to hold onto his post in the government, and so he issued a retraction. On September 9, when the government was in Paris, Grenier was thanked for his "initiative and ardor, courage and energy," and let go.

De Gaulle made no secret of his dislike and distrust of the Communists, including those he was obliged to take into his cabinet as representatives of the Resistance. But that he had abandoned the Vercors just to spite the Communist Party? Not even the Communists have ever suggested that.

What role, if any, politics played in the Vercors decision remains one of the mysteries. Another mystery is how the

Germans knew about the airborne Force C and supplanted it. Another is why the premature maquis mobilization of June 5 was not countermanded or the units, at least, ordered elsewhere. Another is, who sent Mission Pacquebot to clear landing fields for a mythical support force?

Obviously, the liaison between the intelligence people and the military operations staff was snarled in office politics. Obviously, too, the French were asking much of the Allies these overburdened days of two invasions and pursuit of the enemy. And without Allied help, Force C could not move nor be supplied. (A month after Vercors, the French had to force Ike's hand to induce a diversion to Paris. In June, before the Normandy breakthrough, how could they have persuaded him to succor a lone plateau five hundred miles from the combat zone?)

Despite their bitterness, the thousands who escaped the plateau went on to join other maquis, and many eventually joined the regular army. Colonel Zeller, coming from the Vercors, was taken to confer with de Gaulle himself. He spoke his piece, and de Gaulle sent him to Italy to see General Patch, U.S. Army, who was to lead the invasion of Southern France in August. Zeller told Patch the timetable for the southern invasion was all wrong. The planners were not reckoning on the maquis. Colonel Zeller was heard and believed. The plan was changed.

THE CAMPAIGNS

As 1944 flamed on, Supreme Headquarters of the Allied Expeditionary Forces (SHAEF) was becoming aware of how valuable the Resistance could be in the invasion. They created a post for General Pierre Koenig, appointed by de Gaulle in March as commander-in-chief of the French Forces of the Interior (FFI). Then in May, a month before the invasion, they asked him, in effect, to demonstrate the worth of the Resistance fighting forces.

What they wanted was a week-long Plan Vert test in the Morbihan peninsula of Brittany, an exercise, so to speak, but the weirdest in the annals of war games. It was conducted behind enemy lines, and the opposing forces shot at one another in all seriousness.

There was never any question of outside support for the Resistance during the eight days the demonstration endured. The action was contrary to all the counsels of prudence which warned against premature action, but it was carried out by the French to insure an active role for the Resistance in the coming battle for France. Also, by showing that sabotage on the ground was cheaper and more reliable than attack from the air, the French hoped to save the civilian population as much pre-invasion aerial bombardment as possible.

Thus it was that on midnight of May 6, a dozen action units blew breaks in the lines to stop rail traffic. The Germans, already jittery from invasion rumors, responded instantly and wrathfully, but that was only the beginning of the test operation: the rail traffic was to remain halted for a week. Under fire from hugely superior numbers and arms, the Resistance kept up the attacks, carried out the plan, and lost only twenty-two men. Of course, they were Bretons, among the first resistants, and a population who remained granite before the blandishments and the brutalities of the Boches.

When D-Day came, the chief of Free France was left standing in the wings. The Resistance was only partially unified, with two divergent hierarchies at the top and numerous quarreling clans below; ready to take up arms, the Resistance had pitifully few arms to take up.

Nevertheless, the first assignment to the Resistance was superbly carried out. The sabotage planned by the Resistance was executed by the Resistance: Plan Bleu (electricity), Plan Violet (PTT), Plan Vert (railroads), Plan Tortue (roads). This behind-the-lines sabotage, along with military intelligence, was a major military contribution to the liberation of France and the crushing of the German armies.

The signals came from the BBC, and the first — in two parts — was to announce the invasion. The first and second, the fifteenth and sixteenth of every month were the days to listen for it. The first part meant an around-the-clock alert to listen for the second, and the second part meant that the invasion would be launched within forty-eight hours.

The code was an utterly unmartial Verlaine couplet:

Les sanglots longs des violons de l'automne
*Blessent mon coeur d'une langueur monotone.**

The Germans knew the code, apparently through a spy in England. The intelligence section of the 15th German Army at Turcoing noted reception of the first line on the first, second and third of June. The second was broadcast on the fifth of June at 9:15 P.M., at 9:20, 10 and 10:15. The information was sent top-priority to Rommel's headquarters and to von Rundstedt. There was no reaction. Rommel, on leave in Germany, was not recalled. At Hitler's headquarters, Jodl simply did not believe it: "After all, Eisenhower isn't going to ask the BBC to announce the invasion."

There were a lot of other code messages broadcast by the BBC that night: "The dice are on the table," and "It is hot in Suez," and *"Je n'entends plus ta voix."* The general orders for the planned sabotage had been given. These were followed by messages for individual units to carry out their missions as part of each plan.

It was as if trails of powder had been laid crisscross over the map of France. The railroad lines were blown apart, tunnels were blocked, bridges were broken. The lights went out, factory machines were stilled, the telephone was dead.

---

* Long sobs of the violins of autumn stab
Into my heart with a languor drab.

A fifty-train convoy carrying a German armored division arrived from Belgium, but did not get very far into France. Only ten of its trains, much too late, struggled to their final depot, and the soldiers were worthless for battle, because they were unfed and exhausted.

German troops switched from Brittany west to Normandy arrived on stolen bicycles and carts and sometimes on foot. Their route of march was harassed by guerilla fire. One detachment of shock troops made the whole 125 miles to the Normandy front on foot. Not a single train was running in the five *départements* of Brittany.

From the south, with urgent dispatch, the elite Panzer division, Das Reich, took the road for the Normandy front. All the way through Dordogne it was harassed by the maquis. Having lost forty-eight hours in its schedule, it split at Brive, light elements heading for the railhead at Limoges, heavy sections aiming for the railroad at Périgueux. They lost six days reaching Périgueux, and then, finding that all the other rail routes had been systematically cut and re-cut, the heavy units had to entrain on the one line still open, toward Angoulême. Once on this route, there was no way off and no way back. Guided by the intelligence réseaux, Allied bombers let the division — fifteen days behind time — bore its way into the trap, and then pounced. When the bombers finished, the Panzer Das Reich was finished too. Only a few scarred elements with tanks reached Normandy, too late and too feeble to change anything. Swinging around the Dordogne to avoid a similar fate, the Panzer divisions Gross Deutschland and Hermann Goering arrived too late.

Units sent to the front from Nancy, in Lorraine, made it, but it took them two weeks to get there. In the Alps train traffic ceased altogether on June 15. Around the rail center of Dijon, thirty-seven rail lines were cut on June 7, and the passage from the Rhône west toward Germany across Burgundy was impossible by train.

In the *départements* of Avéyron and Hérault, where the rail
lines were sparse, trains derailed in the tunnels effectively
blocked the ways.

In the southern zone, more than a thousand trains were held
up for periods up to the planned two weeks. In the summer
of 1944, the Resistance prevented at least a dozen German
divisions from either reinforcing the Normandy front or escaping toward Germany.

In Brittany at invasion time the maquis was waiting for airborne Force A, as the men of the Auvergne and the Vercors
awaited Force C. Force A was to be composed of four thousand
elite French troops assigned to the newly created Special Air
Services (SAS). The plan called for a mobilization of the
maquis and other FFI, to be stiffened by the SAS troops who
would execute sabotage and assault missions before joining
forces.

On D-Day, the Brittany FFI executed its part of Plans Vert,
Bleu, Tortue, etc., to virtual perfection. When the signal for
mobilization was given in the Morbihan Department, eight
thousand men flowed in from all points to a farm outside the
village of St. Marcel. Planes began dropping weapons and
supplies in enormous quantities. The Germans could not possibly miss the concentration of thousands of men. They began
to probe, while the maquis units were still being formed up and
armed (and in most cases, instructed how to operate the
weapons).

Where was Force A? Force A was right there, its initial
missions accomplished.

On June 18, at 4:30 A.M., an eight-man Feldgendarmerie
patrol came upon the first outposts. Seven were slaughtered,
but one escaped to report. At six-thirty a force of two hundred
Germans deployed and tried to infiltrate the pickets, and was
wiped out, almost to a man. At nine o'clock a whole regiment
showed up and in four attacks failed to breach the defenses.

Then from the other side of the camp, a whole German

division was signaled coming to the attack, and along the original front, tanks were reported. A call to the Allies brought air support, but some of the tanks got through the bombardment.

St. Marcel was being hammered from two sides, and the order for dispersal was issued, to be effective after dark, at 10:30 P.M., five hours away. At 6 P.M. the German strength was increased, and their attack was pressed. The forest began to burn, cutting off advance posts from FFI headquarters. Then there was a new attack from the other side. At 8 P.M. the French counterattacked to relieve the pressure and pushed back the Germans. But a quarter of an hour after that, a new German attack wave crashed in. By nine o'clock there was a full, howling battle, with face-to-face murderous fire and some hand-to-hand combat.

Between 11 and 11:30 P.M. the French managed to disengage and withdraw, blowing up their precious parachuted munitions. The fight had lasted twelve hours. German losses, 560; French losses, 50 SAS, 200 maquisards. St. Marcel is counted a failure as a battle, but a great success as a diversion, forcing the Germans to keep regiments away from the Normandy front, defending Brittany against a landing which did not take place.

June 28, there was a similar mobilization at Saffré, with similar results against fifteen hundred SS and five hundred Milice. At both sides, frightful reprisals were taken against prisoners in jails, civilians and hostages.

But when on August 2 the BBC 6 P.M. broadcast gave the signal for general Breton guerilla attack, it was the start of a lightning campaign in which FFI movements were, through the work of a special staff, carefully coordinated with the plans and movements of the American Army. The Communist FTP accepted orders as part of the FFI, and they swept the countryside, liberating a string of cities by themselves and also fighting on full-fledged Army assignments from the American command. In two weeks, the Germans were swept into pockets, and soon after entirely disposed of, with much Allied thanks to the FFI.

FFI Commander Colonel Morice was decorated with the Bronze Star August 13 by General Hood of the 4th American Armored Division, for "distinguished and meritorious service in present combat, and to thank your unit for direct support it has given the 4th Armored Division in combat operations . . . without which [they would have been] neither so satisfactory nor so quickly accomplished."

In his memoires Winston Churchill saluted "the 30,000 men of the region who played an important role in the rapid clearing of Brittany." Good words for the Bretons were also found by Allied military chiefs Eisenhower ("extremely active"), Montgomery ("excellent work") and Bradley ("worthy ally").

Praise for the maquis in the rest of France for having choked off German Normandy front reinforcements was neither lavish nor rapid. In 1946 former United States Chief of Staff George C. Marshall acknowledged their role: "The Resistance surpassed all our expectations, and it was they who, in delaying the arrival of German reinforcements and in preventing the regrouping of enemy divisions in the interior, assured the success of our landings."

Their work in opening up routes for the Allied forces landing in Provence in August was more quickly acknowledged. Colonel Zeller had persuaded General Patch that sabotage and maquis attack and the urban FFI made nonsense of the invasion timetable: Toulon, D plus 20; Marseille, D plus 40; Grenoble and Lyon, D plus 90. Zeller said the Route Napoléon through the Alps was virtually clear of Germans, thanks to the maquis, whereas the projected route up the Rhône valley was strongly held by the enemy. He urged that a column be sent north by the alpine road.

Having secured their beachhead and the high ground behind it by August 19 (D plus 4), Task Force Butler and the 36th and 45th U.S. Infantry Divisions sprinted up the Alps. The very next day they were before Grenoble, and two days later the last German pockets were mopped up. Grenoble was utterly free and secure at D plus 8, which was two months and twenty-two days faster than foreseen.

Toulon fell on August 26, its outlying fortifications the twenty-eighth, rather than on the estimated September 4. Marseille was taken on August 27, rather than September 24. The liberation of Lyon on September 3 was seventy-two days in advance of the original timetable.

The order for general guerilla warfare all over the South, in support of the landing in Provence, was broadcast on August 17. Subsequently the maquis of the southwest proceeded to liberate their corner of the country. Without the help of regular armies, they set free twenty-six *départements*. Alone, they liberated more than two-fifths of the area of France.

With the Germans' Normandy front broken, the Allies pounding at the gates of Marseille and Toulon, and the maquis erupting into battle everywhere, the Germans ordered all their troops to pull out of France, with the exception of garrisons in the major port cities.

Town after town was evacuated, some garrisons surrendering to the maquis, others pushing on through the hostile countryside. In all there were eighty thousand German troops jamming the roads to reach Dijon before the northern Allied forces took it and get past Lyon before the southern Allied forces arrived and the pincers were closed.

Some of them were cut off and captured in small groups (the figure added up to thousands of prisoners, most of them captured by the FFI). Most of them managed to squeeze, rather damaged, through the gap. But not General Elster's rear guard of twenty thousand men, a collection of units of all kind, organized into three groups.

From one side of France to the other, from the Pyrenees to the Loire, they were nipped and mauled by the FFI, which, using unforeseen masses of men, carried out what amounted to a strategic role.

Two principal groups hung onto the Elster column, the famous *corps franc* Pommiès and the pick-up army led by Colonel Schneider and General Bertin-Chevance. The *corps franc* Pommiès, led by the regular army colonel whose name they took, was twelve thousand men strong, all wearing a uniform of blue shirts, shorts and arm bands. Pommiès, after spectacular military successes, rushed his men to the Spanish border to block the Germans from taking refuge in Spain. The Germans made an about face when they learned that the Spanish would disarm and intern them (they had thought Franco would give sanctuary to fellow Fascists). Pommiès left more than half his men to guard the frontier, and with five thousand men took after the homeward-fleeing Germans.

Colonel Schneider of the FFI had a collection of four thousand men, many from small units which had finished liberating their localities. He too drove headlong toward the north to turn Elster's twenty thousand Germans from the escape gap in the unclosed Allied pincers.

Elster found himself driven northeast into the guerilla territory of Colonel Bertrand, almost exactly in the center of France. Bertrand had already inflicted considerable damage on the retreating Germans who had preceded Elster. Bertrand had five thousand men, the nucleus of which was his original tough 1800-man maquis.

While the Corps Pommiès was involved in the three-day raging battle for the city of Autun (five thousand Boches surrendered to him there), Schneider's column swung around the Elster force toward the pivotal city of Nevers. It was Bertrand's men who closed with the Elster column, which was now traveling only by night, covering twenty to twenty-five miles, harried continually by sniping and by ambushes.

The night movement spoiled some of the maquis tricks for slowing enemy progress and straining his troops physically and emotionally. They were simple tricks: a pile of dung in the road could stop a whole convoy. In the first few patches of horse droppings, the maquis would hide a tiny British contact mine, big enough to blow off a tire or perhaps a wheel. Farther on, another patch, another tire-blower, another accident, and then very soon, at every spread of dung — some of it symmetrically arranged by village children so it would look suspicious — the column would halt, the mine detectors would come out, and long minutes would be lost.

Piles of stone, seen along the sides of every French country road, were used to the same effect. Along the convoy route, piles of selected sharp stones were mounded over a charge of gelignite. The lead truck would trip the pull-wire stretched across the road and the following vehicle and its passengers were slashed to bits by thousands of razor-sharp shards. Every pile of rocks became a threat to be cautiously examined.

But the enemy's night travel meant that the maquis had to content itself with causing rock slides, changing road fences to lead convoys over cliffs, dropping contact grenades from high places, giving a salvo of massed bazookas before vanishing, and mounting the classic moonlight ambush on hills and curves.

Having got only as far as Châteauneuf-sur-Cher in three maddening weeks, Elster surrendered his force, not to the maquis who had beaten him, but to the first Americans he could contact. Colonel Bertrand had the minor satisfaction of having Elster brought to him to read aloud the terms of surrender.

The German reaction to the sabotage and the maquis attacks in support of the Allies was vicious, even for the Germans. It horrified those who had lived through four years of seeing what the Germans and their auxiliaries could do. Where they could not get cattle cars rolling to ship captives from prisons in France to the camps and ovens of the Greater Reich, they exterminated the prison population outright.

The most striking example of the pains they took, first to murder and then to conceal the evidence, occurred at the

prison of Montluc, outside Lyon, on August 20, 1944. Cardinal
Gerlier, archbishop of Lyon, primate of the Gauls, saw what
evidence was left and wrote to the German commander:

I am sixty-four years old, Monsieur le Commandeur, I was in
the war of 1914 and have seen, in the course of a life which has
led me into a good many things, many horrible spectacles. I have
never seen one which revolted me as much as that which I viewed
a little while ago . . .

I am convinced that you have been unaware yourself of the
refinements, the savagery which have marked these atrocious executions. But I do not hesitate to declare that those responsible are
forever dishonored in the eyes of humanity. God deign to pardon
them!

Tied individually, and then two by two, one hundred prisoners of both sexes were loaded onto trucks and driven just
beyond the Lyon suburb of St. Genis-Laval to the abandoned
old fort of Cote-Laurette.

Those nearby heard the firing squads at work inside the
empty fort. Then the guardhouse was seen to smoke and burn.
There was more shooting, probably at prisoners trying to
escape the flames.

At about quarter to eleven, the cars and trucks passed back
through the village. Germans were in the trucks, but the automobiles were full of gleeful Frenchmen flushed with the joy
of killing their fellow citizens. After the convoy had passed,
delayed-action charges blew up the flaming guardhouse at the
fortress.

Red Cross volunteers and the cardinal went out two days
later. They rolled back the huge stones tumbled from the
blackened old walls, but they couldn't find a whole corpse,
only what the Cardinal described as pieces of "human debris,
of which it was just about impossible to determine the exact
nature."

Montluc was just one prison.

And then there were the "executions" of individuals and of groups in all the big cities. And the extinction of whole villages. Outside the Vercors, there were Ascq, Montignac, Montauban, Rouffignac, Oradour and Tulle, to name the best remembered.

At Tulle on the ninth of June, ninety-nine men were hanged. Tulle is the capital city of the Département de la Corrèze. It was taken by the FTP on June 8, and the day after, the guerilla-harried German division, Das Reich, came upon the scene. They took the town back again. Their commander was beside himself with rage. He had been on his way to reinforce the Normandy front for two days now, and he was just about as far as ever from his goal, because of these "terrorists." He was outraged that irregulars could do this to him, and he was afraid that his superiors would not accept the explanation for his delay.

His announcement of reprisals in Tulle opened with the statement that "forty German soldiers have been assassinated in the most abominable fashion by Communist bands." He called it frightful and cowardly and decried the police and gendarmes for "having made common cause with the Communists." It added up to a decision to hang 120 maquisards and to throw their bodies into the river.

From the bridges, the telegraph poles, from balconies and from a few seesaws he hanged ninety-nine men. Not maquisards, most of them, but men of the town. Two months later, the German garrison of Tulle surrendered to the maquis.

The same errant, desperate column passed next day through Oradour-sur-Glane just as school was letting out and the mothers were there to pick up the littler ones. A wave of panic swept the Germans: terrorists! They herded 642 women and children into the church and set it afire. Then they smashed the rest of the village, and resumed their march. It was incredible that anyone escaped, but one did, and so the world knew.

And later, almost three months after the Division Das Reich

had been obliterated by the maquis and the Allied air forces, General von Brodowski was found asleep in a barn. In his personal route journal they found the cold, sparse notes of the good day's work at Oradour. All those burning people "shot while trying to escape." He was captured by regular French forces, who found him a singularly arrogant man. They shipped him off to prison in the fort at Besançon. And he was shot. While trying to escape.

A Moment of Sanity

A MONTH before the people of Paris rose up against Hitler's minions, some of Hitler's generals rose up against Hitler. For a few hours on July 20, 1944, the Paris SS, SD-Gestapo contingent was under arrest in its various establishments, and the Wehrmacht, which had carried out the arrests, awaited word of the successful coup d'état following the bomb assassination of Adolf Hitler. But Adolf Hitler survived.

The Paris Wehrmacht generals, led by Heinrich von Stülpnagel, went ahead with their plan nevertheless. They were going to execute the captured Himmler chiefs and pass to open revolt with their troops. But then Field Marshal Gunther von Kluge, commander of the German Western Front, dropped out of the conspiracy and turned against the conspirators. The Navy establishment at Paris also prepared to take arms against the dissidents. They gave way, and that was all.

Von Stülpnagel attempted suicide, blinded himself with a pistol shot through the head, and, blind, was hanged alongside the others from a meat hook. The investigations and vengeance went on until the end of the war, not quite unto the seventh generation, but far enough so that after the handful of plotters perished, seven thousand more Germans were arrested and five thousand executed.

The new Kommandant von Gross Paris was named August
3. He was General Dietrich von Choltitz, commander of the
84th Corps in Normandy. He reported to Hitler on August 7
in Prussia and was confronted with "an old, bent man with
gray, brush-cut hair" who screamed and foamed. Choltitz said
later he left the interview resolved not to obey the orders of
a madman, "in the interests of my country and my people."
In the same statement he revealed his discovery — after ten
years of Nazidom — that Der Führer was not a democrat: "I
was obliged to disobey the dictator."

On August 10, Choltitz was in the French capital. A week
later he was discussing with Raoul Nordling, the Swedish
consul, the release of political prisoners from Paris jails and
camps and the cessation of deportations. Nordling was also
in touch with the Resistance through Comte Alexandre de
Saint-Phalle. The matter was pressing.

The Gestapo had already shown it was prepared to murder
all Resistance prisoners before withdrawing from occupied territory, as at the Caen prison four weeks earlier, and of dragging
prisoners along to German death camps, as they were doing
now by the thousands from Romainville and Compiègne outside Paris.

Because Paris was now in the battle zone, over which the
Wehrmacht had unquestioned sovereignty, the Nazi police
no longer had power here. Their files had been removed the
week before and most of their personnel shifted east to Nancy.
Still, the prisoners were not Army detainees, but SD-Gestapo
prisoners. Choltitz would not agree to their release without a
covering agreement from the headquarters of the military governor of France, Luftwaffe General Karl Kitzinger.

When Nordling reached the Hôtel Majestic, Kitzinger had
already left, and so had just about everyone else except a
Major Fritz Huhm, who was packing. If the Resistance would
offer twenty German POW's in exchange for every political

prisoner, he would sign a document authorizing immediate release, but quickly, because he was leaving at one o'clock.

Nordling and de Saint-Phalle agreed upon a three-paragraph "contract" which gave immediate delivery to the Swedish consul of all political prisoners from five prisons, three hospitals and three camps as well as in "all other places of detention and all evacuation trains without exception now en route for any destination." M. Nordling for his part "engaged himself to obtain the exchange of five POW's against each one of the above political prisoners," but with no delivery date. Nordling was unable to keep this engagement.

Under instructions from Pierre Laval, the French police had already released the politicals from the Paris prisons of Santé, La Roquette and Les Tourelles. Nordling and the French Red Cross got five hundred from Fresnes, more from other jails, hospitals and camps. But at Romainville, SS Captain Achenbach said he took orders not from Choltitz, but from the Compiègne command, which was outside the Choltitz zone. At Compiègne SD Hauptsturmführer Dr. Peter Illers sent word that if he could lay hands on Nordling and his party, he would add them to the camp population, and they hastened back to Paris in the dark. Next day at dawn, August 17, a death train took sixteen hundred prisoners from Romainville to German concentration camps. (Another, sent off from Compiègne prison on August 27 was halted not far away by a Wehrmacht general and the prisoners released.)

But the day after, August 18, SS-Gestapo chiefs Oberg and Knochen pulled out of Paris, so Nordling tried Romainville again, this time accompanied by Choltitz's chief of staff. The Wehrmacht colonel threatened to send SS Captain Achenbach and his Georgian (Georgia, USSR) guards to front-line duty. The captain thereupon surrendered to Nordling the remaining fifty-seven prisoners, who were thus saved from extermination.

Nordling's "contract" achieved the release of three thousand

Resistance prisoners. Some — those who were still physically able — were out in time to join the fight for the liberation of Paris, which began in earnest the following day, August 19, 1944.

The Liberation of Paris

PRELUDE

A CENTRAL attribute of the French national character is paradox. (It is part of the paradox that the French, unlike most other nations, *have* a national character.) Nowhere was it more gaudily exhibited than during the liberation of Paris. In this tangled series of events can be seen those volatile and peculiarly French compounds of opposites. Dogma was paired with scepticism, logic with impetuosity, opportunism with patriotism, egocentricity with discipline. Added to this mélange were the basic human emotions — love, hate, fear — restored to their primal protency by the free act of killing. There was a further component — the unwritten law that it is the inalienable prerogative of every Frenchman to be absolutely right.

Put them all together, they spell chaos.

Viewed from a distance, the liberation of Paris is a comprehensible picture of struggle and victory. Viewed closely, it resolves into rather frightening fragments in which there is as much stupidity, sectarianism, deceit and distrust as there is of skill, sacrifice, bravery and devotion. There are misty areas of mystery, sharp splashes of irony and big gray blobs of ignorance combined with apathy.

Twenty years after, it is possible to hear from responsible

witnesses entirely reasonable, amply documented first-hand
outlines of the events of July 19–25, 1944. The names, the
places, the actions, the chronologies are the same in each
piece of testimony, but they tell entirely different stories. The
listener is left with the hallucinating impression that each of
these conflicting accounts is unimpeachable.

How is it that Paris did not become another Warsaw, a
field of smoking rubble and heaps of corpses? Was it because
(a) the Resistance beat the Germans, or (b) the Allied armies
arrived to save Paris, or (c) the German commandant was
partly bluffed, partly betrayed into taking, or for his own
peculiar reasons opted to take, only feeble countermeasures
against the uprising? The answer to all is yes, to a degree.

Was the Resistance divided? Were Frenchmen, mortally
engaging the enemy, also fighting each other? The answer to
these questions is both yes and no. It is certainly true that
there was a remorseless struggle in the high councils for control of the fighting, the city, the population. But it was
equally true that despite the bitter debate and the sly machina-
tions, the Germans were confronted with one Resistance,
whether at gunpoint, the barricades or the conference table.

In the months before D-Day the Communist Party gained
dominance in the joint bodies which led the Resistance, the
six-man committee of the National Resistance Council (CNR),
the CNR's three-man Committee for Military Action (COMAC),
and also on the steering committees of the Committee for the
Liberation of Paris (CPL) and its counterparts in the twenty
arrondissements of the city.

The Communist preponderance was revealed when new ap-
pointments were made to fill steering committee vacancies
after a series of promotions of non-Communist leaders to
Provisional Government posts and a curiously coincidental series of Gestapo arrests. Some of the new members from non-
Communist groups proved to have been secret Communists
all along or else fellow travelers. The known Communists,

being thus reinforced, held the majority. CNR President Georges Bidault was no Communist nor was he a tool, but he was often no match for Party polemicists and tacticians.

Inside the liberation committees, the Communists demanded (and obtained) a seat for each one of their front organizations, while insisting, for example, that only a single seat be accorded to Combat, Franc-Tireur and Libération-Sud, since they had fused to form MUR.

The CNR was, after all, the national council of all the Resistance organizations plus the political parties and trade unions. COMAC was in command of the armed forces of all the groups. This comprised virtually an underground government, with an army to enforce its will.

But there was another government and another military command to which the Resistance owed obedience: the Provisional Government of Charles de Gaulle, with its own superb divisions fully equipped by the Americans. How was de Gaulle to enforce the obedience essential to command? For many patriots inside France, the question did not arise: for them all anti-German forces were indivisible.

Here is a painfully clear case of the difference between the fighting French inside the country and the fighting French on the outside.

Many serious and brilliant Resistance leaders — Pierre Brossolette, the ardent Gaullist who died in March 1944, was one — believed that French Communism had been transmuted in the crucible of war. The Communists they knew as comrades-in-arms were brave men of their word, devoted to duty, disciplined and notably fierce in combat. They often admired the Communist insistence on engaging the enemy rather than waiting for attack orders. They shared with the Communists the suffering of being outrageously undersupplied and generally misunderstood by London and Algiers.

But from outside France the Communist strategy was readily apparent to all who wanted to see, for it was the familiar textbook procedure. Taking control of command posts in the trade unions, the executive and the military wings of the movements, they provoke a classic *levée en masse*. Thus the majority of the population is involved in the uprising, making common cause with the Communist minority, and — all unaware — subject to Party control. Victory for the people thus becomes a Communist victory. The Resistance insurrection was to become a Communist revolution.

So the question was there, as subsequent events proved. De Gaulle's answer was the development of three super-commands under his direction: political, military and administrative.

These served as well to circumvent his cool Allies as to shortcircuit his divergent subordinates.

He appointed Alexandre Parodi to be general delegate, a position vacant since the arrest of Jean Moulin in June 1943. As de Gaulle's deputy, Parodi was thus supreme chief of the Resistance inside France.

He appointed new prefects, sub-prefects and chiefs of civil service departments, to take over from Vichy officials as territory was liberated, and to keep the accustomed machinery of government functioning, but under new authority.

He created the FFI, the French Forces of the Interior, under General Pierre Koenig, assigned to Allied Supreme Headquarters in London. The FFI was made up of all the fighting organs of the Resistance. Inside France, under Koenig's command, were national, zonal and regional military delegates.

The national military delegate was the superior officer of the military underground. Below him were two zonal military delegates, one for the North, one for the South. Each zone was divided into six regions, with twelve regional military delegates ostensibly in command over the chiefs of all Resistance units in the region.

The actual authority of these twelve regional delegates (DMR) over the Resistance chiefs was not automatically accepted. They exercised only as much control as they were able to exact from their proud and sometimes resentful subordinates. Some DMR were weak and ineffectual. Some had control of the Armée Secrète and the units of the Organisation de la Résistance de l'Armée, but were barely in contact with the FTP or the independents. Some few were forceful, efficacious, brilliant leaders.

The operation of the imposed super-commands was delicate: the Resistance had pretty much formed and run itself until now. Thus, when the national chief of staff was arrested, the Committee for Military Action (COMAC) named his replacement as a matter of course. At the same moment the commanding officer of the Paris region was also arrested.

The new chief of staff appointed by the Communist-dominated COMAC named Colonel Rol,* a career Communist, as new commander of the Paris region. De Gaulle's regional military delegate hastened to protest that the appointment was illegal, but in mid-protest was himself arrested by the Gestapo.

De Gaulle's difficulties in gaining Allied recognition of his provisional government persisted. Churchill and Eisenhower both attempted to mollify him with every attention and courtesy when he came at their request from Algeria on the eve of D-Day. De Gaulle was not mollified. He had not been consulted in any way about the Normandy invasions; his government remained unrecognized; his Allies were planning to use Army scrip instead of French francs once they were in France, and they had teams of Civil Affairs officers ready to administer liberated territories.

Even his first supporter, Winston Churchill, seemed to mistake de Gaulle's exalted national pride for overweening personal vanity and his intransigence as impossible personal arrogance rather than a desperate defense of France's threatened sovereignty.

* Henri Georges Tanguy, veteran of Spanish International Brigade and 1940 combat (wounded in both). Metal worker and organizer for the Communist Party.

Accordingly, he was not even conveyed to Normandy until June 14, a week after D-Day. He stayed.

In his June 5 meeting with de Gaulle, Eisenhower explained that the United States could make no choice of a French government, since this was something to be chosen by the French people themselves, once their country was free. The American policy-makers, most of all President Franklin D. Roosevelt, simply would not believe what Charles de Gaulle believed: that he was France.

But in spite of initial Allied objections, Gaullist officials replaced Vichy appointees in liberated territory, and de Gaulle set foot back on French soil a week after D-Day. He made a four-hour tour of "France" (Bayeux, Isigny, Grandcamp), making short speeches and leading enraptured citizens in singing the "Marseillaise."

Then he went back to England, then back to Algiers, then to Rome to visit the Pope, then to Washington to visit Roosevelt, to New York, Quebec and Ottawa and arrived back in Algiers for the Bastille Day parade on July 14.

The interview with Roosevelt was surprisingly agreeable, and he won popular acclaim and great support from the press. As he returned to North Africa, the U.S. Government recognized his movement to be the de facto civil government of France.

At that moment, however, almost the whole country was still in German hands. The Americans continued to shop for some other group which could yet emerge as the de jure government of France. In their search they left no stone unturned, and from under those stones wriggled some remarkably slithery specimens.

One of the main anti-Gaullist proposals was the resuscitation of the Third Republic's parliament, dead these four years by virtue of suicide. On this the Americans looked with favor, since it bore an established brand name denoting democracy and respectability, readily marketable with a fresh label.

With the cherished thought of legitimatizing his regime to

continue as the post-liberation government, the notion had been launched by Marshal Pétain himself back in 1943. It had been stamped upon heavily by the Germans and provoked an anguished cry from the Resistance. The December 1, 1943 *Franc-Tireur* published "A Warning to Members of Parliament Who Might Not Have Understood." The warning came from the National Council of the Resistance: "Having abdicated its powers," the parliament had no further part in French life, and the CNR was "the only genuinely French authority constituted on the home soil, the only voice of the national will."

Pétain had not abandoned the idea, and now it had been taken up by Pierre Laval, Pétain's minister and the real governor of Vichy. It was also hot in the hearts of a group of twenty senators led by René Coty (who later became President of the Fourth Republic), and of a group calling itself the Comité des Corps Elus de la République, the Committee of Elected Bodies of the Republic, which passed itself off as authentically Resistance. It was in reality authentically *attentiste* ("wait-and-see"), composed of men who had waited and had seen that they should wait no longer. They planned to keep Pétain as the head of government, supported by a group of parliamentarians who had until now been anti-Pétainist.

But it was Pierre Laval, schemer extraordinary, who proved to be the master planner of (liberated) castles in the air. In his refracted fashion, Pierre Laval was a patriot. He collaborated with the Germans not because he thought they were right, but because he thought they would win. If they won, he wanted France to survive in their orbit. Now that it was clear they would lose, he saw nothing strange in resuming his republican toga and going back to work at the same old stand.

After the war, he would sit in Fresnes prison just outside the gates of Paris, waiting, as so many Resistance patriots had waited in the same cell for the same rattle of the key in the lock to go to death before a firing squad.

While waiting, he would say, "If the Germans had invented

the atom bomb first and if they had won the war instead of losing it, who would reproach me then? Then perhaps I'd be congratulated for having held on right to the end in the interests of France. I would be, according to Léon Blum's formula, 'the clairvoyant man whom events prove right.'"

Thus it did not seem strange, under the very strange circumstances, that Pierre Laval should be in Paris on August 9, two months after D-Day, sounding out the mayors of Paris and its suburbs, the secretariats of the Paris Municipal Council and the Seine Departmental Council, members of the Chamber of Deputies and the Senate about a re-convocation of the last elected national legislature. He found a large body of approval for his actions, and persuaded German Ambassador Otto Abetz to release Edouard Herriot into Laval's custody. Herriot, speaker of the House, had been in prison since 1942 and had been lately removed to a nursing home. Laval brought him to Paris, lodged him in the prefect's apartments in the Hôtel de Ville, and began working to get Senate President Jeanneney to come from his Resistance post near Grenoble to join in the talks.

When Bidault (president, CNR) and Parodi (délégué géneral) heard about Laval's arrangements for Herriot, they surrounded the Hôtel de Ville with three hundred Paris policemen, members of the Resistance. On further reflection they feared that Herriot might be harmed by an extremist from either side, so they canceled the Resistance kidnapping of the elderly leader.

When the fanatically pro-German Vichy ministers heard about it, they ran bleating to General Oberg, the SS-SD chief in France, and Laval and Herriot were both taken by force to the East of France.

All these groups, hopeful of fabricating a new government out of the ruins of the old, as if there had never been a Vichy or an occupation or — least of all — a Resistance, were in touch with American agents. Most of them claimed to have been promised some sort of job or protection or both.

Certainly, during the long exploration by the Americans, conditional promises were made. At least one man whose early, zealous collaboration sickened even Vichy, and who spent some time in a Vichy prison as a consequence (later he claimed he'd been jailed for Resistance activity), emerged with his fortune intact at the end of the war. More than that, he enjoyed the friendship and powerful protection of a British air marshal.

However, in the third week of August, General de Gaulle's success vis-à-vis the Allies was assured by the action of a group he politically feared and morally detested: the French Communist Party. Against his standing orders, they provoked the Paris uprising.

The Allies had broken through the German defenses at Avranches on July 31, occupied Rennes on August 4. Racing east, Patton's armor took Le Mans on the ninth.

The first Germans — civil servants in Army uniform — began leaving Paris.

Patton's armor beat onward, bending an arc around the city. Their mission was to cut off retreating Germans, not to take Paris, as the Allied strategy was to bypass and isolate the French capital. The military reasoning was unexceptionable.

The Allies expected the Germans to hold Paris: so did Adolf Hitler expect them to, but his orders were ignored. But the Allies had a host of reasons, political, cultural, humanitarian and military, for avoiding a house-to-house battle for the city. In such a fight the four-and-a-half million inhabitants of the metropolitan area would be subject to the savageries of combat, and the city would be destroyed. (In Hitler's phrase, "Paris must not fall into enemy hands except as a heap of rubble.") A battle of this sort would divert supplies and troops from pursuit and encirclement of retreating German armies, and Allied casualties would probably be high.

As it was, skirting Paris, they still had a chance to nip the enemy east of Paris and hasten the end of the whole war. Allied forces would be landing on Mediterranean beaches August 15, pushing up the map underneath the Germans: the operational name for the landing was "Anvil."

Militarily, then, there was no reason for taking Paris by storm and many reasons against it. There were also political reasons for military inaction: the American "self-determination" policy for the French. In order to have France, de Gaulle had to have Paris, and the Americans, of all the Allies, were least eager to see him there.

Logistically, Paris represented a ghastly drain on Allied resources, and from an overall view of the battle for France quite possibly an intolerable drain. Paris was virtually out of coal to make electricity and cooking gas, and its food stocks would permit the most meager of rations for a few days only. With the battle raging at its doors, no trains running, roads cut, bridges out, the capital had no way to get more supplies unless the armies provided them.

However, the armies' mission was to kill Germans, and not to feed Frenchmen. This is perhaps brutal and bitter, but one of the ugly facts of war.

The Allies did not move to enter Paris until there was a compelling military reason to alter their plans and go in anyhow. The reason emanated from the Paris uprising and the very odd German reaction to it.

THE BATTLE

It is Saturday, August 19.

The morning mist is lifting from the Seine, and the rooftops of Paris dapple with changing colors as the sun rises. It is the hour when the city wakes and starts another day. But the city does not wake.

No smoke comes from the chimney pots. No buses course the boulevards. No newsboys dash to pick up their bundles of papers. No throngs of workers move toward the factories. No factory whistles blow. No train whistles, either. The stations are empty. The gates across the Métro mouths remain fastened. No barges move upon the river.

Here and there a baker opens his shop, but the other shops remain closed. There are no deliveries of goods. The garbage piles up uncollected. The street sweepers with their twig brooms are absent. There are no mailmen lugging their pouches from door to door. The post offices are closed. There are no policemen on the street. The police stations are closed. The radio gives no news, because the station is abandoned. The city's electric generators are silent.

On that Saturday, there were three million Frenchmen in Paris, twenty thousand of them signed up with the Resistance (five thousand in the previous five weeks). Although German headquarters troops of various services (including the Gestapo) had been pulling out for the past ten days, more than sixteen thousand were left in the Greater Paris Command.

General Dietrich von Choltitz had arrived nine days ago as the new military governor of Paris. He was ordered by Adolf Hitler on Monday and Tuesday of this week to destroy the city's industrial agglomeration, blow up the gas and electric works, wreck the telephone centrals and demolish the thirty-two bridges within the city gates and the thirty in the surrounding suburbs. Choltitz did not obey these orders. He disobeyed partly because he did not have enough men to carry out the instructions and at the same time guard against the approaching Allies and the increasingly aggressive Resistance. Another part of the explanation for his failure to carry out orders was that the bridges of Paris were the only Seine bridges left in German hands. Another is that, smitten with the beauties of Paris, the last military governor did not want to go down in history as the monster who leveled the city to the ground. Further, his recent interview with Hitler convinced him that Der Führer was insane. Those at least are the things he revealed in interviews with Parisian officials, in replies to headquarters, and in his memoirs.

It is entirely possible, however, that von Choltitz never intended to defend Paris, never intended really to fight a battle already lost in a war already lost, for a leader who had made defeat inevitable.

Except for the fact that the city was still standing on Saturday, August 19, there was no sign of what the German command was thinking. In the courtyard of the Senate, three Tiger tanks began to warm up their engines in readiness for the usual morning patrol.

Down by the river the fishermen were at the balustrades with their long poles and their even longer hopes for a catch. Past the anglers, walking or riding on rare bicycles (the departing Germans had taken bicycles from the Parisians as well as everything else that came their way), groups of men headed for the Ile de la Cité, the island in the middle of the city where the first reed huts of the Parisii stood.

People were streaming in from all directions, making for the vast Place du Parvis Notre-Dame in front of the cathedral. Moment by moment the crowd swelled, until there were two thousand of them facing the Prefecture of Police. All policemen who had been out on strike since Thursday, they were three times guilty of capital crimes against the occupation: membership in terrorist groups,* illegal striking, illegal assembly. This would have been the moment for the *place* to be blocked off by tanks, infantry and armored cars and for the roundup or the shooting to have begun. But the Germans did not appear, not a single one.

It was 7:15. The crowd surged toward the Prefecture. One of the men up front hammered on the small door which allows people to go in and out without opening the huge old doors to the courtyard. A guard, an employee of the Prefecture, but not a policeman, opened the small door a crack.

* *Honneur de la Police, Police et Patrie,* and *Front National de la Police.* All Resistance groups were "terrorists" in the German vocabulary.

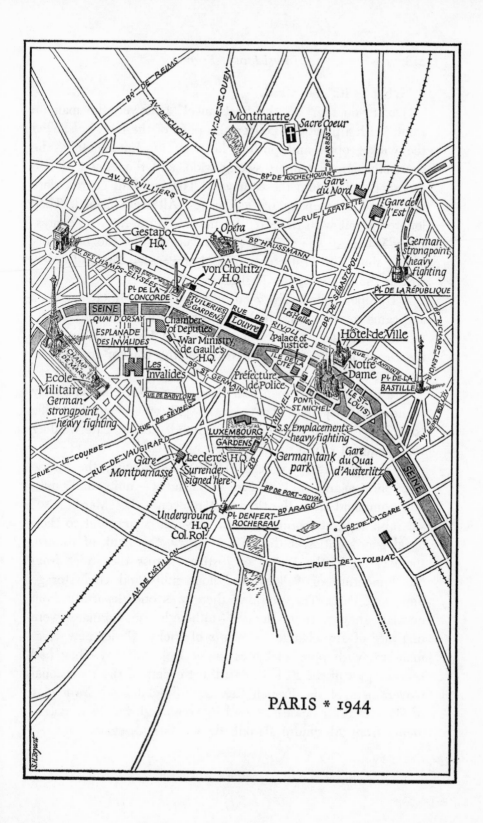

PARIS * 1944

"What is it?" he asked.

"Don't you see? It's the Resistance!" bellowed the man up front. With a practiced policeman's push of the foot, he shoved the wicket open and pushed his way in. Immediately, the great steel-stressed doors swung wide, and the crowd of two thousand boiled into the courtyard. The building guards were there, and a company of gendarmes. All were armed. They loitered about with friendly, if somewhat apprehensive, expressions. When all the striking police were inside, the big doors swung shut. The Prefecture, symbol of Parisian law and order, was in the hands of the Resistance.

A trumpet called. The men whipped off their civilian hats and came to attention. The trumpeter sounded "To the Colors." Up the flagpole, up over the roof of the Prefecture, up over the Ile de la Cité for all Paris to see, the tricolor rose in the morning sunlight.

The two thousand men roared out the "Marseillaise." They sounded exactly like two thousand policemen, mostly traffic cops, but over the still city their proud, defiant caterwauling was beautiful music.

In the principal barracks of the gendarmerie, the Garde Républicaine and the Paris Fire Department — units under military command since the time of Napoleon — the "Marseillaise" was also sung at morning colors. The men swung out to their usual guard duties at the PTT Ministry, the Bank of France, the lock-up in the Palace of Justice (across the street from the Prefecture of Police), the flour mills and cold storage depots of Paris. This morning there was one departure from normal: they were no longer — although the Germans were unaware of any change — servants of Vichy. Under new commanders, with pure Vichyites under lock and key, they had become part of the FFI. Under direct orders of the Provisional Government of the French Republic, they did not form part of Colonel Rol's Ile-de-France FFI command, but took assignments from Alexandre Parodi, de Gaulle's delegate.

By this time other figures were seen in Paris, some dashing along the streets in little groups, others bowling wildly along in forbidden automobiles. They all wore the armband of the FFI. At Les Halles the FTP Battalion Bara set up headquarters in Pavilion 2. When produce and the people who handled it began to trickle in in the late afternoon, the Resistance was in position to control the city's central food supplies — meager in the extreme — and to prevent looting.

The mairies of the First, Tenth and Eleventh Arrondissements were occupied by FFI and local committees of liberation, organized over the past six months. The vacant premises of the daily newspapers were occupied, too, as well as the nearby Central Post Office in the rue du Louvre. It was eight o'clock, and thus far only an occasional shot had been fired.

At the Prefecture, the Vichy préfet de police, Amédée Bussière, sent word that he would like to see a delegation from the men. The delegation, weapons in hand, was already on the way. The prefect received them in his splendid office. Bussière had been a perfectly decent boss, had held out as best he could against the Germans. Although he had not been a zealous executor of Vichy's orders, he was a Vichy civil servant. He had to go. He very sensibly warned in his grand-paternal manner (*Voyons, mes enfants . . .*) the Resistance about the gravity of their revolt, of the terrible reprisals the Germans could take. He volunteered to stand by and mislead Choltitz as long as he could. Nominally under arrest, he stayed at his desk until late afternoon, making and receiving telephone calls.

At nine-thirty the steering committees of the National Council of Resistance (CNR) and the Paris Committee of Liberation (CPL) met in separate rooms of an apartment at 41 rue de Bellechasse. Although, along with COMAC and Colonel Rol, they had been pressing for days to launch the uprising, de Gaulle's delegate Parodi and National Military Delegate Chaban-Delmas held them back. This day the committees were determined to pass the word. Parodi, to avoid an irreparable schism between the external and internal French forces, had already made up his mind to go along with the decision in favor of insurrection should it be taken.

Such a decision would be direct defiance of standing orders from Generals Koenig and de Gaulle, and would fly in the face of military common sense. According to front-line intelligence, several German divisions were falling back on Paris, where they would make a stand. (This, in fact, Hitler ordered Field Marshal Model, commanding Army Group B, to do: "The defense of the Paris bridgehead is of decisive military and political importance . . . In history the loss of Paris always means the loss of France. Therefore the Führer repeats his order to hold the defense zone. . . .")

Even without reinforcement, the Paris garrison had tanks, armored cars, cannon, heavy machine guns, mortars and bombing planes. The Resistance was virtually without arms, munitions, explosives, had no heavy weapons, and only a few stolen civilian automobiles.* Nevertheless, the National Council of the Resistance (CNR) was unanimous: *"Aux armes, citoyens!"* Parodi said, "Gentlemen, I believe that is it." The CNR and CPL (Paris Liberation Committee) produced separate proclamations of insurrection.

This historic act accomplished, they stepped out into the street, less warily than when they walked in, and learned that the insurrection had begun at 7 A.M., without them. Colonel Rol, commander of the FFI, Paris region, heard the same news at the same time. The insurrection had started without him, either.

It had started without orders from anyone at all, in fact,

---

* Official British figures show that of 76,290 automatic weapons (the FTP national commander called them "bad dime-store Sten guns") parachuted to the Resistance, only 114 were for Paris, and only 18 of the 27,961 pistols. Colonel Rol said on August 17, his men had 600 weapons; FTP military advisor General Dassault said 1000. Historian Adrien Dansette estimates 1800 rifles, 240 submachine guns. A black market gangster of the period, who was also an active Allied spy, says that Sten guns could be bought through a bar on the Champs-Elysées before the uprising.

contrary to the orders of all the chiefs. The town halls of several arrondissements, and ministries, schools, newspaper plants, railway terminals, gas works, police stations and post offices had been occupied without a plan, without an order from any headquarters, without the approval of any senior leader.

Colonel Rol's prepared order of the day, not yet issued, was for continued mobilization, strong patrols, and removal of German directional road signs. With a paper package strapped to the carrier of his bicycle, he hurried to the Prefecture. The uprising, no matter how it had begun, was his responsibility, and it was up to him to put the insurgents under his command. From the parcel he took his uniform, changed out of civilian clothes in a Prefecture guard room, and, appropriately clad, approved the measures already taken for defense of the building. Then he waited for the arrival of the new prefect, Charles Luizet, freshly come to Paris from similar duties in long-liberated Corsica.

Luizet had left his hideout and made his way cautiously along the rue du Dragon in the St. Germain-des-Prés quartier. He reached the corner of Dragon and the boulevard St. Germain at eleven o'clock, precisely in time for his rendezvous. As he stepped out onto the sidewalk, two black cars came rocketing up and screeched to a halt, disgorging armed civilians into the street. Had he endured so much and traveled so far only to be arrested at this last moment?

A heavy man stepped up to say, "Monsieur le préfet, the Prefecture has been taken and is at your command. Your car awaits." It was Yves Bayet, chief of Honneur de la Police.

As they drove back to the Ile de la Cité, there was a telephone call from von Choltitz to the prefect. The call was taken by the deposed prefect, Bussière, who assured him that the police would soon be back on the job.

They were on the job, bringing up sandbags from the cellars

and installing them around doors and windows. The best marksmen were stationed at vantage points with the couple of dozen rifles and seven submachine guns that comprised the Prefecture's arsenal.

The new prefect set off with Colonel Rol and Resistance leader Bayet to meet Alexandre Parodi in an apartment in the rue Lowendal, near the Eiffel Tower. Again, they drove through the streets with no difficulty. Parodi formally placed under Colonel Rol's command all the "governmental" forces, such as the police, gendarmes, Gardes Mobiles. Nevertheless, as Parodi knew, these groups would continue to be directly responsible to the delegation. But the gesture underlined the authority of the Provisional Government, while acknowledging the function of the Paris command, and thus enhanced the unity of interior and exterior forces. After which everything went on just as it was before.

At noon, the Germans began to react to the uprising, though not very fiercely. They took back the mairie of the First Arrondissement, which is just behind the Louvre, a few streets away from Choltitz's headquarters at the Hôtel Meurice. They also began clearing snipers out of the Tuileries Gardens.

The town hall of Neuilly, a contiguous suburb, was taken by forty members of the Ajax counterintelligence réseau acting without orders. The Germans, with almost a thousand men installed in a large building nearby, did not react for half an hour, but at one-thirty in the afternoon they responded with a major attack. A machine-gun car, seconded by six tanks, and a wave of SS troopers took the mairie in minutes: eleven dead, thirty wounded resistants; ten dead, ten wounded Germans.

At the Prefecture, at the Sorbonne chemistry labs, at the Ecole Polytechnique, at the HQ of Colonel Lizé, commandant of the Seine Department FFI (he was a white-haired non-Communist career officer,* subordinate to Colonel Rol, com-

* His real name, Jean Teyssien de Marguerittes.

mandant of the Ile de France), the manufacture of Molotov cocktails took place, as it did in other corners of Paris. Colonel Lizé preferred champagne bottles, because an ampoule of sulfuric acid is easily sealed into the depression in the bottom of the bottle. The recipe is three parts gasoline to one part acid, which will explode and burn when exposed to the air in the presence of chlorate of potassium. (Soaking the label in the chlorate of potassium will do it.)

Until one of the *groupes francs* brought a demijohn of sulfuric to the Prefecture, the police were simply putting gasoline into bottles with rag wicks stuffed into the top. The flames from the wick were supposed to ignite the gas as the bottle broke.

On the southern edge of town, German truck convoys were being destroyed by incendiary bottles. As the trucks sped along the boulevard Brune (which changes its name to Lefebvre farther on), the people of the quartier dropped bottles onto them from the overhead trestles of the Versailles railway line. Most of the enemy killed were burned to death, but some died as the flaming trucks went out of control and turned turtle.

Saturday, using an incendiary bottle, the FFI got its first German tank. In one of those broad carrefours onto which eleven streets converge, a tank was poised, machine-gunning the café at the corner of the rue de Courcelles and the rue Pierre Demours. To make sure that the insurgents who had taken refuge in the café had been put out of action, the tank officer opened his hatch. An FFI car, bolting out of one of the side streets, slid up behind the tank and dropped off a shirt-sleeved youth. He scrambled up the back of the tank, slung his bottle into the hatch, and as he jumped off again a nasty orange-red rose of flame bloomed in the open turret. The tank crew was, in the French term, "carbonized."

The mairies of the Fourteenth and the Seventeenth Arrondissements were occupied at 2 P.M. In the streets leading to the town hall of the Seventeenth, which is in the horny-handed Batignolles district, the FFI dumped waste oil and had the

satisfaction of seeing several German vehicles skid out of
control and into captivity.

At the same hour, on the northern edge of town, six hundred
German soldiers tried to infiltrate into the freight yards, but
they were intercepted and then pushed back by the *cheminots*
wearing FFI brassards. As the Germans fell back, the railway
men followed them and continued the exchange of fire through
the streets of the Eighteenth Arrondissement.

There was action at the same hour in the middle of the city
at the Prefecture. A German reconnaissance car coming from
the Right Bank made its way onto the island and rolled along
the boulevard du Palais, spraying the Prefecture with bullets.
While this diversion was taking place, infantry men tried to
sneak across the Petit-Pont from the Left Bank, in order to
flank the Prefecture. From the side windows the riflemen
picked their targets and the bridge was strewn with dead
bodies. Two trucks bulged into the Parvis Notre Dame behind
the Prefecture, but were stopped dead by bullets. The defenders ducked out of the Prefecture and manhandled the trucks
across their end of the bridge as a roadblock. As a third truck
burned, the Prefecture men made another sortie to grab arms
and munitions out of it before it exploded.

Half an hour later, fifty infantrymen brought up in three
trucks made another assault on the front door of the building,
and withered in the cross fire set up from the Prefecture and
from the Palais de Justice across the way. After a few minutes,
the soldiers withdrew, leaving the street littered with German
corpses.

Across the Pont St. Michel on the Left Bank the FFI and
a detachment of police found the war a glorious succession of
easy victories. They were stationed around the Place St. Michel
and up the boulevard, and peering out through the *art nouveau*
iron traceries of the two subway entrances. They had an automatic rifle set up at the Café du Depart, and they were on
watch from the deep doorways of the aged buildings. They

shot the drivers of enemy vehicles, and then, if the thing didn't smash itself to pieces or turn over and burn, recklessly jumped aboard. In the neighborhood, the ambushers managed to capture or to destroy twenty-five vehicles during this single day.

To keep the German drivers from spotting the trap before they were well into it, the trap-setters dragged the corpses off the pavement and down onto the cobbled riverbank below street level. The men and women sunbathing and swimming by the bridge paid as little heed to the stiffening bodies as they did to the bullets whining and whistling above them on both sides of the river.

(Although an unfortunate number of the curious who came out to watch skirmishes were killed when they got into the line of fire, and a number of innocents, some of them sitting in their own apartments, were struck by stray bullets, the sunbathers and swimmers who disported themselves on the banks of the Seine during the fighting seemed immune. Some of them might have been shot dead on the way home, because some frightened German patrols fired wildly at anything that moved. The Germans maintained a few roadblocks and controlled all the bridges except those around the Ile de la Cité and the Ile St. Louis.)

At three-fifteen, immediately after the infantry attack at the front of the Prefecture, there was a new alarm at the back gates. The unarmed men in the Prefecture courtyard — there were no arms to give them — scattered and dived for the subway entrance. Three tanks stood growling on the Parvis Notre Dame. The biggest, a Tiger, loosed two rounds from its 88 cannon. The left door of the giant portal shuddered and sagged, torn almost completely from its hinges. The Prefecture defense telephoned its first call for help to Colonel Lizé, Paris region chief of staff. The colonel had his headquarters across the river a few streets downstream, right next to the Mint.

Léo Hamon, lanky, bespectacled, half-bald member of the Paris Committee of Liberation (CPL), and one of the half-dozen ubiquitous figures of the insurrection, jumped onto a handcart. To prevent panic, he made a stirring "to the last man" oration. The effectiveness of his appeal was enhanced by the mysterious withdrawal of the tanks.

Mysterious, that is, to the apprehensive five hundred defenders, but not totally inexplicable: a phone call had gone out from the Prefecture to Raoul Nordling, the Swedish consul general. Nordling, contacting Major Bender, second in command of the Paris Abwehr, who helped Nordling release political prisoners, learned that tanks were indeed at the Prefecture but had no orders to take the building or to try to destroy it. Nordling hurried to the Hôtel Meurice to see von Choltitz.

Von Choltitz was no longer able to maintain the useful fiction that outside agitators were causing isolated incidents: "the peaceful population of Paris," as he had called it yesterday, was today up in arms. His soldiers had only just finished cleaning out FFI riflemen from the gardens below his windows.

He told Nordling that tanks were at the Prefecture, and said, "The French are impossible." All he wished to do was maintain order and insure the security of his troops. But now the Prefecture was occupied by insurgents killing his soldiers. He said, "I am going to destroy the Préfecture de Police."

Nordling proffered him the frailest logic. . . . "It's a purely French affair, a matter of internal politics. The Resistance is replacing Vichy. The French are just washing their dirty family linen, nothing to do with the German Army."

Choltitz seized on this thought. Urged by Nordling not to attack, but to discuss, the general wanted to know with whom he could talk if he would. Nordling told him, "The Resistance." Thugs, the general declared, terrorists, Reds. Not at all, Nordling assured him. "These are the men from Algiers." He said Choltitz would like them as men better than the Vichy officials they were replacing. He added, "If you were French, you'd be one of them."

At the Prefecture, once the tanks were withdrawn, another convoy of German trucks rolled before the front door, apparently unaware of heated local conditions. The cross fire drummed and cracked once more, three trucks halted and were hustled in through the front portal of the building. They contained some dead soldiers, some guns and gasoline.

It was five in the afternoon before another attack was made against the police headquarters. Infantrymen attempted to slide into position by creeping up the stone stairs from the riverbank. This attack was clumsy and not very serious, but, the defenders asked themselves, what will happen after dark? Another call for help to Colonel Lizé brought another small squad of submachine-gunners, the only reinforcements he had.

This is the moment at which von Choltitz could have crushed the uprising. Any of the FFI-held buildings could have been destroyed by his tanks, had they used exploding shells (but they fired few rounds, and these, armor-piercing shells which only chipped off big flakes of stone from the solid old walls). A handful of low-flying bombers from the municipal airfield at Le Bourget, sneaking through the dusk, could have flattened, for example, the Prefecture. A serious tank-led attack of say two companies of infantry could have overwhelmed the ill-armed and weary defenders of the Prefecture, and even smaller attacks, seriously planned and pressed, could have wiped out the other groups.

And his artillery — Choltitz never used his cannon or even his mortars. Almost all his infantry attacks were small patrol actions quickly broken off. True, when his troops fired, they shot real live bullets which killed real live people. But at this moment, with the FFI about one-quarter mobilized, scarcely armed, and virtually untried under fire, he did not strike the few sharp, brutal blows which could have snuffed out the Resistance.

The leaders, however, did not know that Choltitz would not

swing his hammer, still big enough to smash the insurrection. On the avenue Lowendal, de Gaulle's chief delegate, Alexandre Parodi, held council, and it was gloomy.

They could smell catastrophe. The extremists of the left had ignited the insurrection prematurely, and the moderates had made the insurrection vulnerable by occupying the Préfecture de Police and the Ministries. Jacques Chaban-Delmas, national military delegate, with whose post goes the grade of general (he was a very young inspector from the Ministry of Finance), stopped inveighing against the unauthorized uprising and considered what to do to save it.

If the defenders of the Prefecture were in a bad way, then pull them out, he proposed. The FFI should undertake urban guerilla warfare. It should pass from the defensive, which it was not equipped to maintain, to the offensive of the short shock attack and the swift disengagement, the war of ambush and trap.

General Dassault, military adviser to the Communist FTP, privately gave Parodi exactly the same advice. He undertook to persuade Colonel Rol to order the change in plan. Parodi lifted the title of military governor of Paris from de Gaulle's military delegate and bestowed it on the military adviser of the Communist fighting wing. With the weight of two titles, Dassault's arguments should be more convincing.

Parodi also told the Gaullist civil service chiefs who had occupied their respective ministries to "render your occupation very discreet." By telephone he ordered the besieged Prefecture evacuated.

But the instructions were not followed. The dark streets around the Prefecture were blanketed by German rifle fire. Few of the defenders could make it out alive. They decided that if they were to die, they might better die at their posts, five hundred men with about two hundred and fifty small arms, about thirty of which were automatic.

The German tanks, out of sight of the Prefecture, were still poised at the far end of the Ile de la Cité, ready to attack. At seven-thirty somebody* telephoned from the Prefecture to Swedish Consul Nordling. Was there any possibility of a temporary cease-fire?

The ever-useful Major Bender, still on hand at the consulate, hurried away to German headquarters with the question. In less than an hour he returned with the answer: yes. If the FFI would cease attacking Germans, Germans would not attack the FFI.

If all went well, Choltitz was inclined to discuss an extension of the cease-fire for succeeding days. (The Allies were driving hard on Paris, but Choltitz did not know they planned to by-pass it.)

At eight-thirty Nordling phoned the Prefecture to read the German general's message. The sigh of relief in the besieged building was almost as loud as the "Marseillaise" thirteen hours earlier.

The cease-fire ordained by von Choltitz: eight-fifty-five to nine-thirty. Then minutes after the deadline, he said he was satisfied with the manner of observance and would extend the temporary cessation until 6 A.M. The men at the Prefecture agreed.

Nordling, in relaying the word from the German commander, had not been talking to any member of the Paris Liberation Committee, or the National Council of the Resistance, or COMAC. He had not been negotiating with any commanding officer of the Paris FFI, and certainly not with any of de Gaulle's delegation. He had been talking to a fellow named Edgard Pisani, left at the Prefecture to answer the telephone.

Pisani had done some underground work with Yves Bayet, of Honneur de la Police, and had wandered into the Prefecture in the morning to see if he could be useful. Bayet said he was

* No one who was at the Prefecture ever publicly admitted making this call. The cease-fire notion could have resulted from Nordling's misinterpretation of what someone said.

just leaving with the new préfet de police and Colonel Rol. "Take over the phone," Bayet told Pisani, and through a typically weird efflorescence of circumstances Pisani emerged as the man in charge.

Pisani reported his acceptance of the overnight cease-fire to the delegation. His chiefs assumed that von Choltitz had applied for a truce and had asked for further talks. So far as von Choltitz was concerned, it was he who had responded magnanimously to a plea and expressed willingness to hear more.

By midnight, further truce talks were arranged. Choltitz further extended the truce to cover other buildings occupied by the FFI.

Suddenly, an alert from the Prefecture. The Boches were sneaking up on the building through the Métro! Excited call to Nordling. Nordling, inquiringly, to von Choltitz. Von Choltitz, contemptuously, to the world at large: "If I wanted to assault the Prefecture, I wouldn't take the subway."

It is strange that neither side used the fantastic subterranean network of Paris, even during the worst of the pre-D-Day Gestapo oppression. The sewers of Paris, the subways of Paris, the railroad tunnels, the quarry galleries honeycomb the whole subsurface of the city on a variety of levels. All along the river there are ancient almost-secret doorways leading from the river bank to antique cellars inland. Cellars themselves have earlier vaulted cellars underneath them.

Just before the war, the catacombs at Denfert-Rochereau in Montparnasse had been excavated, reinforced and equipped as a bombproof, gas-proof general staff command bunker. At least this corner of the vast quarry network, under thirteen of the twenty arrondissements and exploited from Roman times until the nineteenth century, was taken over by the Resistance. Colonel Rol used it for his headquarters.

At this moment, the Resistance leaders felt that the cease-fire was really a victory. Without it, they would have lost their strongholds (no military disaster, certainly, but a symbolic and political loss), and many of their finest men.

After dark, a zealous German officer exploded a bargeload of sea mines at the dock in front of the Moulins de Paris. The wrecked mills burned all night, consuming flour enough to give the city bread for a whole day. The firemen, who had spent the past few days distributing arms and transporting Resistance leaders in their ambulances and fire engines, battled through the night to contain the blaze.

The Resistance had begun weeks ago to build up stocks of food (under cover of the Red Cross and National Relief) and to plan emergency truck convoys to bring in what food they could find in the area surrounding Paris. These administrators, planners and transport men are among the many unsung heroes of the insurrection. Their foresight, skill and courage saved Paris from starvation.

The mobile teams of doctors, nurses and volunteer stretcher-bearers were another part of the noncombatant army who were of infinite worth to the cause. Agitating their tiny Red Cross flags, they scooted and squirmed into the thick of combat to rescue the fallen.

Under Father Bruckberger, chaplain of the FFI, teams of volunteers worked around the clock retrieving bodies and attempting to identify them. For several days coffins would pile up at churches and in the morgues, dripping and even bursting in the heat. By Tuesday, things would be more organized, with religious services and mass burials.

Sunday, August 20

Knowing that the truce — should it be arranged — would freeze the positions held by the Resistance, an apprehensive, ill-armed group of men and women marched from the Prefecture of Police to the Hôtel de Ville at six o'clock in the morning. Under the circumstances, the five-minute stroll along the Parvis Notre Dame, across the Pont Arcole and through a corner of the enormous square fronting the City Hall seemed very long.

They were intercepted by a group of armed, uniformed men. These were Gardes Mobiles, governmental shock troops and riot police. They had come to serve as escort. Relieved, Léo Hamon of the Paris Liberation Committee made cordial talk with the leader, asking what the regular duties of the detachment were.

"To protect the life of the head of the government," he said.

"Which head of government is that?"

"Why, Monsieur le Président Pierre Laval, of course!"

Pierre Laval had already been taken eastward by the Germans, and at eight-thirty this same Sunday morning, a dazed Henri Philippe Pétain was led out of Vichy by a column of Nazi armor moving toward Germany.

The Hôtel de Ville is not only the seat of the Paris Municipal Council, but also that of the prefecture of the Department of the Seine (not to be confused with the Seine Department's Prefecture of Police on the Ile de la Cité). Through the series of uprisings which have punctuated its six hundred years, seizure of the Hôtel de Ville has symbolized the re-taking of Paris by its populace.

There was a comic opera scene in the elegant prefectural office in which the Vichy prefect, Bouffet, citing his own sterling efforts to save Paris, rebuked the insurgents for their reckless actions, and wound up asking them for their papers.

The four hundred Resistance defenders of the building included members of the municipal civil service, one hundred twenty police from the Préfecture de Police, fifty Laval bodyguards, some FFI, some Gardes Républicaines, and some squads from the Equipes Nationales. This latter group, officially a police arm of Civil Defense, was Marshal Pétain's Paris guard of honor and 100 per cent enlisted in the Resistance. Staffed by young army officers, its members were seventeen to eighteen years old. The four hundred defenders had few weapons, among them eighteen submachine guns and six automatic rifles.

The terms of the truce sketched out with Raoul Nordling at the Swedish Consulate just after the occupation of the Hôtel de Ville were explained to a brief meeting of the CNR steering committee by Parodi and Chaban-Delmas. All the Communist members of the committee were absent except Pierre Villon of the Front National, and after he offered token objections the other members approved the truce. CNR President Georges Bidault called it a "victory which exceeds our hopes."

Parodi sent his plenipotentiaries back to the Swedish Consulate, where in less than an hour, with Nordling shuttling between the room containing the resistance and the room containing the Germans, the truce was agreed upon. It was noon. Firing continued here and there. Bathers on pneumatic mattresses were paddling on the Seine.

The terms of the truce: German troops crossing Paris (which meant they were retreating from the Allied front) would use the peripheral boulevards; isolated German groups would stop roaming the city, but would "control certain points in the center" to protect their headquarters; public buildings held by the FFI would not be attacked. Sound trucks from the Police Prefecture, in company with German officers in their own vehicles, were to go through the city announcing the truce.

This was the text to be read over the loudspeakers:

By reason of promises made by the German Command not to attack public buildings occupied by French troops and to treat all French prisoners as prisoners of war, the Provisional Government of the French Republic and the National Council of the Resistance ask you to suspend fire against occupation forces until the total evacuation of Paris. The greatest calm is recommended to the population. Please do not loiter in the streets.

As the proclamation was being broadcast, the full CNR and CPL directorates were meeting, with clamorous dissent over the truce. COMAC and the FFI comand condemned the agreement, especially since neither had been notified of the cease-fire which was to apply to their troops.

Though the Communists were the most vociferous in their denunciations — the truce violated both the practical tactics of insurrection and the tenets of ideology — condemnation came not only from the Party. Many non-Communist FFI combatants were enraged at being told to withdraw from a battle so long dreamed of and hoped for. Colonel Lizé, a career officer and far from Communist, thundered, "Any transaction with the enemy is treason." He threatened to have the sound cars seized by the FFI and the crews arrested.

However, the name of de Gaulle was potent and the personality of Parodi powerful. The CNR secretary's notes were headed, *"Le délégué général est absent."* Since he remained absent, both the CNR and CPL meetings finally broke up with any decision put off until he reappeared.

Parodi had been unavoidably detained. Arrested by a German patrol at two o'clock, he had not only admitted who he was, but insisted upon it: "I am the chief of the Resistance, and I am circulating through Paris to verify the truce signed between me and your chief through the good offices of the Swedish Consul. I demand that you notify M. Nordling."

Unfortunately, among the papers in Parodi's briefcase was a general order for accelerated attack by the FFI ("The German armies are abandoning Paris...") prepared in case the truce should fail. To German eyes it was an order countermanding the cease-fire, an effort to use the truce as a trap. Other documents included plans of German military installations in Paris and various intelligence reports.

Having skirted serious threats of summary execution, and having been preceded by his incriminating documents, Parodi was eventually brought before the German commandant.

It was one of those moments when history makes fiction wanly unimaginative. The room was a large one (and luxurious, the Meurice being a luxury hotel) on the first flight up over the arcades of the rue de Rivoli. The windows looked out over the broad Tuileries Gardens toward the Seine. Occasionally, far faint cries were heard: the whoops of youths jumping and diving into the brown river from the Pont du Carrousel.

The cast of characters, like the setting, was somewhat exaggerated:

Generalleutnant Dietrich von Choltitz, Kommandant von Gross-Paris. The caricature of the traditional German commanding general (when a boy he was page to the Queen of Saxony). Shortish, bulging fatly from his tight white uniform, he glistened. Glistening boots, glistening decorations, glistening monocle, glistening shaved head. Face broad and impassive as a dumpling. The general knew the Germans could not win.

Délégué Général Alexandre Parodi, Maître des Requêtes au Conseil d'Etat, prewar director of Labor Ministry. Smooth but sharp, the French intellectual high civil servant. His countenance rather Gothic, with deep lines running from his pointed nose to the corners of his straight mouth. In his own well-tailored way, as haughty as the general. He knew that no matter what happened to him, the French could not lose.

Two interpreters, German officers. The Baron von Poch-Pastor, an Austrian who was probably also an Allied agent, was small, dark, slender, and both physically and socially supple. Major Bender, German intelligence deputy-commander, was tall with a distinguished carriage. His eyes seemed unbelievably blue in the red face under his shock of white hair. His anti-Nazi passion was shown not only by his red-white-and-blue color scheme, but also by his unfailing courtesy toward the French and his undoubted connection with Allied intelligence. Passing through their linguistic mixer, Parodi's tart gallicisms emerged as German confections von Choltitz could swallow.

Swedish Consul-General Raoul Nordling. A Parisian since 1912, married to a Frenchwoman. He was not only his neutral country's consul, but also president of French SKF, a subsidiary of the Swedish ball-bearing manufacturers. The Nazis had obligingly installed his plant underground in Montmorency Forest at Arthenay, with five thousand bombproofed workers. Short but rugged, he had a wide and open Scandinavian countenance with gray hair falling over his forehead. He had all the languor of an expatriate man of the world, and all the wiliness and vigor of an international business executive.

There was one further incredibility in this incredible confrontation: they were all playing the same game, and the name of the game is kaput. Von Choltitz was anxious to save face and give the Gestapo no excuse to harm his family in Germany. He knew that Patton's phenomenal drive around Paris was continuing. The fall of Paris was only a matter of days. Still, Parodi and his men were his prisoners, and he might as well show them some German pride and military exactitude. He asked Nordling if the three prisoners were "thugs" or if they were "messieurs." Nordling said he knew them, although not by name, and they were indeed "messieurs."

Parodi declared, "I am the sole Algiers government minister exercising authority in Paris."

Von Choltitz ignored him and continued to Nordling, "They were arrested before the truce, which was not set to begin until the sound cars made their announcement. For the German command these men constitute the best guarantee of the ceasefire, since they really should be shot on the spot, carrying as they do espionage and insurrectional documents." Indicating the appeal to combat, he said sourly, this time glaring directly across the table at Parodi, "This paper hardly conforms to the terms of the truce."

Parodi replied, "It was written yesterday, before the ceasefire."

Von Choltitz said, "You will permit me not to believe your reply."

"I am a minister of the French Government and I cannot permit my word as such to be doubted."

"Here you are not minister of anything. We know nothing of General de Gaulle. Besides, you have Communists in your group."

For two hours, it went on like this. In the room there were officers of the Feldgendarmerie and some few remaining Gestapo and SD men (they had no legal right to be in his zone, but Choltitz dared not push them too far). To them it was incredible that their chief should treat the terrorists as equals instead of executing them out of hand, as was the custom.

"I want to know if you will enforce the truce," said von Choltitz to Parodi. "Will your men obey you?"

To which Parodi answered, "A population in arms is not to be commanded as are regular troops. You are the head of an army — you give orders, you are obeyed. I have to handle numerous groups of different tendencies; I do not have them all in hand. The Resistance is spontaneous."

This admission tickled the German general's pride, and it pleased him to see that he was dealing not with boot-lickers, nor self-seekers nor go-betweens, but with men who spoke directly for the Parisians, and who spoke up openly. Perhaps it also pleased him that they were in no way afraid.

In his memoires, Choltitz wrote, "For the first time, I was talking with Frenchmen who seemed to have precise knowledge of the overall situation. For once, I was dealing with men of worth and stature."

After the long, disguised wrangle was ended, von Choltitz rose. Everyone else rose. One last question, from the general to the délégué général: "You are a reserve officer?" Parodi said he was. "Well then, between soldiers, such gestures are permitted . . ." said Choltitz, extending his hand. Parodi, hands at his sides, settled for an icy bob of the head. The dumpling face darkened, the glistening boots faced swiftly in the opposite direction, and there was a muttering of German oaths.

It was 6 P.M. Parodi, his aides and Nordling left the Hôtel Meurice. Major Bender followed after them in his car. The SD men followed in their car, submachine guns poking out of the windows. After a few yards, Bender slewed his car around, blocking the SD gunmen. The members of the delegation went on.

Through the night desultory firing went on, in spite of the cease-fire. The Resistance had done well out of this first day of truce: the Hôtel de Ville was in their hands, as were the ministries of Interior, Finance, Health and Public Works.

Monday, August 21

The French Prime Minister's residence-office, the Hôtel Matignon, having been liberated by a youth on a bicycle,* Parodi held a "cabinet" meeting of the civil service chiefs from the various ministries. While they met to conduct government business in the traditional seat of administration, the truce was marked by some stiff fighting.

("There's a truce on, you know," said Préfect de Police Luizet to some visitors entering his office. "Better duck as you pass the windows.")

The contact with Colonel Lizé, broken since Saturday, was re-established Sunday by Parodi, and the Commandant de la Seine was persuaded to accept the truce. He ordered his troops to stop firing, but too late to have the decisive influence this decision might have had the day before.

An afternoon meeting in a tiny, sweltering apartment near the Place Denfert-Rochereau saw twenty sleepless, overworked, worried men from the delegation and the CNR in tumult. The passions aroused for and against the truce had almost achieved what the Germans had not — the rupturing of the Resistance.

---

* "At your orders, M. le Ministre!" said the captain of the guard when the young man knocked at the gate and said he was from the Provisional Government.

The truce supporters wanted to keep the Germans relatively quiet while they somehow arranged for a quick Allied intervention. They wanted liberated Paris to be intact. They wanted time. The truce opponents felt the Germans were already on the run, and that it would be militarily unforgivable, politically stupid and morally poisonous to stop the fight, no matter what the cost in deaths or destruction.

The Communists were more fumingly outraged than other opponents of the truce, because for them it could mean a serious breach in the "leadership of the masses" they had so carefully organized.* Pierre Villon, Front National, cried treason when Chaban-Delmas, the national military delegate, was describing the threat of reported German tank reinforcements. Villon snorted, "It's the first time I've seen a French general who talked like a coward."

After the pandemonium provoked by this historic observation had subsided, Villon apologized. His apology also entered into history: "I didn't actually call Monsieur Chaban a coward. I only meant that he was acting like one." When Parodi began walking out of the meeting, Villon apologized for his apology.

In the end, the CNR adopted a truce-breaking text formulated earlier in the day by the Paris Liberation Committee.

The fight goes on. It must be pursued until the enemy is driven from the Paris region.

More than ever, everyone into combat!

Fell trees, dig anti-tank ditches, raise barricades.

It is a victorious people who will welcome the Allies.

The formal denunciation of the truce was fixed for five o'clock the next afternoon. Parodi, having won the extra respite he sought, approved. He could not have done otherwise with-

---

* The ideological passions of this moment did not die. Charles Tillon, the Communist FTP commander-in-chief, wrote in 1963: "The truce was born of the fear inspired by the sight of a patriotic Paris taking its destiny in its hands . . . The class struggle never stops, no less in the middle of an insurrection."

out fissuring the Resistance. Some part of the movement would have remained obedient to the de Gaulle delegation, but another part would have pressed on in the heat of battle.

Similarly, when he had seen he could not restrain the clandestine newspapers from leaping into full, open circulation, he had given his approval the night before. Today, the presses and papers seized from the collaborationist journals had run off editions for a dozen dailies bearing Resistance names: *Combat, Franc-Tireur, Front National, Libération* and half a dozen others.

News vendors made their way through the streets bawling the titles of the liberated press. The headlines were lyrical: PARIS WINS HER LIBERTY! and EVERYONE TO THE BARRICADES!

At ten-thirty that night, when the half-hour's ration of electricity was fed into the cables, the liberated Paris radio station broadcast a recording of the "Marseillaise." The announcer choked out one sentence, "This is the radio of the French nation."

The truce continued with several notable gaps, such as the taking of the Gare de l'Est from a stubborn German defense. Trucks burned all over town, and the Seine bridges were the scene of miniature battles.

Tuesday, August 22

Colonel Rol, chief of the Resistance forces, arrived at the Police Prefecture to consult with Alexandre Parodi. He had come to report fresh intelligence which Parodi had already received from Chaban-Delmas a few minutes earlier: that the reported column of Tiger tanks was not headed for Paris, and that only one German division was retreating in the direction of the capital, but passing on both sides to avoid the city proper.

The possibilities of heavy military reprisal against Paris and its people had thus been notably diminished. In view of this, Rol said, he had come for an official decision by General de Gaulle's delegate: was the truce to be kept, or broken?

The agreed-upon time for resumption of hostilities was but a few hours away, and COMAC, CNR and CPL were prepared to carry on the fight no matter what. Thus Parodi was somewhat astonished and more than somewhat grateful to have the FFI commander recognize his authority and ask for orders.

Sporadic fighting had continued, street-corner barricades had begun to appear, the Resistance had been collecting supplies, vehicles and arms from German prisoners and casualties. The disjointed neighborhood character of the insurrection had been surpassed, and the uprising had become general. Parodi signed the order to break the truce.

From here on there would be but one aim, to make the streets too hot for the Germans, so that the Allied troops would find them concentrated for easy annihilation.

And where were the Allies? Did they intend to come to the rescue of Paris or not? For General Patton, whose U.S. Third Army was within easy striking distance of Paris, and General Bradley, Patton's superior, and General of the Armies Eisenhower, Supreme Commander of the Allied Forces, the answer remained: not yet, not this week nor any week in August. Vast plans had been made and vast commitments made of vast forces. Paris was a very small spot on the strategic map.

A year ago Eisenhower had promised that Paris would be liberated by French troops. Fretful for a week that he might be engaged elsewhere when the Allies made for Paris, General Leclerc, commander of the French 2nd Armored Division, had obtained the promise all over again, in writing. The 2nd Armored (called 2 DB, for Deuxième Division Blindée) was the sole major Fench unit with the Allies in Normandy.

Leclerc's pleas to be set free to dash for Paris had been made almost daily and rebuffed as often. The same request put Monday to Eisenhower by Generals de Gaulle and Koenig had been refused for the usual solid military reasons.

For four years, starting with a handful of men in the middle of Africa, Leclerc had been fighting the Germans, everywhere on alien soil. Now, at last, he and his men had reached France, only to be tethered one hundred miles from occupied Paris.

Monday, without approval from his superiors, Leclerc dispatched a unit probing toward Paris. The light tanks, ten armored cars and one hundred fifty infantrymen in troop carriers had gone off under Major de Guillebon to scout the enemy and find the best route of attack on Paris for the 2 DB.

The order given, Leclerc wrote to de Gaulle explaining the irregular initiative he had taken. At the same moment de Gaulle was writing to Eisenhower suggesting that if the Supreme Commander didn't send troops to Paris at once, de Gaulle might have to do so himself. In theory, at any rate, de Gaulle was one of Eisenhower's three bosses, on a par with other chiefs of state whose forces were involved in the campaign. The messenger who bore this letter was three-star General Alphonse Juin, which indicated to Eisenhower just how serious de Gaulle's intentions were. At the same time, in response to French pressure, the British were pressuring Eisenhower, who then began to reconsider the immediate liberation of Paris.

Leclerc's unauthorized patrol action had by now come to the attention of his superior, General Leonard T. Gerow, commanding V Corps of the First Army: "I desire to make it clear to you that the 2nd Armored Division (French) is under my command for all purposes and no part of it will be employed by you except in the execution of missions assigned by this headquarters."

Attached were orders for the immediate recall of the patrol in question. Since it was a question of Paris, Leclerc decided to appeal to higher authority and went in one of his spotter planes to Bradley's headquarters.

There he was told that Bradley had just left to consult with Eisenhower on the question of Paris. And there he met Colonel Rol's chief of staff, Major Gallois, who had been on the road, virtually without sleep, since Sunday night, the second day of the insurrection.

Gallois — no Communist — spoke perfect English and had a superior grasp of military matters. This was why, Colonel Rol later explained, Gallois had been sent on this mission, even though he was chief of staff for Rol, whose forces were in mid-battle.

The mission was to persuade the Allies to parachute arms and munitions to Rol. But once arrived, Gallois pleaded for an Allied drive on Paris. He had been persuaded Sunday night, while dodging German roadblocks and minefields, to reinterpret his mission. The man who persuaded him had been his guide and living front-line pass, Dr. Robert Monod, head of the Paris medical Resistance.

He had arrived at Patton's headquarters Monday night, and early Tuesday morning, after a long intelligence interrogation, had been received by Patton. From the general Gallois had received a sympathetic refusal of his request, some champagne, and a long jeep ride. At the end of the ride at nine-thirty Tuesday morning, he had recited his story to a room full of high brass. He had arrived at Bradley's headquarters not long before Bradley was due to fly to consult with Eisenhower.

All day long, Leclerc and Gallois paced the airstrip awaiting Bradley's return. At the same time, another group arrived from Paris, bearing word for Eisenhower. Of the twenty missions which had left Paris for the Allied lines in the past four days, it was the oddest, and next to that of Gallois, the most important.

It was a mixed group of mediators, messengers, warriors and spies and had been dispatched with the approval of von Choltitz and the Resistance through the connivance of Consul Nordling, who told the German general that fixed, unobstructed itineraries for German troops retreating through Paris could be obtained in this way.

In a large car hung with a big Swedish flag, there were: Rolf Nordling, the consul's brother; Colonel Olivier, senior officer of British intelligence in Paris; Jean Laurent, ex-secretary to de Gaulle at the War Ministry in 1940; Comte Alexandre de Saint-Phalle, representing Parodi, and Baron von Poch-Pastor, representing von Choltitz (and probably Allied intelligence). Their guide and bulldozer through the German lines was the singular Major Bender.

One of these men brought Eisenhower word that von Choltitz was prepared to surrender to regular forces after a show of arms, what the French call *un baroud d'honneur*. The Resistance sources were not to pick up a hint of *un baroud d'honneur* from the Germans until Thursday, two days later.

"To make certain that Choltitz understood his role, an Allied intelligence officer entered the city to confirm the 'arrangement' that was to save the city from destruction," is the way an official U.S. Army historian described the subsequent move.

As the agent was being dispatched, Choltitz was receiving the Hitler order which ended, "Paris must not fall into the hands of the enemy except as a heap of rubble." He phoned General Hans Speidel, who was extremely indirect in his responses, knowing the line was tapped by the Gestapo. Choltitz thanked him for passing along "the lovely order" and described how all the Parisian landmarks were about to be blown to smithereens. Speidel understood what Choltitz meant to convey: that the whole thing was idiotic. Sighing, he said to Choltitz, "Herr General, we are really lucky to have a man like you in Paris."

At seven-fifteen that evening Bradley returned to his headquarters. He saw Leclerc and Gallois at the edge of the airstrip and called them over.

"I have just taken a decision which deeply concerns both of you. You, General, because you are going to execute it, and you, Major, because I have made it largely on the basis of your information."

Minutes later Leclerc was airborne. When he landed at his headquarters he called to his chief of staff, *"Gribius, mouvement sur Paris."* H-hour was fixed for 6:30 A.M.

Half an hour after midnight, General Gerow, prompted by his dissatisfied superiors, was on the telephone to ask why in hell the division was not yet on the road. All along the chain nobody seemed happy, except the 2 DB, which was going to Paris.

Wednesday, August 23

At noon, Leclerc had come more than a hundred miles and reached Rambouillet, a twenty-mile Sunday drive from Paris. Ahead of his main body of armor, he was obliged to wait. At SHAEF, General Eisenhower expressed "discontent" to French General Juin. He had expected the 2 DB to march at midnight and he had expected the liberation of Paris to have begun about noon Wednesday.

Ironically at twelve-thirty there came an electrifying announcement on the BBC French-language news broadcast. "Paris is liberated." Despite a harsh correction from SHAEF, the BBC continued to broadcast the "news" at home as well as abroad. The British press printed it. There was dancing in the streets of London. In the streets of Paris, there was blood.

Leclerc's reconnaissance reported that German defenses before Paris seemed "less robust" to the right, at Arpajon. As a consequence, instead of following corps orders to bowl right ahead through Versailles and down the short highway to Paris, Leclerc split his command into two columns of attack and one of reserve. The Langlande Combat Command was sent past Versailles, the Billotte Combat Command through Arpajon with the Dio CC tacked on in reserve. Leclerc would stay with the Arpajon group.

To General de Gaulle, who appeared at Rambouillet, Leclerc explained his new plan. "You are lucky," was de Gaulle's only comment. In receipt of the changed attack orders, General Gerow had a good deal more than that to say, and vaulted into his jeep to say it personally to his insubordinate subordinate. But he arrived too late to catch up with Leclerc.

In Paris throughout the day the barricades had multiplied, some of them authentic Victor Hugo reproductions a full story high. All through the previous night, the *groupe franc* Cevennes had helped neighborhoods build barricades.

The construction workers union, on the promise of red wine rations, came to offer expert help and strong backs. In scenes out of old lithographs, men, women and children labored to erect and strengthen bulwarks. Anything solid, from automobile bodies to park fences, from civil defense sandbags and mattresses to store-front signs, was put to use.

The map of Paris showed hundreds of barricades, scattered like hairs on a barber's towel, even in the beaux-quartiers of the Sixteenth Arrondissement, where there were fewer combatants than elsewhere. The barricades were thickest where Paris history indicated they should be, up on the buttes and in the old faubourgs, the traditionally revolutionary quarters of Paris.

Wednesday, the same tanks that took the mairie of the Fifth the day before punched through the barricade at Gobelins to open the road through the Place d'Italie for a convoy of trucks heading out of Paris.

A *groupe franc* of the arrondissement was called in as reinforcement. The boys of the Fourteenth had attacked a German convoy, rue Jean Dolent and rue de la Fortune, and were in trouble. The convoy got away, finally, but it left behind three trucks and twelve prisoners.

Later in the day it was the turn of the Fourteenth to answer an SOS from a barricade on the rue de Sèvres in the Fifteenth.

At nine in the morning, a German convoy pulling back through Paris from the Allied front turned, by mistake, down the Champs Elysées. There were two armored cars, thirty troop carriers, and two trucks shepherded by two light tanks and a heavy Tiger. As they entered the garden section of the splendid avenue, they were fired upon from the police station by the Grand Palais. The Grand and Petit Palais are glass-roofed exposition halls left over from the curlicued World Fair of 1889. The riflemen killed one German.

The tanks opened fire with their cannon and released two miniature robot tanks, one of which exploded against the police station, which was then attacked with hand grenades. The Grand Palais began to burn.

The frightened horses of the Circus Houk playing there that week were led out. One, hit by a stray bullet, fell dead behind the Palais and was reduced to a meatless skeleton by amateur butchers who sprang from nowhere brandishing their knives.

The Paris firemen in their silver helmets and scarlet-piped uniforms came spink-sponking up, unrolled their hoses, and were fired upon by the outraged Germans. Young ladies carried to safety exhibits from a charity show of work done by French POW's in German camps. The Germans wanted to arrest everybody, including passersby who had absurdly sought refuge inside the Grand Palais. Eventually, some of Choltitz's officers appeared, and the firemen were allowed to extinguish the blaze.

This incident gave von Choltitz a good excuse to bluster. He threatened to destroy the Préfecture de Police, on the grounds that the "truce is not being respected." He also complained about "barricades being pushed toward me." His tanks moved out, knocked down the barricade on the rue de Rivoli and the rue de l'Arbre Sec. They patrolled before the Hôtel de Ville and the Prefecture, but undertook no serious assault (which is not to say they did not wound and kill Frenchmen).

In the canal and stockyard neighborhood around the Bassin de la Villette, German infantry attacked the barricades between the rue de Flandres and the rue Jean Jaurès for an hour and a half but was obliged to disengage.

Around Batignolles, the fighting rolled back and forth across the carrefours of the neighborhood. The FFI swarmed over the huge freight station, capturing two trains and a large supply of gasoline, and taking eighty-four Germans prisoner.

In the Nineteenth Arrondissement headquarters, the only

persons not out fighting when the phone rang were an eighteen-year-old girl and her squad of four teen-age boys. The *cheminots* were calling to warn them that the Germans were moving two trains along the almost-forgotten Petite Ceinture (Little Belt) line, from the Gare de Lyon to the Gare du Nord. There was nobody else to stop the trains, so the youth squad set out with their three pistols, one rifle and several sacks of hand grenades.

They stationed themselves on the overpass at each end of the railroad tunnel. The trains, well guarded, moved slowly along the rusted tracks and into the tunnel. Just before the first train emerged, the girl let fall two bundles of grenades into the tunnel mouth. The trains stopped. A few minutes later, they were heard backing up. The boys at the opposite end of the tunnel tossed their bundles of grenades. Then down the embankment, and rapid fire into the tunnel from both ends. Inside, their bullets ricocheted viciously off the curved walls. Bursts of machine-gun fire from the train whistled harmlessly up the track.

The youths held their fire. A couple of helmets thrust slowly out of the tunnel and their wearers were shot. A squad of Boches started a sortie out of the tunnel and were torn to pieces by a grenade from overhead.

FFI reinforcements arrived. One of the boys slipped down onto the track, glided into the tunnel to uncouple the engines in the dark. A squirt of submachine-gun fire racketed through the tunnel, and the boy did not return.

An old man, a retired *cheminot,* asked the girl leader if he might make a try. He stole down an emergency ladder, and fifteen minutes later clambered back up, grinning, making the "V" sign. More FFI from the Nineteenth and Twentieth arrived, plus the 3rd Groupe Franc. The corner bistro sent out a few bottles of wine (it's hot in the sun) and some patriotic housewives appeared with salamis, worth their weight in gold. Except for those on guard duty, everybody sat on the embankment eating and drinking and waiting for the certain victory. Finally, all hands assembled for one prolonged burst of heavy fire, and the Germans, 137 of them, surrendered.

Thursday, August 24

Leclerc's sixteen thousand men started off from Rambouillet in a heavy rain. His choice to bear east and then swing north to Paris was unfortunate. It led him to the spot where German defense was disposed in the greatest depth. Also, this movement brought him into the operational terrain of the U.S. 4th Division dispatched to enter Paris on his right flank.

Langlande's combat command, following the original route through Versailles, encountered mines and artillery fire, but broke through after a four-hour tank battle. After that, German interference was minor, but the delirious welcome from the French of each liberated town slowed his progress.

Leclerc's main column had a difficult time after passing Arpajon. His American superiors, Bradley, Hodges and Gerow, at first incredulous at his slow progress, were by now furious. They knew perfectly well how much ground an attacking armored division could cover in this territory, since other units had been clearing a circle around Paris all week. They could not understand what delayed Leclerc.

There was an hour's fire fight outside Longjumeau and a five-hour battle at Massy. Reserves had to be brought up against the heavy defense at Palaiseau and artillery massed to force the town of Wissous. There was a street-by-street fight for Antony. The prison at Fresnes was a fortress manned by Nazi fanatics. There were anti-tank weapons at Croix-de-Berny.

Leclerc in his command car whipped up and down and around the columns, jollying, cursing, advising, ordering, being the perfect front-line leader. His frustration was acute. Paris was just over the way.

At five o'clock he sent one of his six spotter planes to Paris. At the Préfecture de Police it swooped and dropped the message: "General Leclerc asks me to tell you, 'Hold on, we are coming.' Crépin, Commander of Artillery, 2 DB."

Out of the capital toward the division flowed dozens of messengers — the Porte d'Orléans is only five miles from Croix-de-Berny. The column had come thirteen nasty miles in one day. And for one day's combat against an overmatched defense, the losses were hardly light: 71 killed, 225 wounded, 25 missing. They had lost 35 tanks, six self-propelled guns and 111 vehicles.

General Gerow, who esteemed the opposition light and the attack lacking in vigor, said later that Leclerc's men were unwilling to "jeopardize French lives and property by use of the means necessary to speed the advance." Bradley said they "stumbled reluctantly through a Gallic wall as townsfolk along the line of march slowed the French advance with wine and celebration."

Gerow asked for authority to send the right-flank 4th Infantry Division (U.S.) into Paris, since Leclerc was not responding to orders "to take more aggressive action and speed up his advance." Bradley concurred, saying he could not wait for the liberators to "dance their way into Paris." He added, "To hell with prestige, tell the 4th to slam into Paris and take the liberation."

At 7:30 P.M. Leclerc spotted a detachment of three of his tanks, eleven half-tracks and four engineer vehicles beating toward the main highway. He halted them and ordered detachment commander Captain Raymond Dronne to start instantly for Paris, avoid combat, and make the eight miles to the heart of Paris as fast as possible, that night. Dronne's group nosed off through the half-dozen suburbs between there and Paris, where fighting still went on around the Luxembourg Gardens and the barracks at the Place de la République.

Dronne pushed his little force across back gardens and through hastily pulled-aside barricades. Guided by suburbanites, he by-passed German forces and ground ahead as ordered. It took him little more than an hour to reach the Porte d'Italie — Paris!

That was fine, but where was the Hôtel de Ville, where he had been ordered to go? In the confusion, there was no FFI guide to show him, and bystanders argued about which streets were open and which blocked, and where the German strong-points were. Finally, through a zigzag of streets, the advance element of the liberating armies followed a man on a bicycle. At the Pont d'Austerlitz, the man told them to cross the bridge, turn left and you can't miss it. Along the Right Bank they raced — Quai de la Rapée, Quai Henri-IV, Quai des Célestins, Quai de l'Hôtel-de-Ville, Place de l'Hôtel-de Ville!

The resistants of the radio began their great moment. Pierre Schaeffer spoke: "Parisians, rejoice! We come to give you news of deliverance. The Leclerc Division is entering Paris! In a few minutes it will be at the Hôtel de Ville! Stay tuned in. You are going to hear the great voice you have been awaiting. We are delirious with joy. The broadcast is being improvised. We operate under poor conditions. We haven't eaten for three days. There are comrades coming to the microphone right from three days on the firing line. We are drunk, maybe, but drunk with joy, with happiness to find our dear city once again. . . ."

From house to house telephones rang. Neighbors shouted to each other. Bicyclists sped through the city shouting the news. Paris, as soon as it heard, as soon as it believed, went mad.

"There they are!" cried the radio voice. "They are here! At this moment, ahead of the troops of General Leclerc, two armored cars pull up in front of the Hôtel de Ville. General de Gaulle should be in one of them. What is certain is that the Allies have arrived, and it is probable that General de Gaulle is with them. Open your windows, hang out your flags. . . ."

Then the radio asked that all the curés of all the churches in all of Paris ring their bells "to announce the entry of the Allies into Paris."

At nine-twenty-two the little squadron was disposed in military fashion in front of the Hôtel de Ville. Thirteen minutes later, Langlande's combat command, having followed the original Versailles route, crossed the Seine at Sèvres and, per instructions, halted. In truth, he was entirely out of touch with Leclerc and could not report his position. The muzzles of Langlande's tanks were virtually on the Paris city line, but without further orders there could be no further progress — the undertaking was too big and too significant for any acts of derring-do, although Leclerc's superiors were fuming at his lack of progress and Leclerc himself was frazzled with impatience, Leclerc, who had troops poised to break into Paris and didn't know it. The powerful combat unit switched off engines at the edge of the city.

Langlande's forward units probably heard the bells. From the heights and from the river islands, the whole Paris basin was filled with the sound of bells. They sang and rang and boomed and shivered from the towers of 146 churches.

Von Choltitz had just finished dining with a few of his staff. He picked up the phone to German field headquarters, and spoke to Speidel.

"Can you hear that?" he asked, holding the phone toward the open window.

"Yes — the sound of bells," said the puzzled chief of staff.

"That's right. The Franco-American Army is entering Paris. Speidel, what are your orders for a commanding general with no troops to command?"

"Herr General, you know very well we must no longer give orders. . . ."

"Well, my dear Speidel, all that remains is to say goodbye. Look after my wife in Baden-Baden. Protect her and the children."

Stiff and weary Captain Dronne was hauled from his tank by the defenders of the Hôtel de Ville. He and a tiny crewman were almost carried into the office of the préfect de Seine. Georges Bidault, president of the CNR, kissed him on both cheeks.

At that instant, the Hôtel de Ville was fired upon. Machine-gun bullets stitched across the paneling and spat bits of crystal from the bottom of the chandelier. Everyone threw himself flat on the floor. Someone finally found the switch and extinguished the lights, the fire was returned, the shooting eventually died away.

But elsewhere in Paris the people were mad with joy. The liberation, the liberation!

Captain Dronne went to report to the delegation at the Préfecture de Police. The police drum and bugle contingent played the "Marseillaise," General Chaban-Delmas gave the command "Attention!" Alexandre Parodi found himself thrust before a microphone.

"I have before me a French captain who has just been the first to enter Paris. His face is red, he is dirty and unshaven, and just the same one wants to embrace him."

Jean Guignebert, secretary general for information, relieved Parodi of the microphone and seized upon Dronne's shadow, the undersized soldier. "And now," he cried, "you are going to hear from one of our own boys, a buck private — *un bon petit Français* — tell me, where were you born?"

A silence, a gulp, a thin, nervous voice, "I was born in Constantinople."

Suddenly Paris, after all these years of darkness, was flooded with light. People turned on all their lights, opened wide their shutters and curtains and windows. Those without electricity lighted the precious candles they had been hoarding. The "Marseillaise" was sung on hundreds of street corners. Strangers embraced. The bells clamored. In Montparnasse they danced in the street around a bonfire. The radio babbled madly.

Then the radio stopped babbling. Earnestly, it advised people to quiet down, to observe blackout regulations, to close their windows.

Why? Because there were thousands of German soldiers in Paris. Because groups of singers and lighted windows had been fired upon. At eleven o'clock the anti-aircraft battery at Longchamps had begun bombarding the city (over-shooting by several miles — perhaps just a warning).

The radio made an urgent appeal for troops to relieve the Eleventh Arrondissement mairie, under attack and almost out of ammunition.

The men of four arrondissements were still in position around the perimeter of the Luxembourg complex, which includes the ancient Luxembourg Palace, the Senate, the museum, the park, the School of Mines and the Lycée Montaigne, plus a fearsome network of bunkers and fortifications. The access streets were covered by a dozen German blockhouses, and the garrison numbered six hundred diehard SS troops with tanks and cannon.

The assaulting FFI was commanded by the FTP's Colonel Fabien (the one who had assassinated the German naval officer in the Métro three years ago).

Across town the units surrounding the pillboxed Place de la République and the fortified Prince Eugène Barracks were punished by German sorties of armored vehicles and tanks. Pushed back, they continued to re-form and to regain their lost ground.

Friday, August 25

Colonel Billotte's combat command jumped off at 7:15 A.M., objective Paris. They roared along, meeting no opposition, since von Choltitz had pulled back the last of his troops during the night. At seven-forty-five they were through the Porte Gentilly, rumbling past the Cité Universitaire, down the rue St. Jacques, the ancient Roman route, to the Ile de la Cité, and on to the Hôtel de Ville. No shot was fired. People poured into the streets, sure at last that this was indeed the liberation. Splendid and heroic in their Sherman tanks and their bristling armored cars, these young warriors laughed away the shame and the fear of the defeat of 1940 and the occupation of yesterday. There was love and pride along the line of march.*

German sentries remained at attention in front of the Lycée Montaigne, part of the Luxembourg redoubt, as the clatter of the column and the cheers of the crowd came clearly through the summer air from a few streets away.

Colonel Billotte established his command post in the billiard room of the Prefecture. Parodi, Luizet, Chaban-Delmas explained the situation (Germans had retired into nine strongholds: the Hôtel Meurice and Tuileries Gardens; the Naval Ministry on the Place de la Concorde; the Palais Bourbon and the Foreign Ministry directly across the Concorde bridge; the Hôtel Majestic near the Etoile; the Place de la République; the Luxembourg; the Ecole Militaire; and several outlying barracks).

From the Senate in the Luxembourg compound, bullets swept the adjacent streets. From the rue de Vaugirard, French tanks cannonaded the Luxembourg Palace, smashing the bunkers of its outside defenses. A group of Leclerc infantry battled into the School of Mines, part of this same strongpoint, but was driven out again by a counterattack.

The barracks at Latour-Maubourg by the Invalides were taken at 11 A.M. by the Garde Républicaine acting as infantry for tanks of the Dio command, which entered Paris by the Porte d'Orléans at 9 A.M. Other Dio elements fanned out to engage in two of the sharpest battles of the day, against the Ecole Militaire and against the block of buildings on the Quai d'Orsay which includes the Chamber of Deputies, the residence of the Chamber president and the Ministry of Foreign Affairs.

To attack this latter block was difficult, because the side toward the Seine was bracketed by German cannon on the opposite bank of the river, and because the inland approaches

* Most of the 2 DB, including Colonel Langlande, went into combat smeared with lipstick.

were studded with pillboxes. The attackers, thus obliged to hit it at both ends, were hit hard in return. After some hours of this, the Foreign Ministry began to burn. Up hustled the firemen to put out the fire. They were dissuaded from such devotion to duty, but not easily.

A motorized regiment of General Raymond Barton's U.S. 4th Infantry Division swung to a halt in front of Notre Dame just before noon. Other elements of the division occupied the railway stations on the east end of Paris, Austerlitz, Lyon and Vincennes.

At half past twelve, a Dio detachment which had been securing the bridges in the western end of the town paused to hoist the enormous tricolor on the Eiffel Tower. Then they swung down to clean out the Ecole Militaire.

Langlande's command rolled in from the Porte St. Cloud to the Arc de Triomphe, pausing to demolish a blockhouse guarding the approach to the Etoile. As the elements entered Etoile by different avenues, they paraded around the great circle surrounding the Arc. At each of the fifteen streets leading into the Etoile, they dropped off a tank to cover the approach.

This disposition made, firemen on the roof of the Arc hung down a huge French flag. As French officers marched to the tomb of the Unknown Soldier under the Arc, a tank farther down the Champs Elysées, a German tank, fired two rounds. One knocked a piece off the statue of La Marseillaise which decorates the front, and the other whistled through the archway.

In the Avenue Kléber just off the Etoile was a large blockhouse, a network of anti-tank barriers, screens of barbed wire and a collection of light tanks, cars and trucks. The Langlande tanks shot them to pieces. The Majestic Hotel, the blockhouse, and scattered other German emplacements surrendered. The crowd tried to beat and kick the Germans. Someone threw a phosphorus grenade into a column of prisoners, killing both French and German soldiers. In the ensuing moments of disorder, shots were fired and there were more dead, including civilians.

Choltitz breakfasted at the Meurice with a few officers, seated as usual with his back to the big windows overlooking the street. Implored to change his seat, he said no. "Especially not today." His communications officer entered with a radio message from Der Führer. Two words — *Brennt Paris?* — Is Paris burning?

Billotte, on the advice of the FFI and delegation officers, composed an ultimatum for Monsieur le Général von Choltitz, and signed it "Commanding General, 1st French Armored Brigade."

Choltitz refused to read the ultimatum, and the peculiar Major Bender made an embroidered reply to the waiting Major de la Horie. Again the words *baroud d'honneur.*

At the Luxembourg redoubt, two platoons of tank destroyers and a company of Marines opened an attack with the FFI.

At the Place de la République, Thursday's battle was resumed at 6 A.M., and now Captain Dronne arrived with his detachment. The *place* itself, whose approaches were protected by blockhouses, was sandbagged, had anti-tank barriers, four cannon, plus heavy machine guns and automatic rifles. The barracks were heavily defended as well.

The fight was a classic piece of street warfare. The blockhouses were knocked out one by one. The attackers moved toward the wide *place* over the roofs and by pouncing from door to door, until they killed off the cannon crews and slowly pushed the defenders back into the fortified barracks.

Major de Lignières, assigned to arrange the residence-office of the minister of war for General de Gaulle's afternoon arrival, arrived from Rambouillet. The guard at the door turned him away. The building, on the rue St. Dominique, was in the possession of COMAC. Just then the Paris firemen appeared and began to unroll the hoses to deal with a small fire somewhere in the building. The major, acquainted with their commanding officer, entered with the firemen. An officer of the gendarmerie who had also come to the scene of the fire argued the COMAC security guards into surrendering a few rooms for the use of the man they claimed to recognize as their chief. During the four years since he had left, nothing in de Gaulle's office had changed, not even the names on the intercom push-buttons.

At one o'clock the attack on the Hôtel Meurice, von Choltitz's headquarters, was ordered, and three columns of tank-supported infantry left from Châtelet for the Place de la Concorde. The center column headed straight down the rue de Rivoli to take the Meurice by the front door. The left was to clean out the adjacent Tuileries Gardens. The right followed the parallel rue St. Honoré, to hit the Meurice from behind and cover the operation from the rue Royale and the Place de l'Opéra.

Fifty-five minutes later, despite a profusion of bunkers and six heavy tanks, the gardens were cleared. Twenty vehicles were afire and 120 more captured. Three hundred prisoners.

The right flank column got 162 prisoners at the Kommandantur on the Place de l'Opera, another 150 from the back door of the Hôtel Continental (these had placed themselves under the protection of an American colonel they had been holding prisoner for three days), and odd groups totaling three hundred more men. They also smashed pillboxes, and set fire to vehicles along the streets between Rivoli and l'Opéra.

The right and left flank columns joined at the Place de la Concorde, where the French lost one of their tanks in a short tank engagement, and the Germans lost all of theirs. The Hôtel Crillon yielded 150 men, the Naval Ministry 380. From the assortment of hotels and public buildings around Choltitz's headquarters, not counting those killed, those hiding and not yet discovered, nor those awaiting capture at the Hôtel Meurice, a total of 1442 soldiers.

Even though protected by the arcades which run the length of the rue de Rivoli, the infantry of the center made slow progress against snipers and hand grenades (the tanks had gone on ahead). After more than an hour, two French lieutenants, Karcher of the FFI and Franjoux of the 2 DB, reached the Meurice and shot their way into the lobby. During their dramatic entrance they improvised a solution to a rare military problem: how to get through a revolving door with a submachine gun.

A gunner behind sandbags in the lobby aimed at them and they cut him down. They threw smoke grenades into the ground-floor passages, and went upstairs to find General von Choltitz. With half a dozen officers in immaculate uniforms, he was waiting for them.

Entering Choltitz's office, Karcher announced himself. He had one of his men, who spoke German, ask if the general spoke French, was told that the general could understand it.

"Do you surrender?" he asked the general.

"*Ja.*"

"Surrender your arms."

As the weapons clicked onto the table, Major de la Horie entered. He told von Choltitz, "You refused the ultimatum addressed to you this morning. You wanted a fight and you got one. However, resistance continues elsewhere and I demand that you order the officers commanding these centers of resistance to cease fire."

As Major de la Horie rode toward the Prefecture with Choltitz and his aide, they met Colonel Billotte coming to find out the reason for the delay. Billotte took the prisoners into his command car, with the German aide on the floor between the colonel's knees.

"You said *baroud d'honneur*. Well, I lost some of my people, too many of my people for your *baroud d'honneur*. The agreement wasn't respected. I don't know what we are going to do with you."

"After the attitude I have shown," countered von Choltitz, "I have a right to some consideration."

While waiting for his men to bring the German commander to the Police Prefecture to surrender, Leclerc was asked to lunch by Prefect Luizet in prewar style with flowers from the municipal greenhouses, silver, napery and an acceptable menu. There was a constant flow of messages from his headquarters in the Montparnasse railway station. Beneath his exterior of professional military calm, Leclerc was perishing with impatience, stayed at table less than ten minutes and went into the prefect's billiard room to wait for the conquered German governor of Paris.

As he sat and glowered, a visitor, General Barton, USA, was announced. There are two versions of this scene, one from French Army sources, one from American Army sources.

French version: Barton and several of his officers entered the billiard room. Barton excused himself "not without *delicatesse*" for intruding. "You should be alone in Paris today." Leclerc responded that a soldier must do his duty. As for the military matter that brought General Barton, that would best be regulated at the map room in the 2 DB headquarters at the Gare Montparnasse. The crowd cheered the *chers Amerloques* as they left the Prefecture.

American version: Holding his napkin and looking annoyed at having his lunch interrupted, Leclerc came out onto the steps of the Prefecture. Directing Barton to the Gare Montparnasse, Leclerc did not invite the hungry American to lunch. Barton, resenting Leclerc's attitude, said, "I didn't come to Paris because I wanted to, but because I was ordered to be here." Leclerc shrugged and said, "We are both soldiers."

In the billiard room, the billiard table was covered, the furniture elegant, and the decor not so informal as it might sound. On a leather divan, Leclerc, stiff with anticipation, sat staring across at the ornate marble fireplace. Alongside him, equally tense, was General Chaban-Delmas, national military delegate. Three of Leclerc's staff, including his intelligence officer and a bilingual captain, were also in the room. Outside rose a chilling swell of booing and whistling. Billotte pushed into the room, passed in front of the divan, muttered, "Here he is," and posted himself by a window, arms folded, glowering.

Beef-red, monocle fixed, von Choltitz entered. He scrutinized the two generals facing him, correctly picked the older, and advanced as if to shake hands.

Leclerc's lean, lined face was fierce. The culmination of four years of hope and combat gleamed there. He was probably unaware of speaking, but from his clenched teeth came, "This is it."

"*Ich bin der General Leclerc,*" he said. "*Sind Sie der General von Choltitz? Setzen Sie sich.*" He made a sign to one of his officers to get rid of all the witnesses crowding in to take up poses for this historical canvas. A small table was brought in and set before the divan.

In the office next door Colonel Rol and M. Kriegel-Valrimont were telling Préfet Luizet, "You can't do this to us." The prefect agreed. There was already enough dissension among the French, and these men certainly had had a good deal to do with the German surrender. He spoke to Chaban, who spoke to Leclerc. Leclerc nodded yes for the colonel, but made a face regarding the civilian. Chaban indicated that the presence of Kriegel-Valrimont, COMAC Communist, would be politically expedient, and he too was admitted.

Choltitz contended that signing a capitulation would be redundant, since his chief of staff was working out the surrender details at the Meurice with French officers. Leclerc said, oh, he hadn't heard. Choltitz said, oh my yes, just leave these details to my chief of staff.

Leclerc cut him off icily. "No matter what, it is necessary that you sign this."

The paper was headed "Provisional Government of the French Republic." It annoyed many Americans later, who said it should have been headed "Supreme Headquarters Allied Expeditionary Forces."

The fat, red face of Choltitz was now blanched white. Sweating profusely, he mopped his forehead with a handkerchief he took from his sleeve. Subject to cardiac spasms, he looked unwell.

Colonel Rol, big, blond and forthright, spoke up for the FFI.

He spoke up quietly and honestly, and as a self-educated man, with more elegance than many an expensively schooled career officer. Rol habitually avoided argot and never swore. He pointed out that his men as well as Leclerc's had liberated Paris, and on behalf of these men, Rol should sign too. Leclerc replied that he, Leclerc, commanded all French forces in Paris at the moment, and his signature therefore stood for all those who fought.

But as the entire group rode to Leclerc's command post at the Gare Montparnasse to put the terms of surrender into force, Kriegel-Valrimont buttonholed Chaban-Delmas: there were two armies, there should be two signatures, etc. As a Resistance product himself, Chaban could not help but agree that the years of clandestine combat should be recognized. He and Kriegel-Valrimont spoke again to Leclerc, who not only shrugged his shoulders, but changed the text, and even put Rol's name ahead of his own.

Convention of surrender concluded between Colonel Rol, commander of the FFI of the Ile-de-France, Major General Leclerc, commander of the 2 DB, and General von Choltitz, military commander of German forces in the Paris region.

On the way through the station, Choltitz's heart acted up. He took a pill case from his pocket, and a French interpreter gasped, "Oh, General, I hope you aren't . . ." The general said, "Oh no, young man, we don't do that sort of thing."

Upstairs, he signed the order for surrender of the strongpoints. Franco-German teams of officers were assigned to accept the surrender of each. At the Place de la République, the Ecole Militaire, the Palais Bourbon–Foreign Ministry, the Luxembourg and some other spots, fighting was still in progress.

At this moment General de Gaulle arrived. This was his first stop in liberated Paris, but he was not pleased: the appearance of Rol's name as co-acceptor of the German surrender was not only inaccurate, he said, but totally improper, since the senior officer alone is responsible for victory or defeat of his troops. And besides, the whole idea was a Communist trick, or, as the general put it, "It comes from an unacceptable (political) tendency."

As de Gaulle"s party proceeded to the War Ministry, it was fired upon, but arrived unharmed. Alexandre Parodi, whom de Gaulle had never seen, was waiting to outline the political situation. He tried to explain why de Gaulle should go to the Hôtel de Ville and meet the CNR. He did not succeed.

De Gaulle knew that the CNR thought of itself — and with reason — as a sort of Provisional National Assembly (it would ask in vain to be assigned the Chamber of Deputies as its meeting place), a council guiding the growth of the New France. He also knew that it was Communist-dominated. The General had at his command troops, funds, the whole French empire and the apparatus of a Provisional Government. But a false move now, and the France he had envisaged would never emerge.

He too had had four years of living on hope and willpower in a struggle with powerful forces, and he was the first for Free France and was alone.

He wanted to avoid traps proffered by political groups, in which he had had small confidence before 1940 and less since. The Communists dominated the CPL, the CNR and COMAC, and they too had their own army. He knew what they wanted: France, his France.

His final word to Parodi — it was not for the Head of State to call on the CPL and CNR in the municipal building, but rather for Resistance leaders to pay their respects to their Chief in a State building.

Parodi called for help. He phoned Charles Luizet, préfet de police, an old friend of de Gaulle's who had been there through the whole uprising, who knew the mood and the structure of the Resistance and who knew how to choose the words which could persuade the General.

Luizet hustled over, repeated Parodi's argument that the

Resistance had fought in de Gaulle's name and deserved the recompense of his presence. He added that for hours the vast Place de l'Hôtel-de-Ville had been black with people, the people of Paris waiting for a glimpse of Charles de Gaulle, the last hours of four years of waiting. Could he disappoint them, rob them of this final joy?

De Gaulle finally said, "Well, if go we must, then let's go."

General de Gaulle stopped first at the Préfecture de Police, a State building, to greet Luizet's men. The defenders paraded for the General as the police band played. From the Prefecture, the General insisted on walking to the Hôtel de Ville through the screaming, laughing, weeping mob. Inside the building, he ascended the grand stairway, each step of which was guarded by a member of the youthful Equipes Nationales. They performed prettily, having practiced so much for the arrival of Marshal Pétain. De Gaulle's préfet de Seine greeted and accompanied the General.

At this same moment, at the Place de la République, about a dozen streets away, there was some difficulty in making both sides understand that the battle for Paris was over and the shooting must stop. Finally the five-hundred-man garrison surrendered. At the Luxembourg, after long parley and some force, the sobbing, cursing SS men obeyed Choltitz's orders and surrendered too.

As de Gaulle entered the prefect's office in the Hôtel de Ville, the mystique of the Resistance crystallized. The combatants, tears in their eyes, presented arms. Cries of *"Vive de Gaulle!"* echoed and re-echoed. De Gaulle was as deeply moved as any of them.

Then came the formalities. Georges Marranne, the big, bluff Communist who had come north to Paris for the fighting, and was everywhere in the insurrection, fearless and inspiring, spoke for the CPL. His speech was short, simple, warm and patriotic. Then Georges Bidault, for the CNR, produced an allocution fraught with historical allusion and stiff with overwrought phraseology.

De Gaulle responded: "Why should we dissimulate the emotion which grips us all, men and women, who are here at home in Paris, a Paris risen to liberate itself with its own hands? No! We will not hide this sacred and profound emotion. These are moments which surpass every one of our poor lives."

And then, from the sublime to the meticulous, he made a short peroration calling for national unity under the stamp of the authority of the State, and said that national renewal must be built "legally and fraternally."

No word of thanks to the Resistance, without which he would not have been here. He did not meet the members of the CNR or the CPL. Georges Bidault asked the General if he would not like to step out on the balcony and (as prescribed by last night's CNR meeting) proclaim the Republic. The General said, "No, the Republic has never ceased to exist."

He did, however, step to the balcony and raise his arms to the loving crowd. And then he returned to his quarters at the Ministry of War. He did not invite the CNR to accompany him in the next day's victory parade down the Champs Elysées, though many showed up and marched with him nevertheless.

The combat for Paris yielded eleven thousand German prisoners. There were, all told, 2788 Germans killed and 4911 wounded. The FFI and the regular forces lost 901 dead and 1455 wounded. The civilian population had 585 dead and 2012 wounded.

When the liberation was over, the authorities added up the total of those claiming recognition as Paris FFI. It came to more than 123,000, an impressive increase from the 20,000 when the insurrection had started August 19 and the 10,000 just before D-Day.

Out of the Paris Resistance came enough volunteers for the regular army to make almost a full division, including three thousand "working-stiffs" recruited by Colonel Fabien, and a whole battalion of students from the Lycée Janson-Sully.

SOME UGLINESS

There are thousands of Frenchmen to whom the word

"maquis" has an ugly sound twenty years after the liberation. For the most part, these are people whose homes or shops were sacked or whose innocent relatives were executed either by maquis bands gone sour or else by gangs who emerged in the last anarchic moments around the period of liberation.

And there were, in isolated spots, miniature wars between rival factions. The civilians caught between these two fires (and sometimes three, if Germans were still in the region) were often seriously maltreated in the process. If they refused help, they suffered, and if they gave help to one, they suffered at the hands of the others.

And there were the lynch-minded idiots, filled with false-patriotic frenzy, to whom every stranger was a spy or fugitive collaborator. Yves Farge, de Gaulle's representative at Lyon, was arrested six times in one day by so-called maquisards who wanted to shoot him as an enemy because he did not carry a pass signed by himself. Other Resistance leaders who had out-smarted and outrun the Gestapo for four years found themselves in the worst danger of their lives when arrested by such vigilante bands.

For weeks, the self-liberated territories were out of touch with the rest of France, their only links to the outside world being the clandestine radios to Algiers and London. In many places it was a grim showdown between rival forces. Some of these were eager for power because they were tasting it for the first time, because at last they were important and could make everyone realize it. Some were there by "right": they had fought for the village or town or *département*, they had saved it, and it was theirs to hold against "outsiders." There were some who were simply brigands, there to take what they could and live high for a while. There were some commanded by SOE officers who saw themselves as reincarnations of Lawrence of Arabia and would obey no orders not emanating from the British High Command. Some groups were Communists obeying Party instructions and carrying the banner of their own special new world. Some were the officially appointed Gaullist authorities, and they succeeded, by bluff and maneuver, in dislodging the other contenders.

It was now clear why the Allies had refused to drop heavy weapons to the Resistance. During these bad weeks, one great Resistance chief observed, "It is not going to be a question of demobilizing these people, but of *disarming* them."

Tribunals of various sorts, most of them with no authority but that of their weapons, held court all over the country, mechanically sentencing suspects to die. Just how many, nobody knows. Almost no one in France wanted to know, because what happened was beastly, stupid and painfully needless. For the good of the country, for the preservation of national unity, they deemed it best forgotten.

Robert Aron, one of the handful of serious historians of the occupation and Resistance, estimates from all available sources that summary executions in the name of post-liberation *épuration* (purification, purging) totaled thirty to forty thousand.

The French had had experience with this sort of thing before in their history, and a warning that it always bears bitter fruit: *Un pur trouve toujours un plus pur qui l'épure.* [A "pure" will always find a "more pure" to "purify" him.]

Another ugliness, more in the threat than in the action, was the Communist upsurge. Charles Tillon, chief of the Communist armed forces, wrote in his recent history of this Resistance movement, "It is sure that only the Front National with the Communists possessed in August 1944 in several regions of the country the means of imposing itself on the entire Resistance, had it pursued goals divergent from those of the National Council of the Resistance, or if it wished to conquer the territory to install its political control.

"This was done nowhere."

Why was it not done? The Communists controlled great chunks of territory. They were either directly in control of several major cities, or in a position to wrest control from those who had it, but they did not take the last steps in Limoges, Bordeaux, Toulouse or Montpellier.

Was it because they had failed in Paris and in Lyon to turn the liberation into a revolutionary uprising controlled by the Communist Party? It was clear that this had been their objective in Paris, and the Party ranting since about the "sell-out" at Lyon indicates it was the plan for that city, too.

General de Gaulle made it plain at the time and since in his memoirs that he feared a Communist attempt to take over. He asked, Eisenhower recorded in his memoirs, for the "loan of two divisions in order to make, as he said, a show of force to assure his position." The best Eisenhower could do was to hold a "parade," reviewed by himself, Bradley and de Gaulle, of two U.S. divisions marching through Paris on their way north to do battle that very day.

As soon as he could, during the month of September, de Gaulle visited the principal cities in the southern half of the country. In each, he acted much as he had in Paris, brusquely, at times rudely, toward many of the Resistance chiefs. He brought military commanders in from the colonies to reorganize some districts. In Montpellier, he assigned Colonel Zeller to be "associate" commander of the Communist-inclined military chief.

At the end of November, the arrival of Maurice Thorez was announced. Thunderbolt. Scandal. Thorez had decamped to Russia in 1939, and, since he had not reported for military service back in France, had been declared a deserter. Now, by de Gaulle's authority he was back, free, and still the boss of the French Communist Party.

In December, de Gaulle was in Moscow, talking to Stalin. Another thunderbolt. More scandal. He wrote that he went there to obtain "from the Communist Party the year's respite I needed to get the situation back in hand."

In January 1945 Thorez told the Central Committee of the Party it was time to dissolve the Milices Patriotiques, the armed shock troops that the Party had been recruiting for almost a year, even more intensively since the liberation.

France had trembled on the brink of civil war. There had been a good chance of repeating the story of Greece, the possibility of Prague. De Gaulle, with remarkable assistance from subordinates in the field and the weakness of Party loyalty of some of the Communist chieftains, had prevailed. The Communist plot had been mounted, as de Gaulle correctly diagnosed, but the signal to go ahead had never been given.

No matter what blend of circumstance, zeal and shrewdness brought it about, Charles de Gaulle again saved his country.

And saved it for what? De Gaulle himself was no less disgusted than many of the Resistance veterans, and he withdrew while France resumed its futile round of feeble and transitory governments.

It was as Will Rogers had described it before the war: "I always go down to the Quai d'Orsay to watch the changing of the government."

The true resistant of the occupation period had been, just by risking movement membership, a hero. In carrying out his missions, he had been many times a hero, every day. He had few fellows. (At a review of the Marseille Resistance the day after liberation, there were fifteen hundred in the line of march, three times the number inscribed when the fighting had begun a few days earlier.)

The Resistance had said it many times in its newspapers, in the studies of the Comité d'Etudes, in the CNR "Charter," in meetings with de Gaulle and his staff in London and Algiers: they were fighting for a new France. De Gaulle agreed and spoke often of the coming *renouveau.*

This shining goal, what they felt to be the real reason for liberation, eluded the Resistance. Their highest hopes were deceived. However, they had fought and they had won their horrible, silent, misunderstood war. They had kept faith with France, and France was free. And they were, as they had never ceased to be, free Frenchmen.

Et Après?

Once more France rises, proud and ardent before her destiny, ready to resume her mission, ready to make her voice heard, the voice of a great and independent nation.

> Paris Liberation Committee, in a poster distributed after the capital was freed.

You are accomplices in one of the great crimes of history. I die for having loved my country too much.

> Pierre Laval to French firing squad.

Imbeciles! I am dying for *you!*

> Victor Feldman to German firing squad.

> *It was not fraud, nor foolishness*
> *Glory, revenge or pay*
> *We came because our open eyes*
> *Could see no other way.*

> C. Day Lewis, quoted by Jacques Bergier, Réseau Marco Polo, as "an admirable description of the French Resistance."

The Resistance was the expression of a civic virtue on which the salvation of a nation depended. . . . The capital merit of

the interior Resistance was to have rendered possible, within
the discipline of definite missions, the mass rising of the French
people which restored the honor scuttled in 1940.

Charles Tillon, Commander-in-Chief, FTP.

. . . Justly proud of your efforts and of the sacrifice of too many
of your comrades, you will have a tendency to expect gratitude.
You believe yourselves to be liberators. No doubt about that, but
don't forget that the French who remained in France have also
suffered, an obscure suffering, but often as great as yours and
perhaps as useful . . . Above all, you will find before you, alongside you, those of the French Forces of the Interior. Take care
not to underestimate their hardships. More lately come into
the fight, their role is no less decisive; they will speak to you
of their exploits; speak to them all the less of your own. You
are sons of the same mother and soldiers in the same cause.

To his troops upon landing in the South of France,
from General de Lattre de Tassigny, rescued the
previous year from a Vichy prison by the Resistance.

I confess that I am full of disappointment . . . I do not find
what I expected — I expected something that was both purified
and imbued, and in many respects I have the impression of
finding myself in the middle of a country that is — how to put
it? — corrupted. . . . I have the impression of a sort of weary,
nonchalant, lazy convalescence just right for the development
of every kind of malady.

Léon Blum, on his return to France from German
capitivity, May 1945.

We could not stir an inch, eat or even breathe without becoming
the accomplices of our enemy. . . . Not a drop of blood formed
in our veins but he took his share of it. . . . The whole country
both resisted and collaborated. . . . Everything we did was

equivocal; we never quite knew whether we were doing right or doing wrong, a subtle poison corrupted even our best actions. . . .

No doubt during that time (the occupation) France — the Resistance Movement being excepted — did not always display greatness of conduct. But it should be remembered that active resistance was necessarily limited to a minority. And I think that that minority, by accepting martyrdom deliberately and without hope, has more than redeemed our weakness.

Jean-Paul Sartre, Resistant, in *France Libre*, 1944.

Nothing that I expected of the Liberation was realized. . . . It was, by definition, the era of the false: the false combatant, the false decent man, the false patriot, the false lover, the false brother, the false false. In the world of false noses, I was one of those whose nose was real and it seemed to me, as it did to all the Reals, that in reality we were real *cons*.

Dominique Ponchardier in *Les Pavés de l'Enfer*.

Index